AMERICA'S FIRST WESTERN FRONTIER: EAST TENNESSEE

A story of the early settlers and Indians of East Tennessee.

Written By
Brenda C. Calloway

Edited By
Jay Robert Reese
East Tennessee State University

Illustrated By
Tamara Geisert

The Overmountain Press
JOHNSON CITY, TENNESSEE

ISBN 0-932807-34-8

TABLE OF CONTENTS

LIST OF MAPS

LIST OF ILLUSTRATIONS

This book is dedicated posthumously to my grandfather, Loyd B. ("Andy") Anderson. Together we tramped across many farms reclaimed by the wilderness, surveying remnants of any structure. We traversed backroads, explored early towns, and visited in old homes. All the while, he related tales of the past about each, making the people and their way of life come alive once again. From him, I gleaned much regional and local history. Herein, with you, I share some of it.

In my distress I cried unto the Lord, and he heard me. Deliver my soul, O Lord, from lying lips, and from a deceitful tongue.
What shall be given unto thee? or what shall be done unto thee, thou false tongue?
Sharp arrows of the mighty, with coals of juniper. Woe is me, that I sojourn in Mesech, that I dwell in the tents of Kadar!
My soul hath long dwelt with him that hateth peace. I am for peace; but when I speak, they are for war.

—Psalm 120

APPALACHIA, MY MOUNTAIN HOME

The cradle of my ancestors, Appalachia, cradles me;
She is a warm and generous mountain-mother whose
Cradlesong is sung in quaint Elizabethan words.
From the beginning through glacial ages to today,
She has been a shrine and sanctuary to all forms of life;
Lofty, she and her sisters extend from Canada to Georgia.

With her feet planted firmly upon the ground,
Her majesty rises far above the level of the sea,
Where her noble head occasionally brushes the clouds.
There she stretches her loving arms for many miles,
Cradling her children in the cleavage of her bosom.

As you go up "Cripple Creek" by the "Wildwood Flower,"
There's tassled corn, half-runner beans, turnip greens,
Grape vine swings, leather breeches, and smoked hams;
Old time religion, hardwood benches, dinners-on-the-ground,
"Amazing Grace," creek baptisms, "Onward Christian Soldiers;"
Where else except in Appalachia, could all of this be found?

Southern Appalachia is my home, my mountain-mother;
Planted here by Scotch-Irish and German ancestors,
My roots grow deep, I thrive, and I will ever stay,
Secure in her fertile valleys, by cool rushing waters;
        Appalachia is mine and I am Appalachia's!

ACKNOWLEDGEMENTS

The author would like to thank the following people for their helpful suggestions, encouragement, and for reading portions of this manuscript: Brad Jolly, city editor of the Johnson City Press, Richard Blaustein, Center for Appalachian Studies and Services, and Dr. Elery Lay, local historian. I also thank Peggy Hensley and Lucille Deakins of the Gray Library and June Presley, Reference Librarian, of the Kingsport Library who helped me acquire important research materials and gave me pertinent information on the area. Too, I wish to thank those whom I interviewed for their time and valuable information, and for the copies of useful materials which a few gave to me. I wish to express my appreciation to Archer Blevins and the staff of the Overmountain Press for their time, helpful suggestions, and the special efforts they put forth in the publication of this book.

Special thanks to Dr. Jay Reese, English Department, East Tennessee State University, for his editing of the work and his valuable aid in expanding the text, as well as the final proofreading and typing onto disks to interface with typesetting equipment. I also thank Dr. Melvin Page, Department of History, East Tennessee State University, for reading the work and writing an introduction.

Finally, I deeply appreciate the patience, financial help, constructive criticism and continued support of my mother, Opal Bates, and grandmother, Dora Anderson, as well as the support and assistance given to me by friends and other members of my family.

EDITOR'S FOREWORD

There are many "if onlys" in history. If only the arrow which struck Harold at the Battle of Hastings in 1066 had fallen short, the invasion of William the Conqueror might have failed and the history of England would be entirely different. If only President Lincoln had decided not to visit the theater that night, would not the bitter history of the Reconstruction have to be rewritten? If only one of the early plots to kill Adolph Hitler had succeeded, how many thousands would have lived? But when the history of the early American frontier is examined, it is difficult to find pivotal "if onlys" which would have changed the outcome of the American Indian-white struggle. The conflict between the two was too great, too basic. Perhaps the only true "if onlys" would have been if Columbus had discovered the Americas five hundred years later, now that it is unpopular for Europeans to invade populated countries.

Once America was found, the needs of Europe made the outcome almost inevitable. We cannot today understand the tremendous compression of humanity that existed in Europe when America was discovered. It was not just a compression of bodies, but one of minds, ideas, and social structures. For a man born without land—and almost all were—there was no way to acquire it. No landowner would think of selling off his estates, subdividing for money his heritage and power into bits and pieces. Land was wealth, respect, power; and all that was on the land—the houses, the oxen, the gardens, the tools, and for practical purposes, the people—belonged to he who owned it. In the country money was only of secondary importance. It was to own something—anything—that caused the rural populations of Europe to flee to the cities. There they found poverty, disease, starvation, greed, and the same unequal laws. In the cities, gold was power, education, and opportunity; for most it was just as unobtainable as the land they had fled.

Then they heard the at first unbelievable tale that a world lay across the waters where the land and all it contained were unowned. It could be taken, used, and possessed by any who were desperate, brave, and lucky enough to cross the seas and live. Upon it were a people they saw as wild, un-Christian savages whom their laws nor their churches protected.

Thus the explosion of humanity to the New World began. With it also began the bloody struggle between those who had lived in paradise for centuries, and those who saw possessing it as their only hope of achieving what they thought God had promised them.

In the telling of such a history, it is difficult to find the truth of the conflict, to present it with balance, and to reflect the great sense of drama and tragedy that the reality deserves. Brenda Calloway has succeeded admirably in doing all three. She researched and worked on **America's First Western Frontier: East Tennessee** for a number of years, and she and I have written and rewritten it over the past year. I am certain you will enjoy reading **America's First Western Frontier: East Tennessee.**

Jay Robert Reese

INTRODUCTION

When I came to Johnson City, friends told me I must feel fortunate, as a historian, to be moving to such a historic region as northeast Tennessee. At first this puzzled me. Certainly, I recognized the many well known aspects of the area's past: Daniel Boone, the "lost" State of Franklin, the traditions of the overmountain men, and so on. Yet surely, I thought, all regions have their history. No area of the country, indeed of the world, where there has been continuous human habitation is without its history.

After all, one of the most appropriate and useful definitions of history is simply "a story about the human past that is intended to be true." For many professional historians, the intention of truth may not be enough, but in reality it is about the best that we can do. And given the element of human nature and interest, it is important that history also have a story to tell, not simply to keep our interest but also to carry the message that we wish to get across.

My experience since coming to northeast Tennessee is that there are a whole host of stories told here about the past. It is, I think, this seemingly never ending supply of such stories which give the region a reputation as being in some way more historic than many other parts of our country. What I have discovered, however, is that a great many of these stories are intended to be true, and even by the tests of truth which professional historians administer, many of them are.

This emphasis on true stories about the past, as well as a carefully nurtured sense of place which has encouraged the canonization of more historic shrines than I have seen in similar sized regions, lends credence to that conception that ours is a most historic area. So, despite having no more history than any other region, northeast Tennessee is an exciting place for a historian to live and work, just as I was told when I arrived.

In part this was made clear to me as I read Brenda Calloway's fascinating account of this first American frontier. This is a story intended to be true, and it meets all the tests of truth to which it might be put. Indeed, this account seems more moving, more real, than any I have seen. Why? I have pondered this for some time, and think that I have found the answer.

This is not simply an account of the westward expansion of a people, the winning of land for a new nation. Certainly, that is a major part of the story. But this is truly the account of a frontier, "a border between two countries" or peoples as Webster prefers to call it. Ms. Calloway has not forgotten this in a rush toward the all too common hagiography of the rugged frontiersmen—and later frontierswomen—who did so much to "open up" the trans-Appalachian west to European settlement. Instead, she presents a more balanced picture of "a dramatic contest between two races who differed so radically that any accommodation was inconceivable."

This truly is a story of a frontier, a moving boundary of two peoples with divergent ways of life. The one, native to the whole of north America, feeling at home with nature, as Calloway says "depending on the woods" which it saw as an integral part of its life and not merely its livelihood. And the other, newly arrived across the mountains, seeing the land and environment not primarily as an ally but more as a challenge to be overcome, to be conquered and, in many ways, to be exploited.

Ms. Calloway tells this story well, capturing our interest and attention. But she does much more, for deep within her intended truth we can see the message that Newton's third law of motion—for every action there is an equal but opposite reaction—applies as well to peoples as it does to inanimate objects. On the first of America's vast frontiers it is a story that is especially clear, and profoundly troubling. For as we remember the great achievements of those who spread a new way of life west, we see the cost: an old way of life shattered in the balance.

While perhaps a sad story, it is also true. We may be tempted to say it was inevitable, the price of the steady march of progress. But as the east Tennessee frontier pushed back the border between these two ways of life, it also pushed us away from the boundaries of our understanding. Removed two hundred years from those days which Ms. Calloway reminds us were so vital and remain so fascinating, we would do well to remember the way of life that was lost, especially as we struggle to maintain an environment with which we can now live in peace and harmony, just as did that now lost culture of our first frontier.

Melvin E. Page
Department of History
East Tennessee State University

PREFACE

Many volumes have been written concerning the history of America's first western frontier and the people involved in it; but, surprisingly, among all these works of non-fiction, only scant information can be found pertaining to the southeastern Indian tribes, particularly the Cherokee, and the interaction between them and the early white communities of East Tennessee. This stark fact became obvious to me while preparing a series of historical articles concerning the early settlements of Upper East Tennessee for the **Johnson City Press Chronicle**, and I casually mentioned it to the city editor, Brad Jolly. After discussing my ideas with him concerning the lack of published information on this topic, Mr. Jolly encouraged me to write a book about the subject. Thus, this book which puts together in one volume, the historical facts of the early years of America's first western frontier, especially those lesser known ones.

America's First Western Frontier: East Tennessee is a history of this primitive wilderness; an account of Indians, explorers, pioneers, soldiers, and politicians. It is a narrative of the Old West across the Appalachian mountains, and the many "first" that occurred here. It is a statement of courage, dreams, and determination; a record of challenge and change.

The historical data has been gathered from works of other authors and personal interviews, with other facts gleaned from early maps, magazines, newspapers, and pamphlets. In order not to break the flow of the historical drama which took place between the whites and the Indians, there are no footnotes and internal references have been kept to a minimum. Seldom did I rely on a single source for any specific data, but rather I combined reports from several accepted accounts. I have provided internal references whenever I thought that the reader might desire more information concerning an event, or when I relied specifically on an individual historian's interpretation of an event. Whenever possible, I attempted to reconcile conflicting reports.

The history of the Cherokee Nation is so closely interwoven with the story of the white settlers of Tennessee and the white man's expansion westward that to separate the two belies the historical reality of America's first western frontier. Therefore, my purpose has been to write, as far as I was able, a definitive history of both races, bringing as needed into the volume pre-historical information on the Cherokee with which the reader might be unfamiliar. Neither time nor effort has been spared to attain this end.

I concentrated my recital of events which took place primarily within the period between 1600 to 1839—a span of time which vividly presents the westward sweep of the pioneers along buffalo and Indian trails as they moved across the eastern mountain barrier into the heart of the Cherokee country. The work includes sketches of some of the episodes of the first explorations west of the mountains and information on two decisive wars: the French and Indian and the American Revolution. It provides details of the "backcountry" settlers—those hardy traders, hunters, adventurers, and homeseekers—who encountered not only hardships and terrors in the unknown, mysterious wilderness, but who also found proud, independent, stubborn and resentful Indian tribes who resisted the ruthless advance of the white men into their forested domains.

Above all else, the purpose of this book is to promote an understanding of the role played by the inhabitants of America's first western frontier in the period of discovery, the years of settlement, the hardships of the Revolution, and during the aftermath of Independence which led to the achievement of statehood in 1796 and to the removal of the Five Civilized Tribes in 1838. It is the story of how an ambitious and venturesome people acquired, settled, and defended the land; and how a courageous and intelligent race fought that settlement and struggled for their own survival, finally being driven from their ancient homeland.

The greedy push of the white man onto Indian lands increased the Indians' resentment and brought much suffering and death to the Appalachian frontiers. What made history for the whites meant horror to the Indians. The inability of the whites and Indians to live in peace is truly shameful. The harsh treatment the Indians received and the unfortunate fate of the Five Civilized Tribes is indeed a sad part of the Southern Appalachian past. But, the story is not an isolated one; however, the United States is the only nation in history that paid the natives for the land it took from them.

The Appalachian frontier was a land soaked by much sweat, blood, and tears; a land ravished by young settlers who could not resist her beauty, the forests that perfumed her air, nor the fertility of her soil. It was a natural environment with the most ancient of titles, having a birth date beyond the reach of human record and a validity confirmed by possession. It was a land that Indian rivals fought many wars to keep, a land in which they were finally defeated and exiled.

The story of East Tennessee in the period covered is an exciting and eminently human drama—one full of heroes and villains, and of men and women not so easily classified. The story of Tennessee shows the gratitude which we owe past generations, and it is a reminder of the obligations we owe future inhabitants of the great state. Understanding our roots gives us an appreciation of the past and a valuable perspective on the future. Therefore, to those who enjoy local history and life in the mountains, those who gather their strength from the Mountain Mother, who defend her domain and see her secrets, I proudly offer **America's First Western Frontier: East Tennessee**, a narrative of the fascinating life-styles of those remarkably diverse individuals of the two races who traversed her land, settled on her fertile soil, and fought battle after battle to keep her from one another.

Love and Peace
Brenda C. Calloway
Kingsport, Tennessee
December, 1988

I
THE LAND AND ITS EARLY PEOPLE

Though occasionally darkened by a flight of wild fowl, the highland air was temperate and clear. In the forests crisscrossing the vast region there was an abundance of fruit and nut-bearing trees, covered with gnarled, woody vines whose grapes were fairly large and very sweet. The extremely fertile land was watered by numerous brooks, streams, and rivers which rambled deviously between floral banks, through the wild wood, and around romantic bluffs. The highland was indeed a limitless and beautiful country, bountifully supplied with fish, game, and fruits to satisfy one's needs as well as to delight one's senses. Commonly referred to as the **back country,** this was the western wilderness beyond the crest of the Appalachian mountains.

The original Appalachian range rose from the ocean floor about 500 to 600 million years ago during the Mesozoic era, and during long, patient centuries its tall peaks and plunging valleys have been sculpted by nature through the action of ice, lava, and water. Today's range, lower than centuries before because of erosion, begins on Canada's Gaspé Peninsula as a limestone finger only one and a half miles wide and grows to be the great Appalachian mountain system that dominates the eastern United States. It consists chiefly of a plateau fifty to two hundred miles wide which slants 3,000 miles southwest across New England and the Atlantic border states into northern Georgia and Alabama.

This great mass of plateaus, long lines of ridges, fertile valleys, and wooded mountains taken together make up the Southern region known as the Appalachian Highlands. It is often suggested that the mountains were named for the Apalachee Indians of northwest Florida because early explorers incorrectly believed this tribe lived in the highland to the north. But whatever the origin of its name, this great mountain system of the eastern United States includes several ranges and mountain groups of which the most important are: the Alleghenies, the Blue Ridge, the Cumberlands, the Black mountains, the Catskills, the White mountains, and the Green mountains of Vermont. Most of the highest peaks in the chain are located in East Tennessee.

The Great Valley of East Tennessee, America's first western frontier, is part of a larger valley—the Great Valley of the Appalachians—which extends from New York to Alabama, and consists of a broad, broken succession of many river valleys blocked from each other by crossing ridges. The Great Valley of East Tennessee, formed by a large inland sea which once flowed through the middle of Tennessee, lies between the Appalachian and Cumberland mountains. When the early colonists first entered the valley the area was the treasured hunting ground of the Cherokee Nation, but the Cherokees were not the first to live here. Primitive Asians, remote ancestors of the Cherokee, ventured into the untrodden wilderness of what is now Tennessee over 10,000 years ago, while the last great Ice Age still held the world in its grasp, but when the giant glaciers had begun to decline. Only a few hundred families of these nomadic hunters survived the long, difficult journey from the north. They were the first inhabitants of the Tennessee region and lived here longer than any other group of people. Living along the rivers and streams throughout the vast wilderness in small, isolated family groups, they progressed by trial and error. Today we call these ancient wanderers the Paleo-Indians—most ancient of the American Indians—and their culture, the Paleolithic (Old Stone Age). Evidence of their habitation has been found at a camp site known as the Lecroy site in Hamilton County. Elsewhere in Tennessee, so far thirty-one counties have yielded spear points made by these most ancient inhabitants. Nine of these counties are located in East Tennessee: Bledsoe (1), Blount (1), Hamilton (28), Johnson (1), Knox (2), Meigs (2), Roane (1), Sullivan (1), and Unicoi (1).

These Ice-Age immigrants came into North America during the Wisconsin Ice Age when massive glaciers blanketed a third of the earth's land. It was during this period, between 25,000 and 8,000 B.C., that intermittently the floor of the Bering Strait stood high and dry, forming a thousand-mile wide, land bridge linking present-day Siberia and Alaska. Small family groups seeking to keep themselves alive followed herds of wild, prehistoric mammals such as bison, saber-toothed tigers, and mammoths across the broad, rolling plain into the New World. Like a gigantic fan of humanity, these wandering clans and their descendants traveled far and wide, pursuing the ever-moving groups of land and sea animals, settling in various regions of North, Central, and South America. This Asiatic and Mongoloid division of mankind (both belong to the same racial stock) who moved unknowingly over the threshold of two huge continents, utterly devoid of human habitation, were not yet American, and not at all Indian. They were simply Old-World hunters from Siberia.

The progression of the ancient ones was not rapid; hoards of Siberians did not pour into and through the Americas. Instead, there was a slow, steady process through the glacial corridors. The inhabiting of the New World required nearly 25,000 years to spread from Alaska to Cape Horn at the southern tip of South America.

At that time, because of the great glaciers throughout the northern latitudes in both the Old and New Worlds, the shapes of the continents were different and the ocean levels were lower. In North America much of Canada and the present Great Lakes region of the United States were covered by a single, ice mass hundreds of feet thick. Immense glacial lakes around the southern borders of this ice were drained by the Mississippi river system. In the western United States, smaller ice masses capped the highest peaks of the Rockies and many of the present dry, or almost dry, basins were lakes and marshes. Tundra near the ice fronts was rich in vegetation, and the Great Plains were lush. In the eastern United States, much of the northeast, from the Great Lakes region down into the Ohio River Valley, was covered by yet another glacier thousands of square miles in width. Smaller ice masses capped the more southerly mountain chains. The plains were grassy, the valleys lush, and the forests flourished in a climate somewhat cooler than the present.

As time passed, the massive glaciers of the Wisconsin Ice Age melted, the sea levels rose, and the Bering land bridge disappeared. The Great Plains and the Desert West began to dry up. The forests of other regions were drastically altered in their composition as ranges of the large animal species were being greatly reduced. By 5,000 B.C. the ecological pattern in North America had changed completely. Thousands of generations had lived and died. The exotic Ice Age animals no longer existed. Kin of the scattered first Americans had fragmented into different tribal and linguistic stocks. Later, the Iroquois, inhabitants of what are now the North Central and Atlantic states, would become one of the most distinctive of these stocks.

The heyday of the first Americans, the "Paleo-Indians", as we call them, was 14,000 years ago during the period 12,000-8,000 B.C., and evidence of their lifeway in North America is scattered over most of the continent. Forced to adjust to new, post-glacier conditions, the Paleo-Indians developed new hunting techniques, increased incipient agriculture, and began their reliance on vegetal food stuffs. Each family was largely self-sufficient, providing for their own needs.

There were many stages of development, marked by numerous local and regional variations, through which these early people advanced. Their culture was made up of many tribes who spoke different tongues, but shared a basic way of life that formed an every-changing design. Most of the time, the cultural areas which evolved were large, and their boundaries hard to define because the lines between neighboring peoples were vague and changing. People of the same language family, moreover, were often found in more than one geographical area; conversely, individual areas contained groups who spoke different languages.

One such early culture was the Archaic, whose people became the settled hunters of the post-glacial forests. This culture was made up of numerous tribes who spoke different tongues, but shared a basic way of life. These hunters and fishermen spread far and wide throughout North America, settling along coasts, on the shores of glacial lakes, and along the banks of the great inland rivers. The Archaic era was a long one which lasted many thousands of years, beginning before the Paleo-Indian era ended and lasting, in isolated places, up to the coming of the white man. In the Tennessee region, the era is characterized by that of the "Eva" group, so named for one of their settlements near the junction of Cypress Creek and the Tennessee River in Benton County, near the present hamlet of Eva.

For the period of 8,000-5,000 B.C., the Archaic lifeway, whose major language family was Muskhogean, was primarily a southern one because at this time the northern forests offered little food for herbivores or carnivores. By 3,000 B.C., the northern forests were beginning to change, and by 5,000 B.C. much of the northern section was covered with a mixed forest that attracted both game animals and man. There in the north the major language families were Iroquoian and Algonquian.

By 3,000 B.C. the free-roaming nomadism of the early Americans had given way to a pattern of regular, seasonal movements. The Archaic Indians experimented with cultivating plants such as squashes, certain beans, peppers, and corn, but they were still essentially gatherers of wild plant foods who complemented their diet by hunting and trapping. Regular meetings of the different clans held in predictable seasonal rounds fostered the growth of social and economic ties that went beyond tribal limits. Through these meetings the cultures of the Archaic period begin to form a dynamic network that would later lead to the development of extensive trade between the tribes.

The Eastern Woodlands, an immense area extending from Canada to the Gulf of Mexico, has been the setting for a diverse array of cultures. The name indicates the main area in which the culture occurs, and the phrase "Woodland Indians" is a broad, general term for the numerous tribal groups in the region. This vast territory has its eastern and southern boundaries clearly defined by the Atlantic and the Gulf of Mexico. Elsewhere, the boundaries are somewhat obscure. In the north, the region extends to the southern limits of Canada's coniferous forests, a vague and uneven line running east to west, north of the St. Lawrence River and the Great Lakes. The western boundary is a ragged line parallel to, but generally a few miles west of, the Mississippi River.

Four of the major language families had reached this region by 1,000 B.C.: Algonquian—from north of the St. Lawrence River in the Hudson River Valley to the Ohio River Valley, and east of the Mississippi River to the Atlantic Coast; Iroquoian—from the southern limits of Canada to below the Great Lakes, then east to the northern Atlantic Coast; Siouan—from below Lakes Superior and Michigan and extending to the coasts of what is now the Virginias and the Carolinas; and the Muskhogean, in the heartland of the south—present-day Georgia, Alabama, Mississippi, and parts of Louisiana and Tennessee. As the population increased, subdivisions began to appear in these families.

In the Eastern Woodlands, for the first time, we find fixed settlements comprised of small villages. The use of the bow and arrow—which may have been invented much earlier—and grooved axes made from thick green slate obtained in the mountains were common tools of the period. There were a few domesticated plants, such as a primitive type of maize and a wild form of wheat. About 3,500 years ago, Indian corn, domesticated in Central America very early but whose origin is shrouded in mystery, reached the Eastern Woodlands. The most ancient of this grass-like wheat was a small pod-pop type whose kernels came in assorted colors— black, yellow, white, red, and blue. Special kinds of maize were used for meal, for flour, for popping, and for corn-on-the-cob. It is during this period that pottery appears for the first time. The clay containers were created with a stamping pattern, which continued as an artistic tradition practiced by the Cherokees in the Southeast until the nineteenth century. The Woodland Indians had no domesticated animals except the dog which had been domesticated about 5,400 years before.

In East Tennessee, a Greene county site found at the junction of Camp Creek with the Nolichucky River represents one of the early phases of the Woodland

4

culture—the Camp Creek phase. Here, a section of a two-thousand-year-old arrow shaft was found, proving their use of the bow and arrow.

By 1,000 B.C., in much of the Eastern Woodlands the Archaic lifeway had been abandoned, giving rise to a new way of life and to the creation of Tennessee's first permanent monuments—temple and burial mounds. During this period, which would continue until recorded history, most regions had their own individual, but interrelated, culture. The era is characterized by the construction of uncounted thousands of mounds which sprinkle the east. For the purposes of this book, this period is referred to as simply the Mound Era, and its people as the "Mound Builders." Mound building reflected the beginning changes in the increasingly complex social and religious systems of the Woodland Indians. There was a vast network of trails crisscrossing the forests, serving as channels for the spread of farming techniques, fashions, mound building, and rituals. For example, the idea of mound building, which began in the Northeast, spread far and wide among the people of the Eastern Woodlands, who built altar, burial, and temple mounds.

One culture of mound builders, beginning about 1,000 B.C. and lasting to perhaps 200 A.D., was the Adena culture, exemplified by the increasing custom of burying the dead in high places away from settlement sites, such as on sandy knolls or high ridges. Placed with the deceased were various personal objects to accompany the spirits of the dead on their last journey. This early stage of mound building was centered in present-day, southern Ohio and adjacent portions of Indiana, Kentucky, Pennsylvania, and West Virginia. It is in these burial mounds for the first time we find the tobacco pipe of a familiar shape. The pipes were made from steatite, pottery, or soapstone, and were of simple shapes with almost no decoration.

Tobacco, all species of which originated in South America, was used throughout most of the New World, being either chewed, snuffed, dipped, or smoked, depending on local custom. The smoking of tobacco by the Indians was mainly for magical or religious purposes, and only secondarily to pass time. That smoked by the Indians of the East appeared in North America by way of Mexico. Among the historic Southern tribes, wild tobacco was a carefully tended plant; its flowers as well as leaves were used in rituals. During councils, ceremonial pipe-smoking formed an integral part of the formalities as a pledge to bind peace treaties and as a rite to invoke the high gods. The English, who introduced a West Indies species into Virginia, quickly adopted tobacco after 1600. It was this Virginia tobacco, not the hardy wild species, that came to be so popular with Europeans.

In the Ohio Valley, by 100 B.C. a new culture spawned by the Adena had developed. Lasting until about 700 A.D., the "Hopewell," or "Hopewellian," stage—named for one of its sites in the Ohio Valley—was one of the most impressive ages of native people that ever existed on the continent north of Mexico. Centers of it were also in the Illinois, Mississippi, and Tennessee river valleys. Farther south, an outpost of a Hopewell-type culture existed along the Gulf Coast, and evidence of its existence is found scattered here and there inland as far west as Oklahoma. Even the early Woodland Indians, living on Camp Creek in the remote foothills of the Smoky mountains in East Tennessee, had rare objects whose inspiration was Hopewellian. Later, the culture became the initial stage of the eastern Iroquoian culture.

Though numerous, the burial mounds of East Tennessee were not as large as those of other areas. The mound builders of this section are called Hamilton Indians, being named for Hamilton county where the new culture is well represented. Even though these burial mounds are in groups, the Indians lived in straggling villages extending a mile or more along the river bank.

The culture of the mound builders in Middle Tennessee was called "Copena," a word coined from copper and galena—two minerals frequently found in the mounds of this area. The Copena people, in contrast to the Hamilton Indians' preference for shell, preferred copper ornaments. This culture was more advanced than the Hamilton and reflected a closer relationship to the Hopewellian.

Passing downstream from the Copena province, the mound era had still another expression in western Tennessee—the Harmon's Creek Indians, named for one of their sites at the mouth of Harmon's Creek in Benton county. Burial customs revealed by these mounds resemble very much those of the historic Choctaws.

In death as well as life, the Woodland Indians wore red ochre paint made from hematite, an iron ore which occurs in crystals and in a red, earthy form. Using a mortar and pestle, it was ground into powder and mixed with grease or water. Because the color of red ochre so closely resembles the color of fresh blood, most early Indians attributed magical powers to it, and used it for body and face paint, as well as to decorate all sorts of objects. Because of this red body paint, early Europeans called the Indians "peaux-rouges," or redskins.

The two centuries leading up to 700 A.D. were a dark age, perhaps connected with the fading of the great Classical Indian centers of highland Mexico, for much of the Eastern Woodlands. It was during this period that a stream of Mexican traits began to gradually flow into the region. The Mexican temple mounds, in a scaled-down form, were readily adopted by the Eastern Woodland Indians and used as altars, temples, and houses for chiefs. This widespread, temple mound building gave rise to a new, broad regional culture, the "Mississippian." It was facilitated by a general climatic change that occurred in the Mexican highlands, which narrowed the desert barrier separating Mexico from the Eastern Woodlands, allowing a population expansion northward.

The heartland of the new culture lay in the bottom lands of the Mississippi, Louisiana, Tennessee, Ohio, and Illinois river valleys. The climate and rich soil of these areas were ideal for the newly available strains of maize and Peruvian type of lintless cotton which were being grown.

Perhaps a natural route for the flow of Mississippian culture, especially its "Southern Cult" stage, into the vast Tennessee wilderness was via the Mississippi River itself. All the streams and rivers throughout Tennessee eventually reach the waters of the Mississippi. This vast network of channels, navigable by watercraft, made water transportation easy throughout nearly all times of the year.

The Tennessee, or "River of the Big Bend," is the largest avenue passing through the state. Named for an old Cherokee village, Tanasi, it is a majestic river—one of a romantic and tragic history. It was a natural communication and transportation route for the Indians and the Europeans. Beginning in the rich valley of East Tennessee, it swings southwestward in a great arc through Alabama; then, reversing its original direction, it flows northward to join the Ohio. This winding, and sometimes treacherous, river is over one thousand miles long. It divides the state of Tennessee into the three divisions of East, Middle, and West, and is its most important waterway.

When referring to the Mississippian people, we may define them—like the Woodland people—as those who shared a similar culture, regardless of what tribe or nation they belonged to, or what languages they spoke. But above all, most of them built temple mounds. The two major language families spoken in the vast Mississippian cultural region were Muskhogean, to the east of the Mississippi River, and Caddoan, to the west. No one yet has been able to trace either of these languages back to a definite place of origin; however, the traditions of the Muskhogean-speaking Indians contain legends of their migrations from some unknown, earlier homeland west of the Mississippi River. They were a numerous people who spread rapidly over the Southeast to later become the dominate southern Indian nation. The Mississippian Indians living in the Illinois and Iowa river valleys spoke the Siouan language.

As the Mississippian Culture spread to the Southeast, it was accompanied by a diffusion of elements. After about 1,200 B.C. there is running through all the later local expressions of Mississippian culture a common thread, usually called the "Southern Cult." Painted pottery, restricted to the peoples of the Eastern Woodlands, makes its appearance during the Mississippian period. Many are in two colors and apparently the techniques necessary to produce the pottery came directly from Mexico.

In Tennessee, local Mississippian artisans produced some of the finest stone sculpture of the prehistoric Eastern Woodlands. Examples of this statuary made during the area's Lamar stage of mound building are also found outside of Tennessee at sites such as the one at Etowah in northern Georgia. The temple mound age in Tennessee is characterized by Mississippian traditions and the culture's changing customs, whereas the burial mound age represents the earlier Hopewellian culture. Stemming from the Southern Appalachian Indian traditions, and combining elements of the Mississippian culture, the Lamar stage was the way of life of the Lower Creeks and Cherokees at the time that the white men first entered the Southeast. After 1600, the Lamar culture spread down to and along the Gulf Coast, giving rise to the new Pensacola cultures, and later became the way of life of the Apalachee Indians.

Throughout western Tennessee, temple mound sites are numerous along the Mississippi River and its small tributary streams. One of the most impressive sites, covering more than twenty-five acres, is on the headwaters of the Obion River in Henry County. Middle Tennessee also has its temple mound sites in the valley of the Cumberland River. One of these, the second largest in the nation, is located in Cheatham County. Lying where the Harpeth River, a branch of the Cumberland, makes two adjacent bends, it has two divisions. The entire area is over three hundred acres.

The best known, but by no means the largest, temple mound sites in Tennessee are located in the eastern part of the state. From Chattanooga northeastward into the remote valleys of the headwaters of the Tennessee River, flowed the tide of Mississippian immigrants. The Indians established medium-sized towns along the Clinch, Powell, French Broad, Pigeon, and Little Tennessee rivers, as well as along the main Tennessee. Reflecting the results of interaction that took place between the Mississippian and Woodland people, some were settled early and others much later.

One site in particular, located on Hiwassee Island at the confluence of the Hiwassee River with the Tennessee, furnishes a fairly complete picture of Mississippian life. Hiwassee Island, about seven-hundred acres in extent, had eight successive major stages of mound building which in their entirety represents four hundred years. This places the founding of the town back in the twelfth or thirteenth century, depending upon when mound building ceased. Generally, because there are no records existing of mound building in Tennessee during the early eighteenth century, the period of British colonial trade, 1700 A.D., is taken as a terminal date. The town of Hiwassee is but one of many in East Tennessee which spans the whole temple mound building stage. Although much is known of this era, one question remains unanswered concerning the people who lived on the island; "Where are their graves located?" As yet, no graves of these early Mississippian Indians have been found in eastern Tennessee, and today, whatever the reason, their whereabouts remain a mystery.

The age of temple mound building with its Mississippian traditions firmly rooted in agriculture and a strong Mexican flavor to its arts continued well into the full light of recorded history. The numerous trails and river roads which had long laced the continent would continue to be used for increased trade and contact—and inevitably pestilence flowed along them.

Such was the nature of eastern North America at the dawn of Europe's discovery of the New World.

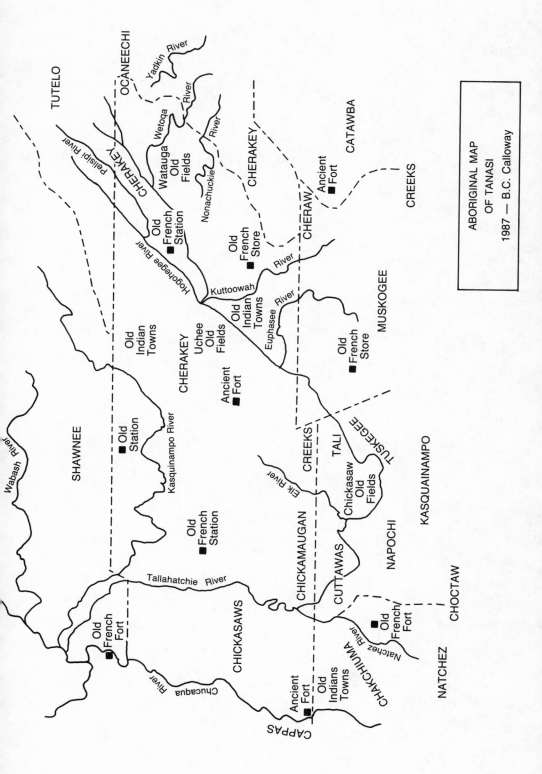

ABORIGINAL MAP
OF TANASI
1987 — B.C. Calloway

TUTELO

OCANEECHI

Yadkin River

Wetoqa River

Pelisipi River

Watauga Old Fields

CHERAKEY

Nonachuckie River

CHERAKEY

CHERAKEY

CATAWBA

Ancient Fort

CREEKS

Old French Station

Old French Store

Hogohegee River

CHERAW

River

Kuttoowah

Old Indian Towns

Euphasee River

MUSKOGEE

Old Indian Towns

Uchee Old Fields

CHERAKEY

Ancient Fort

Old French Store

Kasquinampo River

Old Station

CREEKS

TALI

TUSKEGEE

SHAWNEE

Wabash River

Elk River

Chickasaw Old Fields

KASQUAINAMPO

Old French Station

CHICKAMAUGAN

CUTTAWAS

NAPOCHI

Tallahatchie River

Natchez River

Old French Fort

CHOCTAW

Chucaqua River

CHICKASAWS

CHAKCHIHUMA

Old French Fort

NATCHEZ

Ancient Fort

Old Indians Towns

CAPPAS

9

II
EARLY INDIAN-WHITE CONTACT

Although the white man came as the last of many migrants to the shores of the Western Hemisphere, his effect was one of the darkest chapters in human history. No one will ever know how many native sons and daughters were enslaved, tortured, massacred, and exterminated. The stain is made even darker by realizing that the conflict was forced upon those who suffered; the aggressors were the whites and the scenes of tragedy, the very homeland of the victims. In this narrative of man's suppression and near annihilation of his fellow man as the whites spread through the New World, no single European nation or special group of white men was more—or less—blameworthy than others.

In fairness to the white man, there is another side of the story. From time to time, there were many individuals, groups, and even some governors of the provinces, who fought courageously on the Indian's behalf—and attempted to place white relations with the Indians on foundations of fairness. Several monarchs issued royal measures against the enslavement of the New World's natives, and religious leaders of home churches spoke out loudly and labored earnestly in efforts for them to be treated humanely. But the enforcement of such decrees issued so many thousands of miles away was often impossible. Most of the explorers and conquistadors, having braved the oceans to get rich, simply ignored the royal commands.

The Age of Discovery, which began in the latter fifteenth century, was a time of great turbulence and unrest in a Europe which had just begun to emerge from the feudalism of the Middle Ages. Protestants, profoundly influenced by the Protestant Reformation started by the German Martin Luther, were leaving the Roman Catholic Church in large numbers. And the invention of the printing press (1450) facilitated the spread of scientific knowledge.

Countries such as Portugal, Germany, and the Italian city-states were torn by political and economic strife. Spain had only just succeeded in freeing itself from nearly eight centuries of Moorish domination. The newly formed kingdom of France had internal turmoil and external warfare. England was burdened with surplus population and a period of increasingly hard times. By the end of the sixteenth century France, Spain, Portugal, and England would be attempting to establish colonies in the New World, and this relentless onslaught of European explorers, traders, and armies would take its toll on all Indians.

The Indians themselves were not wholly innocent in the complex, long conflict and intense struggle that followed Columbus' arrival in the New World. A fundamental, often overlooked, cause of the conflict was the warlike nature and bold provocations of some of the tribes which led to violence and injustice that otherwise might not have taken place. In repeated instances native leaders appealed for help from the whites against rival chiefs and clans. Indians themselves became slave catchers of their own people, overseers of other Indians, fighters in the employ of white men, and bitter enemies in tribal wars for monopoly of the traffic of European trade goods. Often they destroyed other Indian groups with relish.

Warfare and hunting were the primary occupations of Indian males. Before whites, warfare was as much a ceremony as a deadly business. Until the white man's weapons changed the character of woodland warfare, that combat was more for sport and practice than to subdue enemies. To touch a live enemy and not kill him was a great honor. It was through war that Indian men proved valor and won status. Boys were not considered men until they had participated in combat. At puberty or anytime thereafter no male was ever forced to fight, but joined his fellow comrades in war only when he felt he was ready. However, until he became a warrior no male could marry, for no woman wanted to marry a boy.

Even before the coming of the white man, societies of the woodland people were in constant change. Social and political changes came as the different groups of people gradually shifted from nomadic lifeways to a more structured way of life in permanent villages. Cultural changes resulted from the increasing trade in copper, wampum, salt, tobacco, and other items.

The Southeastern people usually had an abundance and variety of food, and their culture thrived in the pine and hardwood forests of the area. The "Great Valley" of the Appalachians teemed with wild game—buffalo, elk, bear, deer, panther, wolf, wild turkey, and many small animals—and abounded with grapes, berries, currants, wild mustard, and a variety of nuts. The trees of the forests, except where fires had produced barrens, grew thick and tall, producing deep shade. Beneath them was a heavy matting of tall grass, large ferns, and snarling vines. On the mountain heights and sides grew thick, tangled, masses of laurel, briers, and rhododendron. By reason of size and tough skin, the animal best suited to penetrate such a terrain was the buffalo; his hooves and compact weight served to beat out a trace. They were lured here by the vast meadows, extending beyond sight, the unlimited fields of cane, and the far-separated salt licks. By instinct, they chose the line of least resistance over the ranges, around mountains, through valleys, and along and across waterways. These buffalo traces were not wide—two or three feet—but served well the Indians, early explorers, wartime militia, later long-hunters, and then settlers.

The towns, fortifications, and societies of all the woodland people were a source of wonderment to the Europeans who saw them in their pristine state before the introduction of alcohol, pestilence, and guns—before their dependance upon the white man's technology. In their confrontations with whites, these indigenous people paid a dear price for progress, especially in loss of land.

The widespread Mississippian Culture continued into the full light of recorded American history; therefore, many of its people can be identified with known Indian tribes. Very few of the numerous Indian tribes in the Americas have ever been known by the names they called themselves—most names used by the whites were given by neighboring tribes. Often, a single tribe had as many different names as it had neighbors. Since the early explorers, missionaries, traders and others who came to the Americas were from different European countries, tribal names appear in many variant forms in their recorded histories of the Indians. Here the saga of the American becomes not only the archeologist's story but also the historian's.

According to ancient legends, Norsemen from Scandinavia were the first Europeans to visit the New World. Sailing from the coast of Greenland, Norse navigators chanced upon the northeastern shoulder of North America about the year 1000 A.D., where they built a temporary colony at a place abounding in wild grapes, which they named Vinland. After a short time, the settlements were abandoned and the discovery forgotten, except in Norse sagas and songs. It would be almost 500 years before other Europeans crossed the oceans to discover the unknown and unsuspecting continents of the Western Hemisphere.

The first of these Europeans to come was Columbus in 1492, seeking a cheaper route to the treasures of the West Indies. Land was sighted off the Bahamas and being certain he had found the territory he sought, Columbus named the near-naked natives "Indians." Actually, he had chanced upon a new route to the New World.

The giant bulge of South America was discovered eight years later by the Portuguese navigator Pedro Cabral. Portuguese empire builders who had acquired immense wealth from their flourishing trade routes in the East subsequently erected a large empire in the Brazilian wilderness. In 1513, two spectacular exploits were achieved by Spanish explorers. One was when, wading into the foaming waves off the Panama coast, Vasco Nunez Balboa discovered the Pacific Ocean. The other was Juan Ponce de Leon's discovery of Florida, which he thought was an island. Another Spaniard, Franciso Coronado, wandered in 1540-42 with clanking troops through present-day Arizona and New Mexico as far east as Kansas in quest of golden cities; on route the expedition discovered the Grand Canyon of the Colorado River and massive herds of bison. A few years later they would also discover Mexico. At this early date neither France or England was sufficiently unified to challenge Spain seriously as a colonizer; yet the two countries did manage to send out a few navigators who explored the coast of North America, from what is now North Carolina to Newfoundland. In the mean time, as the Spanish groping continued, rumors of golden cities and treasures, greater than any yet found, drew the conquerors to Mexico and the upper mainland.

In May, 1539, Hernando de Soto, Spanish governor of Cuba, landed on the west coast of what is now Florida with an army of six hundred to one thousand men, and they immediately struck off to the north, seeking gold and silver.

Mounted on horses, de Soto's armor-plated cavalry rode in front of the expedition; behind them, in rich silks and velvets, marched the foot soldiers; and behind them, dragged along in chains with iron collars around their necks, were several hundred

Indian slaves who carried supplies. In addition, there were numerous pigs, fowl, cattle, and ferocious Spanish hunting dogs (Mastiffs).

Lured in an errant fashion by constant rumors of riches just ahead, the expedition floundered through marshes and pine barrens from Florida through the Creek country into what is now Georgia and up the Savannah River, past the farms and villages of the Lower Cherokees. Their route was circuitous and sometimes they were lost.

The expedition wandered for three years through the Southeast, meeting Creeks, Cherokees, Chickasaws, Yuchi, Mobils, and numerous other Indian tribes. These woodland tribes received the army with ceremony and gifts, but in return the soldiers looted and burned villages; tortured and murdered native chiefs; made slaves of hundreds of hostages; and slaughtered thousands of people.

After circling through parts of what are now Georgia, South and North Carolina, Tennessee, Alabama, and Mississippi, the expedition crossed the mighty Mississippi River, wandered through present-day Arkansas and returned to the lower Mississippi, where after a short time, de Soto died of fever and wounds. His remains were secretly buried at night in the waters of the Mississippi lest the Indians mutilate the body of their abuser. In 1542, the survivors managed to make their way through Texas to Mexico.

The news of the white men's coming spread rather quickly among the native Americans and by the early sixteenth century almost all Indian tribes knew of the coming of a strange white-skinned race of men to the shores of their land, who had come in large canoes with white wings spread to the winds. As wave after wave of armed Europeans bent on riches and glory, descended on the Americas, they brought with them numerous diseases against which the Indians had no immunity. The natives were helpless before the foreigner's guns and cannons. On both continents, epidemics of smallpox, measles, influenza, dysentery, typhoid, tuberculosis, as well as other diseases, wiped out whole tribes and decimated others.

Indian traditions demanded that strangers be given hospitality, and at first they welcomed the newcomers with delight, willing to share whatever they had with them. But, in short order they saw their hospitality repaid with treachery, pillaging, slavery, rape, and slaughter. The Indians were bewildered by the ferocious hostility and lust of a people to whom they had done nothing. They watched in horror as their people died from the effects of war, disease, and persecution.

European cruelty to the Indians was motivated by their staunch religious beliefs as well as greed. Indian customs, such as ritual cannibalism, homosexuality, and human sacrifice were misunderstood and, therefore, considered abominations by the strict European Roman Catholics and Protestants who could not comprehend any religious rituals other than their own. Native languages were just gibberish to most white traders and explorers. Overdressed Europeans were shocked by the nakedness of the Indians. Considering the Indians subhuman, thousands were enslaved and forced to act as translators, porters, and servants on European expeditions. The natives were not only robbed of their gold, silver, and other treasures, but were forced to work as slaves digging out precious metals from their own mines.

To tribes in North America, the arrival all at once of European expeditions such as Hernando de Soto's with hundreds of armed men, with numerous horses, dogs, and livestock, and Indian prisoners in iron collars and chains must have seemed as devastating as Genghis Khan's invasion of the people of China four centuries earlier.

Chroniclers of the de Soto expedition in 1539-42—over half a century before the first permanent English colony was established in North America—recorded the first detailed European impressions of the Southeastern Indians, and these records furnish glimpses of the extent and influence of their Mississippian culture. At this time there were five identifiable Indian tribes living in the vast wilderness of what is now Tennessee.

The Yuchi, or Euchee, were a small group occupying the southeastern section of the Great Valley of East Tennessee and, according to some legends, parts of Middle Tennessee before the invasions of the Creeks and other Muskhogean peoples. They called themselves Tsoyaha, or "Children of the Sun." The first recorded historical mention of them is in the de Soto chronicles; the next in connection with a battle between them and Spanish soldiers in 1566. By the end of the seventeenth century, Carolina and Virginia traders operating beyond the Appalachian mountains did business with both the Yuchi and Cherokee villages in eastern Tennessee. The sudden disaster which befell the village of Chestowee on the Hiwassee River in 1714 in which every Yuchi there was killed by an invasion of Cherokee, and the ever present threat of the Cherokees and Creeks caused the Yuchi to abandon southeastern Tennessee. Some settled in what is now Georgia, while others went to present Florida.

The second group were The Shawnees, whose name in their own language means "Southerners." They were a war-like tribe who originally had dwelled near the southern shores of Lake Erie, but who were forced by the Iroquois into the Ohio Valley sometime before 1500. A later migration took them to the Cumberland River Valley in present Tennessee and to the eastern side of the Savannah River in present Georgia. The Cumberland and Tennessee rivers were sometimes shown as a single stream on early maps and labeled with the name of different tribes who lived along its banks, e.g., Hogahegee, for the Honga tribes, the Callamaco, the Acenseapi, and, sometimes, the Warioto, meaning "river of the Shawnees." The Cherokee united with the Chickasaw in 1715 to drive the mighty Shawnee out of the Cumberland region into an area beyond the Ohio River. Thereafter, both the Chickasaws and Cherokees used the Cumberland Valley area for fishing, hunting, and grazing preserves.

The third were the Chickasaws, a vigorous fighting tribe who had established themselves in what is now northern Mississippi and present western Alabama. There is evidence that in earlier times the tribe had a landing for its canoes at the Chickasaw Bluffs, near present Memphis, and two other landings higher up the Mississippi River. It is known that they had many hunting camps scattered throughout West Tennessee.

The Creek confederacy, organized long before Columbus, included more than a dozen Muskhogean and other tribes. Among the peoples who shared the Mississippian culture, theirs was the largest pre-historic intertribal alliance. Creek is not an Indian name; it originated from "Ocheese Creek," which was the English traders' name for the Ocmulgee River in what is now Georgia where the Ocheese tribe lived at the time. Gradually, the English traders, who at first referred to the tribe as "Ocheese Creek Indians," dropped the Ocheese part and merely called them "Creeks." Since this tribe was one of the most important in the confederacy, the name "Creeks" eventually was used for all tribes that belonged to the alliance. Most of the Creeks lived in present Georgia and Alabama but there were a few of their villages in what is now southern Middle Tennessee. The defeat of the Creeks and their allies was largely the result of the Yamassee War in 1715-16, a revolt against the abuses of the English trading system. When the Cherokee, who had an age-old enmity between the confederacy and themselves, were finally induced to join the British, the power of the Creeks was broken. Outlying villages were abandoned, and many Creek tribes migrated south to Florida to become the nucleus of the Seminole nation.

The fifth tribe in Tennessee during de Soto's expedition were the Cherokee, a tribe discussed more fully in a later chapter. It was the largest single tribe in the South, and one of the largest of all tribes north of Mexico. In the early 1500's, they had an estimated population of over 15,000. By the mid-sixteenth century nearly all tribes other than the Cherokee, had been driven out of what is now Tennessee; therefore, the Cherokee claimed all of this vast wilderness as their sacred hunting ground, and they were the tribe in possession of the land when the first Europeans entered the Great Valley of East Tennessee.

But regardless of the claims the various tribes made to portions of the Southeast, de Soto took possession of the new territory and its inhabitants in the name of the Spanish Crown. Thus through the explorations of de Soto and other Spaniards, by the end of the sixteenth century Spain had succeeded in Peru and Mexico, made beginnings in what is now Florida, and claimed a tremendous empire spreading from California to the Floridas on the north, to the southern tip of South America. She had become the dominant colonizing and exploring power, and would remain as such until the seventeenth century. By 1574—thirty years before the first English settlers—there were about two hundred Spanish cities and towns located in North and South America.

In the far Northeast the situation was different, for the French met the Indians in a friendly manner and opened trade with them. France relinquished all claim to the Floridas in 1565 after the Spanish destroyed the French fort at St. Augustine, killing or capturing nearly all the Frenchmen in that territory. Having failed in their attempts to settle in established Spanish territories in the Floridas, France turned toward the Northeast, but it still would be thirty-eight years before they succeeded in establishing a permanent colony in the New World.

The French, with their proverbial aptitude for diplomacy, managed to make themselves as loved and accepted by the American natives as the Spanish had made themselves feared and hated. Frenchmen, keeping all promises made to the Indians, established themselves as trustworthy; thus, they were permitted to pass safely through tribal territories, and even to live among them as traders.

The permanent beginnings for a vast French empire was finally established in 1608—the year after Jamestown—at Quebec, the rocky sentinel commanding the St. Lawrence River. The leading figure was Champlain, who later became known as the "Father of New France." He and other Frenchmen entered into friendly relations—a fateful friendship—with the Algonquian Indians. Later, yielding to their pleas, the French would join them in battle against their foes, the federated

Iroquois tribes of the upper New York area, thereby earning the lasting enmity of all the Iroquois tribes.

By 1676, France was firmly entrenched in Canada. During the seventeenth century, "New France" (Canada) gradually spread outward from Quebec, along the St. Lawrence, the Great Lakes, and the Mississippi River as far as the Gulf of Mexico.

England, at first content with her fisheries in Newfoundland, was relatively slow in joining the steady stream of newcomers to the New World. Although several attempts at colonization were made, it was nearly one hundred years after the voyages of Columbus before she seriously took any part in the affairs of North America and created a permanent colony.

Early in the seventeenth century, after the death of Queen Elizabeth and peace with Spain was obtained, the seeds of a mighty nation were planted. England finally established her first permanent colony in 1607, at Jamestown, in what is now the state of Virginia. On the wooded banks of the James River, the spot was easy to defend against Indians and Spaniards. The area was ruled by Powhatan, the powerful chief of an Algonquian-speaking confederacy whose borders extended from the Potomac River almost as far south as Albemarle Sound in what is now South Carolina. Here, the English sought neither gold nor slaves, only to tame their new and frequently hostile environment. Nevertheless, frequent conflicts, often as the result of the colonists' greed, arose as they sought to take possession of more and more land.

Over the span of thirty-one years, England would colonize the entire Atlantic Seaboard, and in 1733 she would plant the inland colony of what is now Georgia, making a total of thirteen colonies. As a buffer colony, Georgia served to protect the more valuable Carolinas from the vengeful Spaniards in the Floridas, and the hostile French in Louisiana. It would be a vital link in imperial defense when later wars broke out between Spain and England. Thus, unknowingly, the British Crown, with its thirteen colonies, had made the first notable milestone on the long and rocky road toward colonial unity and the formation of a new nation.

Between 1660 and 1763, the Spanish controlled what is now Florida, and the French held the Mississippi Valley. British subjects were not welcome in the domain of the two Roman Catholic powers. Therefore, the British confined their exploits to the tribes living between the Floridas and the Ohio Valley and between the Appalachian mountains and the Atlantic Seaboard.

The newly arrived Europeans, by conquest and pestilence, in short order had destroyed the rich and flourishing culture of the Eastern Woodlands. By 1660, the Algonquian tribes had greatly declined in number and importance. Many tribes from the Atlantic to the Mississippi River were simply dispersed west or destroyed by the European invaders and the diseases they brought with them. The Cherokees had located in the Appalachian mountains, in the region where the present states of North Carolina, South Carolina, Georgia, and Tennessee nearly join. The Lower Creeks inhabited the Piedmont of Georgia. The Woodland Indians, as well as other tribes, realized their world was slipping away, their customs eroding, and their numbers diminishing. Recognizing their way of life was being destroyed, they bewailed the inevitable loss of identity.

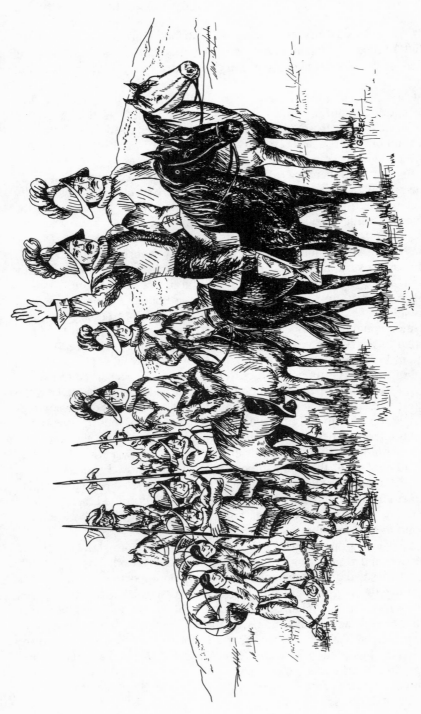

De SOTO'S EXPEDITION

Amid the marshes and pine barrens of the Southeast (1540-41), de Soto's soldiers and their "native" slaves march north in search of rumored gold. The expedition, begun in Florida, wandered through the Southeast for nearly three years meeting numerous Indian tribes, in their search for "riches". De Soto's armor-plated cavalry—mounted on horses and walking—with Indian captives dragged along in chains, numerous farm animals, and ferocious hunting dogs, was a terrifying sight to any natives who encountered them.

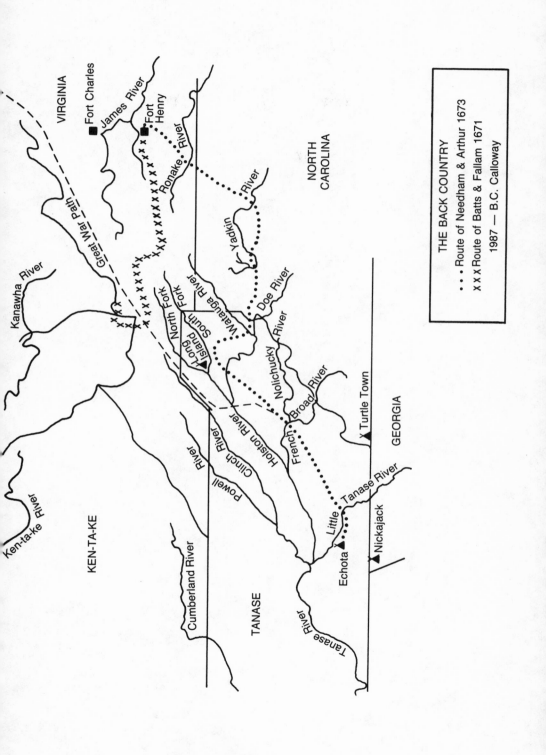

THE BACK COUNTRY

• • • Route of Needham & Arthur 1673
x x x Route of Batts & Fallam 1671

1987 — B.C. Calloway

VIRGINIA

Fort Charles

James River

Fort Henry

Ronake River

NORTH CAROLINA

Yadkin River

Doe River

Kanawha River

Great War Path

Ken-ta-ke River

KEN-TA-KE

Cumberland River

Powell River

Clinch River

Holston River

North Fork

South Fork

Long Island

Watauga River

Nolichucky River

Broad River

French

TANASE

Tanase River

Little Tanase River

Echota

Nickajack

X Turtle Town

GEORGIA

III
THE TENNESSEE BACKCOUNTRY

The Appalachian mountains, stretching from New York to Alabama, form a natural barrier which separates the Atlantic seaboard from its vast interior valley. During the American colonial period, this Great Valley of the Appalachians was known as the "Backcountry," or "Old West." Here, in the first half of the eighteenth century, poured stream after stream of German and Scotch-Irish immigrants. They moved into the backcountry of New England, the valley of southeastern Pennsylvania, central and western Maryland, the Piedmont of Virginia and the Carolinas, and the Valley of Virginia.

The Great Valley of East Tennessee was the southern section of the Old West and where the first permanent settlements were made. Its rich soil, swift streams, mild climate, and boundless forests were irresistible attractions to the early colonists on the Atlantic seaboard.

As far as records disclose, James Needham and Gabriel Arthur were the first Englishmen to see the Great Valley of East Tennessee. They were in a party sent out by Colonel Abraham Wood in 1673 from Fort Henry, a fortified trading post he maintained in the Virginia colony which served as a combination of frontier town, military fort, and trading post located at the falls of the Appomattox River on the present site of Petersburg, Virginia. The purpose of the expedition was twofold. Needham and Arthur were to explore the mysterious frontier which lay west of the Southern Appalachians, and they were to establish a trading path with the Cherokees between the Overhill's capital of Echota and the Virginia colony.

The route they traveled followed buffalo and Indian trails leading southwestwardly along the well-established Occanoechi path; thence passing from the waters of the Catawba to the Yadkin; up Buffalo Creek; past the site of the present town of Boone, North Carolina; along another well-worn Indian path, coming into the Tanasi territory at its northeastern corner through a gap in the Alleghenies to the Watauga; down that stream; up the Great Buffalo Trail which follows Buffalo Creek and goes around the end of Buffalo Mountain; past the bold spring (on the present Tipton-Haynes tract in Johnson City, Tennessee); down Cherokee Creek to the

21

Nolichucky; and down the valley to and over the French Broad; thence on to the Cherokee Indian town on the Little Tennessee River.

Their arrival in Echota greatly excited the Cherokees, and they were well received by the chief. The horse they brought was a curiosity to the Indian because horses would not be introduced among them until the beginning of the next century. Needham and Arthur visited and traded in the Cherokee villages for several weeks; then, needing more trade goods and wanting to report to Colonel Wood, Needham in the company of twelve Cherokees returned to Fort Henry, leaving young Arthur with the villagers to learn their language.

After a short rest, Needham with his Cherokee friends and an Occaneechi guide, Hasecoll or Indian John, set out on the second outbound journey. One night while encamped at the fork of the Yadkin River, Indian John quarreled with Needham, shot him in the head, quickly scalped him, ripped open his chest, tore out his heart, and holding it up in his bloody hand as he turned eastward, shouted defiance at the whole English nation. He then flung the still-convulsing heart at the feet of the startled Cherokees, and commanded them to kill Arthur when they reached home as he himself rode off to his people on Needham's horse.

The frightened Indians hurried to their village and reported what had happened. In the resulting confusion, some friends of the Occaneechi seizing on the absence of the chief, grabbed Arthur, bound him to a stake, and heaped dried cane about him. A Weesock Indian living among the Cherokees threw his lit torch onto the pyre. At that moment, the chief with rifle on his shoulder walked into the village and killed the Weesock. He then stamped out the fire, cut Arthur's thongs, and sent the young man to his own hut for safety.

A short time later, promising to escort Arthur home in the spring, the chief sent him out with a war and hunting party. They roamed as far south as the Apalachee country in West Florida, then trekked northward to Port Royal on the Carolina coast, from there to the valley of the Great Kanawha (in present West Virginia), and returned to Tanasi on the ancient war-trail through Cumberland Gap. Because of this excursion, Gabriel Arthur is credited with being the first white man to see the land of Kentucky (called Ken-ta-ke by the Iroquois, meaning ''Prairie'' or ''Meadow Land''). The last journey made by Arthur was one of ten days down the Tennessee River; thus, he was also the first white man to navigate this great waterway, so far as extant records indicate. Finally, in May of 1674, Arthur was taken back to Fort Henry by the friendly Cherokee chief.

A coincidence—one of the most striking in the history of Tennessee—is the fact that at about the same time the Needham party first pressed a foot on Tanasi soil, two Frenchmen, Marquette and Jolliet, caught their first view of the region from their birch canoe at the mouth of the Arkansas; they were the first Europeans to see the entire coast of West Tennessee. Another Frenchman, La Salle, arrived at the Chickasaw Bluffs in 1682 and there built the first fortification on Tennessee soil, Fort Prudhomme, at the mouth of the Hatchie River (present-day Memphis). This courageous fur trader claimed for France all of the land drained by the Mississippi River, which of course included present-day Tennessee.

Close on the trail of these early explorers followed ambitious fur traders, adventurous long hunters, and courageous settlers. The glowing accounts given by these transients about the paradise of the west only served to whet the pioneer's appetite for land. The beauty of the Appalachian West beckoned to their souls just as the seductive singing of the Grecian sirens lured the ancient mariners, and they would find her just as irresistible.

The stage was set, the script prepared, the players selected, and the play began to unfold. The plot would be a dramatic contest between two races who differed so radically that any accommodation was inconceivable. It was to be a conflict from which even surrender could bring no release, and would climax when both victor and vanquished would realize too late what both were losing. Although we already know the outcome of this story and how inevitable that outcome was, the drama is still worth the watching.

The year 1760 opened the decade of the "long hunters," men dazzled by tales about the new country who burned with a desire to see it for themselves. To them the wild land of the first Old West beckoned with an irresistible fascination. The typical long hunter was a product of the outer frontier; essentially he was a farmer-hunter, knowledgeable in the ways of the forest and trained at an early age to the use of the long rifle and other hunting skills. In hunting he combined sport with utility, adding meat to the larder with profits coming from the skins, tallow, and meat of animals slain or trapped. Deciding to leave home, he did not have to make great preparations. He only picked up his rifle, bullet pouch, powder horn, knife, and hatchet and stepped from the edge of his corn patch into the woods. From there on he was in the wilderness, on his own, and could live off the land indefinitely. Usually long hunts occurred during the winter months so that the meat could be more easily preserved. The long hunters went alone, or in pairs, on treks which lasted from several months to as long as a year. For some this restlessness and great love of adventure became an engrossing passion.

The daring and courageous Appalachian frontiersmen who ventured on long and longer hunts became famous pioneers in both Tennessee and Kentucky. Knox, Stone, the Crocketts, the Bledsoes, and others spent many months in the treasured hunting ground of the Cherokee—hunting, exploring, and trapping. Numerous rivers, mountains, and other sites were named by them and in honor of them: the Holston River for Stephen Holston; Duncan Clinch named Clinch River; Eaton's Ridge honors Amos Eaton; Boone's Creek was named for Daniel Boone; Powell River and Valley were named for Ambrose Powell; and Stone's River for Uriah Stone. The first settlers who made the break over the mountains were distinguished from the long hunters only in that they brought a family along, built a cabin instead of a lean-to, and planted a corn patch.

Without a doubt, the principal routes used by the Indians and later by the white men date back to the ancient traces where the sagacious buffalo broke the way and made location. Indians adopted these paths as their trails, and the pioneers made them their roads. Early traders, hunters, and settlers would sometimes blaze trees along a path so seasonal changes could not confuse them if they decided to make the return journey by that route and guide others outbound.

Perhaps the greatest buffalo-Indian trail was the Great War Path, also called the Great Warrior's Path, which was the major artery joining the northern and southern Indians. From the accounts of early French traders and long hunters, this route was the one taken by the northwestern Indians when going to war with other nations in the south, and by the southern tribes on retaliatory raids. After

This is where the first skirmish of the Battle of Long Island Flats occurred. Leads toward Eaton's Fort site and the Long Island Road.

South fork of the Holston River. Vicinity of present-day Kingsport, TN.

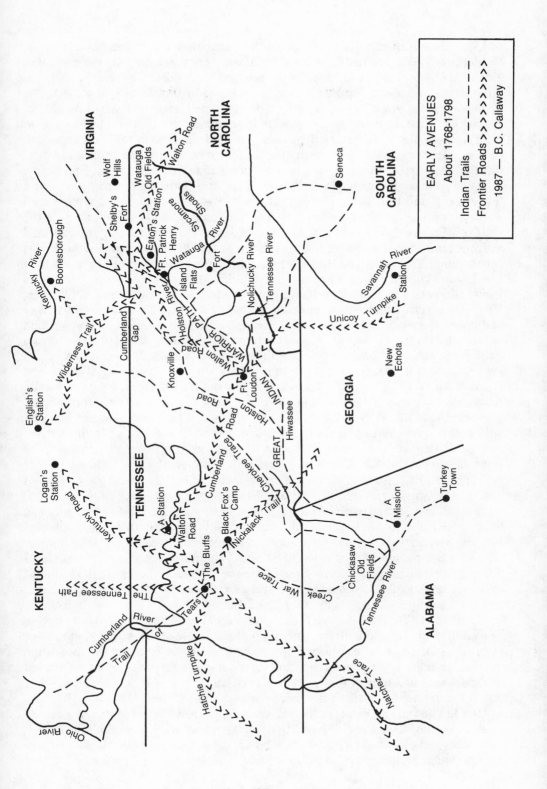

EARLY AVENUES
About 1768-1798
Indian Trails — — — —
Frontier Roads >>>>>>>
1987 — B.C. Callaway

VIRGINIA

NORTH CAROLINA

SOUTH CAROLINA

GEORGIA

KENTUCKY

TENNESSEE

ALABAMA

Kentucky River

Boonesborough

Wolf Hills

Shelby's Fort

Watauga Old Fields

Eaton's Station

Ft. Patrick Henry

Walton Road

Sycamore Shoals

Watauga River

Island Flats

Fort

Nolichucky River

Tennessee River

Seneca

Savannah River

Unicoy Turnpike

Station

English's Station

Wilderness Trail

Cumberland Gap

Holston River

PATH

WARRIOR

Knoxville

Walton Road

Holston Road

Ft. Loudon

INDIAN

GREAT

Hiwassee

New Echota

Logan's Station

Kentucky Road

A Station

Walton Road

Cumberland Road

Cherokee Trace

Black Fox's Camp

Nickajack Trail

A Mission

Turkey Town

The Bluffs

Cumberland River

Trail of Tears

The Tennessee Path

Creek War Trace

Chickasaw Old Fields

Tennessee River

Hatchie Turnpike

Natchez Trace

Ohio River

25

1775, a section of this path was given the name Boone's Wilderness Trail, or Wilderness Road, and as the white settlements crept southward, the road was extended by the settlers until it finally reached Knoxville, Tennessee, in 1792. Another war trace much used by the Cherokees led from the mouth of the Little Tennessee to the French Lick on the Cumberland, the present-day site of Nashville, Tennessee. Passing over the Cumberland mountains, leading southwestward to the Tennessee River, it became the pioneer's road from East to Middle Tennessee. In West Tennessee there were many trails of the mound builders connecting their fortified villages. These trails were used by later Indian tribes and by the Europeans.

There were many other traces, some minor, too numerous to mention, but a few are referred to at other places in the text. Every one led to some other trail passing north to the Great Lakes, south to the South Atlantic seaboard, or to the Gulf of Mexico. Nearly every trail described above became a wagon road, and many became the route of later highways or railways. No wagon reached the Tanasi country until 1761 when the Virginia militia under the command of Major Andrew Lewis cut a road for the transporting of supplies. Prior to the completion of the Island Road, as it was called, reliance was upon packhorse. Starting in Chilhowie, Virginia, several hundred axemen at the head of the expedition cleared the way and traced the road. Behind them followed a caravan of packhorses, wagons and cannon. It was the fall of the year and autumn had begun to transform the forests into a hugh canvas of brilliant colors with ever changing hues and tones. The green laurel and somber pine contrasted magnificently with the golden sugar maple and crimson sumac. The axemen forged among the dangerous cliffs, over creeks and rivers, up the rocky masses of hills, and over lofty summits into and through the inner depths of the wilderness. At last, the militia reached a broad valley covered with buffalo grass and studded with chestnuts and pawpaws. For a few more miles they continued west, marching directly to the sacred island of the Cherokees, the Long Island of Holston. There they paused for the lengthy and arduous task of building Fort Robinson—the second English fort built on Tennessee soil—, located nearly opposite the east end of the Long Island on the north bank of the Holston. Afterward, hunters and explores came in even greater numbers, and families began to come in order to till the soil of the rich fertile valleys and to establish homes.

It was the early explorers, fur traders, wartime militia, and later long hunters who told the people of North Carolina and Virginia of the natural paradise of America's first western frontier—East Tennessee. Thereafter, every ragged colonist in Virginia and the Carolinas (and some as faraway as Maryland and eastern Pennsylvania) increasingly saw the Appalachian West as a veritable pot of gold.

In the fall of 1763, one hundred-fifty four years after Jamestown and only twelve years before the Revolution, the American colonies were still but a long, threadlike strip along the Atlantic seaboard. Colonial settlement had halted at the foot of the mountains; there was no more free land for the taking. After numerous wars most of the Indians had moved to the other side of the Appalachians, and France had ceded her immense North American dominions to England.

After the Fourth and Final conflict between England and France during the decade of the long hunters, King George III issued a proclamation forbidding British settlement and colonial land grants beyond the crest of the Appalachians: a natural barrier which divided English America into two parts, an eastern and a western section; a rampart between the seaboard and the great interior valley. The royal edict stated that beyond the crest of the Appalachians, from Maine to Georgia, on territory washed by the "western waters" the land was reserved for the Indians, and Europeans already beyond the Line were to remove themselves. Thus, England hoped to avoid the expense of recurrent Indian wars and to nip in the bud any great migration of colonists into the western wilderness.

Several nations applauded. As a result of the war Spain had inherited the entire region west of the Mississippi, including the French city of New Orleans established by de Bienville in 1718. She realized any movement of colonist across the mountains posed a tremendous threat. The Indian Nations, although often at war, were all in contact with each other, and were united in their fierce opposition to any further advance of the white frontier. France which still retained residual advantages over the Indians, a French town on the St. Lawrence, and traders living in wilderness villages scattered throughout the interior resolved to recover her empire. She knew, however, that intrusion by settlers into the central valley would close the way forever.

In the colonies, the average person saw the boundary as a way of forestalling Indian wars and as a way of keeping the vengeful Indians back. But needless to say, on the whole this "Proclamation Line" was highly unpopular. Some colonies claimed vast territories in the west and colonial legislatures, behind which were the interest of land speculators and western settlers beyond the Line, rejected the edict. Those few beyond the Line, refused to move back.

Fringes of English settlement in the Carolinas had reached the Appalachian foothills, and those in Virginia were spilling over into the Kanawha and Holston valleys. After the Proclamation of 1763, these border people hesitated, but only briefly, as they stepped across the invisible boundary line at the crest of the various ridges to take up land washed by the western waterways. Thus fifty miles west of the Line in the vast, unexplored wilderness of what would later become Tennessee, a small group of permanent buildings was being raised on land already cleared by the Indians not far from the Watauga River on the Watauga Old Fields, near present-day Elizabethton, Tennessee. The Watauga is a stream which flows from the Allegheny mountains and empties into the Holston River from the south. Its name is from the Creek word "Wetoga," or broken waters. Near its junction with the Doe River above Sycamore Shoals was a rich open valley—ancient Indian fields which had been cleared by them in remote times. This locale was commonly known as the "Watauga Old Fields," so called because when the first settlers arrived there early in 1769 the bottom lands were found to contain graves and numerous ancient remains of a former Indian town. Tradition ascribes these remains to the Cherokee, whose nearest settlements were then many miles southward.

Living on the Watauga was not safe, and land holdings were not legitimate. Those who went out into the unknown, mysterious Tanasi wilderness did so at the peril of their lives. Sometimes whole families disappeared without a trace ever being found. Many paid the extreme penalty for their hardihood, such as Jesse Duncan who is credited with being the first white man to die and be buried on Tennessee soil. In 1765, while traveling with a scouting party from Buffalo Mountain toward the Boone's Creek area, he lagged behind. After a time, realizing he was no longer with them, the hunters went back to search, and found that he had been killed and scalped by the Indians. Today, just a few miles north of Boone's Creek, Tennessee, a marker indicates the site of his grave.

Clearings were widely scattered and neighbors were miles apart. A few settlers were at Wolf Hills (present-day Abington, Virginia); some were at the Long Island of Holston where Fort Robinson had been built in 1760; and later in 1768 an exploring expedition moved down the Holston as far as present-day Rogersville, Tennessee. Before long, these pioneers were filtering south toward the Watauga and beyond. All of the newcomers were squatters on Indian land, just as the earlier long hunters had been poachers, and the surveying parties had been trespassers. In a brief span of time, a transition had brought about the mysterious materialization on the border scene—men and women of a sort hitherto unknown now existed, the Frontier People.

Credited with being the first white man to die on Tennessee soil in 1765. Gravesite is approximately 2 miles east of Rocky Mount.

MURDER OF JAMES NEEDHAM

While encamped at the ford of the Yadkin River Needham and his Occaneechi guide, Indian John, quarreled. Quickly, Indian John shot Needham, scalped him, and tore open his chest. Then ripping out the heart, he turned eastward; shaking the still pulsing heart, Indian John shouted defiance at the whole English nation. Frightened, the Cherokees and other Indians with the party ran to their village to report what had happened. Indian John rode off on Needham's horse.

IV
THE CHEROKEES

By the time of the coming of the Unakas, or white men, the prehistoric Cherokee people had developed an advanced culture probably exceeded only by the Mayan and Aztec groups of the Southwest. This mysterious tribe—whose origin is lost and whose name is inexplicable—were the aborigines of present Tennessee, or at least the tribe in possession of this land when the first Europeans came. The history of the Cherokee Nation is so closely interwoven with the story of the first white settlers in Tennessee and the white man's expansion westward that to separate the two would be ludicrous. It would be almost impossible to relate the Old West story without inclusion of that of the Cherokee.

Between 1540 and the early nineteenth century the people of the Cherokee Nation reached a higher peak of civilization than any other North American tribe. For the most part, however, the Cherokee's conquest of civilization was an agonizingly slow, erratic, and grievous process. These Indians of the southern Appalachians, fiercely devoted to their mountain homeland, were forced by circumstances to forego their ancient lifeway and to concentrate on the problems posed by the whites. For following their first encounter with Europeans (the de Soto expedition in 1540), Cherokee recorded history is fused with the problems initiated by the white man. Being forced to cope with these unwanted problems at a time of sudden thrust towards cultural growth and progress led to the near annihilation of the whole Cherokee Nation. From the silent recesses of the past, down the corridors of time, the lamentation of the Cherokee—a dirge heralding the infinite pathos of a vanishing race—echoes and re-echoes throughout the hills and valleys of the southern Appalachians.

Over ten thousand years ago, when the giant glaciers of the last Ice Age had begun to wane, remote ancestors of the Cherokee drifted from Asia to the North American continent across the dry sea bed of the Bering Strait, now called Beringia. The inherent need of survival, not a pioneering spirit spurred these wandering hunters of Siberia. They came seeking to keep themselves alive by following herds of now-extinct prehistoric animals. It took thousands of years for the forefathers

31

of the Cherokee to reach what now constitutes the Eastern United States. Today, the seas roll again over the ancient land where the Indian saga began.

The obscurity of Cherokee tribal origin suggests their ancestors were not mindful of history; therein they differed from other ancient North American tribes who before the coming of white men pictured their history on Walam Olum, an ancient hieroglyphic bark record, wove it on Wampum, i.e., strings or belts of wampum beads arranged into significant designs, and instilled it in the memories of shamans, those men singled out in childhood and trained in the revered mores of the tribe. But even though the Cherokees cannot explain their origin, they once had a dim oratory of a long, mass migration. Until the nineteenth century, shamans, or priests, recited the saga of Cherokee tribal migration every August at the Green Corn Ceremony. Then, for unknown reasons, the migration tradition was deleted from orations delivered by the shamans, and by the early nineteenth century, this facet of oral history was barely remembered by the eldest member of the Cherokee Nation. Today it is lost in the ages of time. Lacking records of their origin, the tribe is not easily identified with any prehistoric culture of the Southeast; therefore, the Cherokees are compelled to reconstruct their pre-recorded past from extant traditions, archaeological facts, and linguistic data.

The proper name of the Cherokee, that which they call themselves, is **Ani-yun-wiya**, signifying principal people. The name Cherokee by which they are commonly known has no meaning in their own language (although there were three different dialects), and seems to be of foreign origin. Used among themselves the form is **Tsa'lagi** or **Tsa'ragi**, which may be a corruption of the Delaware word **Talligewi**. There is other evidence that the name was derived from the Choctaw word **choluk** or **chiluk**, signifying a pit or cave, and this theory is borne out by the Iroquoian name for the Cherokee, **Oyata'ge ronon**, signifying "inhabitants of the cave country." Perhaps the name came from the Portuguese word Chalaque, used in the narratives of de Soto, or from the French word Cheraqui, found on a French document; or even perhaps it comes from the English word chera. One or all of these words could have been corrupted into the name Cherokee by the English-speaking people. Although there has been much dispute concerning the name itself, there seems no longer reasonable doubt as to the identity of the people.

The most ancient tradition concerning the Cherokees is apparently that recorded in the Delaware's Walam Olum, which mentions both a prehistoric migration of the Cherokee and an account of that tribe's expulsion from the north. According to the Walam Olum and legends of other northern tribes, the Cherokee originated in the country of the upper Allegheny and Ohio rivers. At one time, the rivers of the Allegheny and Ohio were considered as one, and were named for the tribes living along their banks, the **Alligewi** or **Talligewi**. The Cherokee were the largest, most advanced, and except for the Iroquois, the most powerful of all the northeastern tribes. In the Walam Olum we find the Delawares advancing from the northwest until they come upon a river, probably the upper Ohio. On the other side were the **Talligewi** who possessed the east. Desiring the eastern land, the Delawares decided upon war. The independent and willful Tallegewi, or prehistoric Cherokees, defended themselves so well that at last the Delawares were obliged to seek the assistance of their northern friends, the Iroquoian tribes. The warfare continued for many years throughout the reigns of four successive Delaware chiefs before the **Talligewi** finally received a crushing defeat. The survivors fled south down the river into the cave country of the Allegheny region. The land they had abandoned was parceled out amongst the invaders—the allied Iroquoian tribes took the northern portion about the Great Lakes while the Delaware took possession of that south of the lakes. Later, under continued hostile pressure from the north, the Cherokees would again be forced to remove themselves farther to the south. The traditions of the Cherokee, as far as they have been preserved, supplement and corroborate those of the northern tribes, thus bringing the stories down to the Cherokees' final settlements in the southern Appalachian Highlands. The ancient remains of the Cherokee tell us that they were long-time inhabitants of the Southeast, and archaeological evidence reinforces the ancient northern traditions of the Cherokee and indicates that their culture—as we know it—developed in the Appalachian mountains.

Linguistically, the Cherokee are related to the Iroquois, but their languages are so dissimilar that linguists believe the two tribes have been separated for a very long time (at least 3,500 years). Basic similarities do exist, however, indicating that both languages descended from a common tongue. It is assumed, therefore, that the Cherokees and the Iroquois were once a single people who separated from each other in the distant past.

The original Appalachian frontier of the Cherokee Nation covered about 40,000 square miles, embracing portions of eight present states: the northern parts of Alabama, Georgia and South Carolina; western North Carolina and Virginia; the southern section of West Virginia; and the eastern portions of Tennessee and Kentucky. The territorial claims of early Indians were not always definite because there were no fixed boundary lines. On every side the Cherokee claims of land were contested by rival claimants. On the northeast, the Cherokees were held in check by the Powhatian and the Monacan. To the east and southeast, the Cheraw, Tuscarora and Catawba were inveterate enemies of the Cherokee. In the south were the Muskogee and a hereditary war with the Creeks, who claimed nearly the whole of upper Georgia. Toward the west and southwest, the Shawnee on the Cumberland River and the Chickasaw on the lower Tennessee River repeatedly turned back the tide of Cherokee invasion. In the far north, the powerful Iroquois held an almost unchallenged claim from the Ottawa River of Canada southward to at least the Kentucky River.

Before the intrusion of white men, the population of these "mountaineers" (as Cherokee were called by the Iroquois) numbered 15,000 to 25,000 people who lived in some fifty-five to eighty-five settlements on both sides of the Appalachian summit region. Their villages were located on the headwaters of river systems flowing west, south, and east out of the mountainous area.

Cherokee men were of medium height and muscular. Their complexion was bronze with a copper tint, but the "red man" label given to the Indians by the Europeans was because of the red paint used on their faces and bodies during war and at certain ceremonial dances, not because of their complexion. The men had a long face, with a broad forehead; a flat or aquiline nose; high, prominent cheekbones; and a square jaw. Their heads were shaved except for a patch of hair—ornamented with beads, feathers, porcupine quills, or other trinkets—which was left dangling from the crown. There was little or no hair on their faces or any

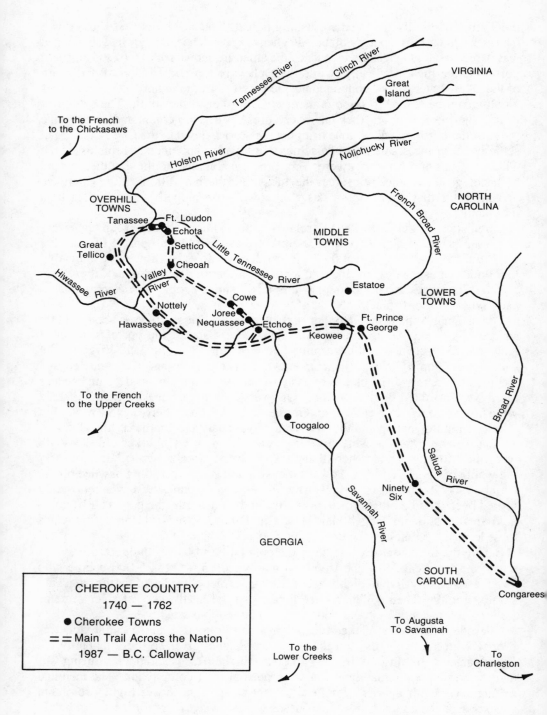

To the French
to the Chickasaws

VIRGINIA

Great
Island

Tennessee River

Clinch River

Holston River

Nolichucky River

NORTH
CAROLINA

OVERHILL
TOWNS

French Broad River

Tanassee

Ft. Loudon

Echota

Great
Tellico

Settico

Cheoah

Little Tennessee River

MIDDLE
TOWNS

Hiwassee River

Valley
River

Cowe

Estatoe

LOWER
TOWNS

Nottely

Joree

Nequassee

Etchoe

Ft. Prince
George

Hawassee

Keowee

To the French
to the Upper Creeks

Broad River

Toogaloo

Saluda River

Savannah River

Ninety
Six

GEORGIA

SOUTH
CAROLINA

Congarees

CHEROKEE COUNTRY

1740 — 1762

● Cherokee Towns

═ ═ Main Trail Across the Nation

1987 — B.C. Calloway

To Augusta
To Savannah

To the
Lower Creeks

To
Charleston

34

other part of their bodies. Both sexes shaved their pubic region. Several of both sexes tattooed their faces and other parts of their bodies, filling the lines with ashes or gunpowder. At home the males wore a shirt of buckskin hanging to the knees, which became known among whites as the "Cherokee hunting shirt." They wore an undergarment, a breechcloth or flap, of animal skin; sometimes this was their outer garment as well. They wore deerskin moccasins which occasionally were made like short boots, reaching to mid-calf. While on hunting trips or in cold weather, they also wore leather leggings that resembled loose trouser legs. A large, mantle-type, long coat was draped over their shoulders. Because the Cherokee wore only the barest necessities when on the war trail, these clothes and any jewelry were left at home.

Cherokee women were usually tall and delicately built with small hands and feet. Their complexion was somewhat fairer than that of the men. Their faces were oval shaped and their straight, jet-black hair was worn long. They either braided their hair or folded it into a club at the back; trinkets such as ribbons or beads were used for adornment. Except for their eyelashes and the hair of their head, women plucked the hair from their bodies. In summer, they wore short, leather skirts, a short waistcoat, and deerskin moccasins; sometimes they went without the waistcoat. In winter, the buckskin skirt was longer, reaching to mid-calf, and a shoulder mantle was added for warmth. They also wore leather leggings or short, boot-like moccasins reaching almost to the knee. In addition, both sexes had a number of ceremonial costumes and clothes made from feathers, or furs for cold weather. Dignitaries in all the towns had elaborate apparel befitting their official offices. Cherokee children when small went unclad. At about age ten, the females— and males at puberty—began to wear clothing similar to those of their parents.

There were three main geographical divisions of the Cherokee Nation which corresponded roughly to the three principal dialects of their language. The Lower Towns were along the Savannah and Tugaloo rivers and their tributaries in north-eastern Georgia, as well as at the headwaters of the Keowee River in northwestern South Carolina. The now extinct Lower, or Eastern dialect, (properly the Elati dialect) was spoken in this division until the late nineteenth century. The Middle Towns—the very heart of the nation—were located in the Smoky mountains, along the Tuskasegee River, and the upper Little Tennessee and its tributaries in western North Carolina. The Middle dialect (properly designated as the Kituhwa dialect) was originally spoken in this division, and is still spoken by a great majority of Cherokees on the Qualla Reservation in the Smokies. The Upper Towns were located in East Tennessee along the Little Tennessee, Hiwassee, and Tellico rivers, as well as the Cheowa River in western North Carolina. These were called the Overhill settlements. In this division, the Upper or Western dialect (properly the Otali dialect) was spoken in all the towns of East Tennessee, upper Georgia, and upon the Hiwassee and Cheowa rivers in North Carolina. It is considered by some the most musical of all the dialects and it is also the literary dialect. It is spoken by most of the western Cherokees on the Cherokee reservation in Oklahoma. The differences in the dialects were mainly in pronunciation, rather than vocabulary.

Although the early Cherokee culture belonged to the Woodland tradition, the late prehistoric Cherokee culture was essentially Mississippian. Each village was a self-governing body, with its own system of government patterned after the national one, with its own chiefs, advisors, medicine men, and minor officials. Thus, every settlement group had units of political, military, and religious life, and functioned on its own except in emergencies, such as war, or for special national ceremonies.

Cherokee society was largely a matriarchal one wherein women enjoyed a freedom not usually exercised by other tribes. They owned the home, had control over the children, and had a full voice in council. Women of rank were identified by such formal titles as Honored Woman, War Woman, or Beautiful Woman.

The Cherokee's preoccupation with uninhibited personal freedom, indoctrinated from his earliest years, was the principal Indian weakness and one which accelerated their downfall. From boyhood onward, males were self-indulgent, oblivious to the passage of time, inclined to postpone decisions and shirk irksome tasks, and if they chose to spend their days in idleness, they did so. The lowest military rank among braves was slave catcher, followed by Raven or Colona, then Man Killer or **Outacite**, with the highest status being Great Warrior. Before receiving a title, boys were called gunmen, or simply boys.

War-women and old warriors who could no longer go to war but who had distinguished themselves in their younger days were called Beloved, and were greatly venerated by all the Cherokees. Although too old for active service, this group of revered elders had garnered during their lifetime the experience which made them the chief's main counselors.

Closely linked to the family institution was the clan organization. Cherokee clans, like all clans, were extensions of the ordinary family group to include persons who considered themselves related by descent from a remote ancestor. These clans—Wild Potatoe, Paint, Blue, Deer, Bird, Wolf, and Long Hair—were basic to the social structure of the tribe. All children belonged to their mother's clan, and inherited clan membership was retained for life. Each clan had its own symbol, and clan membership was indicated by the color of feathers one wore. Inter-clan marriage was forbidden; each person was expected to marry into either their paternal or maternal grandfather's clan. Members of each of the seven clans lived in every town throughout the nation; therefore, each generation within a clan considered themselves brothers and sisters, and all members had obligations toward each other. These kinship ties formed a bond linking all the Cherokees, and this kinship link also formed a network of personal relationships and community ties which strengthened the political bonds that made up the national government.

Even though tribal organization was loosely knit and the Cherokee empire vast, the national government was effective and efficient. It was divided into a Peace and a War Organization. The peace, or civil organization consisted of a Peace Chief, two assistants, and five counselors. The Peace Chief, who was head of the nation in both civic and religious affairs, ruled during times of peace. The capital of the nation changed according to the residence of the paramount chief. The war, or military organization, consisted of a principal War Chief, three main advisors, and seven counselors. In time of war, the War Chief and his organization replaced the Peace Organization.

In addition to the above chiefs and their designated officers, there were delegated headmen chosen from the individual towns who made up the Tribal Council—the supreme law, but not absolute authority of the Cherokee Nation. The women also had their own clan council with delegates chosen from the local towns. The chosen leader of the National Women's Council was called the "Ghighau," i.e., "Most Honored Woman" or "Cherokee Woman Chieftainess." The chosen female leader could sit with the Tribal Council, had a vote in deciding whether or not war would be declared, and had the power of life or death over captives. If death, she chose the method of torture; if life, one of the head women of one of the clans was required to adopt the captive into her family and clan.

The last woman of the Cherokee Nation to hold this office was Nancy Ward; one of the greatest among Tennessee's celebrated women. She was greatly respected and revered by the Cherokees. Nicknamed "The Wild Rose," called "Beloved Woman," known as "Princess and Prophetess" to the Cherokee and as "Pocahontas of the West" to the whites, and often referred to as that wise, beautiful, resourceful woman, Nancy Ward—with connections on both sides of the frontier and influence among both races—was responsible for saving the lives of many settlers, and devoted her life to reducing the tensions between the races.

During the Cherokee-Creek war of 1755, at the Battle of Muskogee, Nancy Ward's first husband, Kingfisher, who was a noted war chief was killed. After he fell she took up his rifle to fight side by side with the warriors. For her personal heroism, she was elevated to the highest rank among Cherokee women, Ghigan, with the authority to speak in councils, delegate death sentences, and pronounce pardons. Her symbol of power was a swan's wing.

Nancy Ward was related by blood to many distinguished figures in the Cherokee drama during the eighteenth century. Her mother was Tame Doe, a niece of Kana-gatoka (Standing Turkey) of Echota, Principal Chief after Old Hop. One of her great-uncles was Oconostota (Groundhog Sausage), War Chief of the Nation. She was the niece of Attakullakulla, himself the nephew of Old Hop, who later became Peace Chief. The great warrior Dragging Canoe, or Tsugunsini, was her cousin. In the white world her prestige was as notable as among the Indians. Her second husband, whose life she saved using her power as Ghigan, was Brian (Bryant) Ward, a prominent English trader from South Carolina. Of her children, a daughter Betsy married General Joseph Martin who later became Virginia's Indian Agent to the Cherokees, and another daughter, Nannie, married Richard Timberlake, a descendant of the explorer and trader Henry Timberlake. Two of her sons became prominent chiefs. Nancy's father, except for being her father, had little importance in the Cherokee drama. His race is questionable. It is the consensus of most historians that he was a much respected English officer; however, some Cherokee historians contend that he was a Delaware chief who married Tame Doe, becoming a member of the Wolf clan.

The individual tribal villages varied greatly in size—ranging from fifteen to one hundred houses, with approximately two to five hundred Indians. The settlements, connected by a network of trails, generally were located in fertile bottom land along the mountain streams and rivers, but sometimes they extended for several miles into the woods. Each home site had its own vegetable garden, orchard, hog pens, poultry coops, and hot-house. The Cherokee did not live in tepees; those were the homes of the migratory Plains Indians. Cherokee houses were one-story log cabins; the logs were stripped of bark and notched at the ends, and grass mixed with smooth clay was plastered over the walls. They were roofed with bark, long broad shingles, or thatch. Usually windowless, the dwelling was partitioned to form two or three rooms, and an animal skin or mat covered the small doorway. Adjacent to the dwelling was a smaller, partly subterranean winter house where the family slept during the cold weather. White traders called these structures "hot houses" because of their stifling heat and smokiness. The floor of the house was dug two to four feet below ground level and was twenty to thirty square feet in area. Large upright logs formed the framework, which was covered with clay plaster. Cane couches for sleeping were built around the walls, and a small, scooped-out fireplace which often burned day and night occupied the center of the floor.

Hot houses, i.e., "sweat houses," were used by medicine men as a method of treating certain diseases and for purification rituals. Another use of the hot houses was for the secret meetings of the "myth keepers," an order of shamans. Inside they discussed the lore of the tribe, and instructed chosen young men as future myth keepers.

The focal point of the community was the seven-sided Council House, each side representing one of the seven clans. It was the largest and most important structure in any Cherokee settlement. This sugar-loaf like structure was large enough to seat several hundred people, and it was here that religious, civic, and war matters were discussed. Inside the Council House, elevated tiers of benches encircled the walls to form an amphitheater. The entrance, on the east side, faced the square and was constructed as a narrow, winding corridor to keep the interior from being seen from the outside. Opposite the door, at the west side of the building, was the sacred area where all the ceremonial costumes and paraphenalia were kept. This also was the area where all the main officials sat. During times of peace the "sophas," or seats, were whitened with a mixture of clay, but during war periods three additional seats were installed; all were painted red to symbolize war. In the central area, in front of the officials' sophas, was a small altar of clay where a perpetual, sacred fire burned. This was the area reserved for speakers. Among the Cherokees speech making was a greatly admired art, and no chief could be successful without possessing oratorical gifts. The people occupying sophas on each of the seven sides of the Council House were clansmen; custom decreeing that members of a clan sit together.

On a flat ground by the river near the Council House was an area called "The Square." Oblong in shape, it encompassed about half an acre. Community life centered about the square which was used for ceremonies, games, dances, and social gatherings. It was the basis of local government where the men spent much of their time each day, assembled in council to discuss town affairs. Near the Council House and the square were the public granary and the community gardens. Surrounding this public area were the private dwellings of the Cherokees. Each town, or **talwa**, had its own special emblem, and each town's warriors could be recognized by the special designs that were used for face painting.

The stream close by provided the water for the prescribed plunges during or after ceremonies. Believing that immersion in water alone kept them pure in body and spirit, the Cherokees participated in some rituals requiring whole communities to march in procession to bathe in the river.

Early each morning after bathing, the men congregated in the public square for a purification ritual called the **asi**, or "white drink" by the Cherokees, which the early traders called the "black drink," or "black tea." This was a strong, black liquid with white foam on top made by boiling roasted leaves, tops, and shoots of the cassia shrub (Ilex Vomitoria), a member of the holly family. We know the shrub by its common name, Winterberry. The concoction was a very strong purgative, and its almost immediate effect was to cause vomiting. The Cherokees believe that the drinking of this liquid cleansed and strengthened their bodies, made their minds powerful, purified them from sin, and made them invincible in war. The ritual, strictly for men, was governed by a rigid set of customs. It is often suggested that the black-drink rite was one of the surviving elements of a ritual practiced by the Southeastern tribes, especially the Creek and Cherokee, during the "Southern Cult" stage of the Mississippian culture. The Cherokees usually drank the black tea from gourds, but during some council meetings after the lighting of the sacred fire, the drink was served in special cups made from conch shells. These beautiful drinking vessels were engraved with intricate symbols and were so cherished by the Cherokees that they were seldom used except during the **asi** ritual.

The European recorded history of the Cherokee begins in the year 1540, by which date they were already established in the southern Appalachian Highlands. The first white entry into their country was made by the de Soto expedition advancing up the Savannah in a fruitless quest for gold. Other Spaniards followed, including Juan Pardo who led an expedition to the mountains in 1566-67 in search of reported Cherokee gold mines. After these expeditions, over a century of Cherokee history passed unrecorded by white men and only orally recited by the Cherokees.

Sustained European contact with the Cherokee did not begin until the close of the seventeenth century. In 1673, James (Jems) Needham, a gentleman from Virginia, and Gabriel Arthur, an indentured servant, made contact with the Indians, and became the first Englishmen to investigate the vast eastern Tanasi wilderness. Their purposed trading path between Echota and the Virginia colony, however, did not materialize until the following century; then it was developed by Eleazer Wiggans, one of the first English traders in upper East Tennessee.

French traders were the first Europeans to see the entire coast of what is now West Tennessee. Like the Spanish, they did not want to colonize the vast wilderness because it was too far inland, and there were too many Indians. Still, these "runners of the forest" operated throughout the Tennessee region and were so active in upper East Tennessee that one mighty river was called the French Broad.

As early as 1673, two French explorers—the Jesuit Father Marquette—a Catholic missionary—and Louis Jolliet—a fur trader—were exploring the west coast of present Tennessee. Then in 1682, La Salle—another French explorer who was the first European to travel the entire length of the Mississippi River—arrived at the Chickasaw Bluffs in what is now West Tennessee. La Salle claimed for France all of the land drained by the mighty Mississippi, which included the region of Tennessee. La Salle built a small supply base on the first Chickasaw Bluff for French traders traveling the Mississippi River. To honor the French king, this large area was named Louisiana. Seventeen years later the French would take possession of the immense Louisiana territory by planting a French settlement at Biloxi.

The Frenchmen took to the Indian's way of life from the first, and traded widely with all Indians across the interior. They lived among them, were adopted by them, took Indian wives, and soon were scarcely to be distinguished from Indians. This French influence over the Indians with whom they were so intimately associated gave them a strategic importance to be retained for years.

European traders who visited for the first time an inland Indian community such as the Cherokees usually opened their visit by distributing presents—goods of the kind which later would be used in barter. The custom of exchanging gifts was an ancient one among the Indian tribes, especially upon meeting friends for the first time. The Indians, who never before encountered many of the articles presented, would give a few pelts in return. After the trader's gifts had been used, broken, or lost, the tribesmen clamored for more. Then, however, only a few gifts were given to important members of the tribe; all other Indians were told they must exchange furs for new merchandise. Thus, a cycle was set in motion.

No event was more intriguing to a remote Indian village than the arrival of a trader with his string of packhorses, each equipped with a string of merrily, tinkling bells. It was a cause for celebration, a gala affair with much dancing and feasting, enlivened by the trader's distribution of rum. The Indians could hardly wait for the trader to empty his packs which they knew were filled with a glittering store of treasures—needles, mirrors, knives, bolts of calico, spirits, glass beads, ribbons; everything the Indian intensely desired. The item most valued above all others was a gun, the possession of which instantly raised the status and prowess of the warrior.

Guns were introduced among the Cherokee about 1711, presumably by Charles Town officials on the condition that they help in the colonists' war with the Tuscarora. The Cherokees, being hereditary enemies of the Tuscarora, eagerly agreed to help the South Carolina volunteers. During 1711-13 the English, with the assistance of the Cherokee warriors, succeeded in driving the Tuscarora out of the Southeast and to the North, where they became the sixth nation of the Iroquoian confederacy.

The English, envying the French, wanted good trade relations with the Indians, but their fierce appetite for land involved them in numerous tribal wars and, therefore, they were denied the familiarity which the French enjoyed. Nevertheless, British fur traders were accepted by the Indians because of their compelling desire to swap furs and deerskins for weapons, blankets, red paint, ammunition, and other useful items. The Indians had begun to depend upon these items which made their lives easier and gave them effective weapons with which to dispel their enemies.

In 1721, English merchants disturbed by inroads the French were making on the Indian fur trade invited the Cherokee to a treaty council at Charles Town (present-day Charleston), South Carolina. At the conclusion of the treaty, the English had secured a trade agreement with the Indians for most of their furs. The Cherokees also made their first cession of land to the British; a fifty-square-mile tract of land between the Santee, Saluda, and Edisto rivers. This was land the Cherokee seldom used, but which was extremely valuable to the expanding Charles Town colony. The cession was the first step toward the loss of the Cherokee homelands, their culture, and their eventual removal to the West.

Both the French and English traders, like almost all Indians, became experienced voyagers and well acquainted with ancient avenues and bypaths. In dress they adopted the costume of the Cherokee warrior; knee-length buckskin hunting shirt, leather leggings like loose trouser legs, deerskin moccasins made like short boots reaching halfway up the leg, and a large mantle-type coat draped over the shoulders.

By 1730 there were trading posts—under strict regulation because the Cherokee did not want permanent settlers on their lands—stationed throughout the Cherokee Nation. Before the eighteenth century, the French dominated the trade with the Cherokee, but soon after the English drove them away. It was this fierce competition between the two that brought on the French and Indian War; thereby, opening the door to American Independence—a climatic situation wherein both races would be losers.

Traders varied. Some married Indians, sired Indian children, and became Indians. Several kept their cultural identities, but were good representatives of their country. There were others who took Indian scalps for the bounty and exploited, abused, and deceived the Cherokee. Although the Cherokee, as well as the other southeastern tribes, requested that no whiskey be sold to their warriors, exorbitant amounts of rum, whiskey, and brandy were forced into their villages. Rum was one of the main reasons for the traders' success. Negotiation for the sale of furs was often made in the heart of the forest, and a trader could easily induce the tribesmen to have a free dram of rum before the business of barter began. This was often a fatal step for the Indians—one dram called for another and before long the warriors were thoroughly drunk. Then the trader could literally steal their skins and furs, slipping off into the night with his ill-gotten spoils. Traders who wished to establish a long-term business of trade with the Indians did not resort to such tactics because the Indians were unlikely to be deceived in this manner twice and were prone to seek revenge.

One of the most bizarre events of Tennessee history occurred in 1730 with the appearance of Sir Alexander Cuming in the Cherokee Overhill towns. Some historians claim he was an emissary of Britain, but others believe he acted on his own. Either way, on March 13th of that year Cuming decided to leave Charles Town where he was staying with a friend and visit the Cherokee Nation. Ten days later he and his party arrived at the Lower Town of Keowee (near present-day Clemson, South Carolina). There, heavily armed, Cuming boldly entered the council house where some three hundred Indians were meeting, and with eloquent words veiled with threats and intrepid gestures, he demanded that all the headmen present kneel and swear allegiance to the king of England. Whether by luck or because of the Indians' admiration for such bold courage, Cuming achieved his purpose. Messengers were sent to all the towns of the Overhill country, Middle towns and Lower towns, telling all the chiefs and headsmen to meet in two weeks at Nequassee (located near present-day Franklin, North Carolina). Nonchalantly, Cuming departed on a brief tour of the Nation. At each place he stopped, Cuming elicited the same allegiance from the inhabitants by the same methods he had used at Keowee.

The climax of Cuming's dramatic exploit came at the Middle town of Nequassee on April 3, 1730. There, among dignitaries from throughout the nation, he arranged to have the Head Warrior of Tellico, Moytoy, crowned "Emperor" of the Cherokee

Nation and Old Hop of Chota designated as "King." Further, he lay plans to take seven warriors and an English trader who was a trusted friend of the Cherokees across the ocean to Great Britain for a visit with King George II. On May 13th, accompanied by the white trader Eleazar Wiggam, affectionately called "The Old Rabbit" by the Cherokee, to serve as interpreter, they set sail from Charles Town to London aboard the man-of-war **Fox**. Their arrival in Great Britain was the cause of much excitement, and soon the seven warriors were the rage of London. They met King George II, exchanged gifts, and signed a treaty of friendship and trade. They also promised to aid Britain in time of war.

The hundred year period—1700 to 1800—was one of misfortune for the Cherokee Nation. The price the Indians paid for their new commodities was high. The guns and whiskey introduced by the whites shortly after 1700 proved disastrous to thousands of Indians. The demand upon the Cherokee for animal skins to pay their debts to the English traders increased yearly until Indian hunters, forsaking their ancient ways and customs of protecting nature's balance in the animal world, began to kill for profit rather than food. This led to a massive slaughter of wildlife. An epidemic of smallpox, contracted from a slave ship anchored at Charles Town harbour, swept through the Nation in 1738-39. The Cherokee **Adawehi** (medicine men) knew nothing of this highly contagious disease, but nevertheless they attempted to treat the scourge in several ways. One method, according to Alderman, was a sweat bath in the hot house, followed by a cold plunge in the river, but this proved to be a fatal remedy (13). Waves of this mysterious, unknown disease incurable by the strongest medicine passed through the Nation in plagues so horrible that many Cherokee men killed their families and then committed suicide. It is estimated that half of the Nation perished. Finally there came the settlers. Land-impoverished and freedom seeking, they saw a country where even depleted game was plentiful; a land seemingly free for the taking.

The Cherokee of this era were proud and independent. A people who at first resisted the lures of European civilization, clinging tenaciously to their homeland and their own culture. Content with their lifeway, the Cherokee probably would have remained in mysterious darkness but for the English, French, and Spanish colonists who in the last decade of the seventeenth century, and throughout the eighteenth century, kept the Cherokee Nation in a furor.

The English were encroaching daily on Cherokee lands. The Cherokee hunting grounds were being depleted. The colonists continued to deal in the deplorable, enforced slavery of the Cherokee. And the Indians had begun to realize they were losing their homelands, but did not understand why or how.

By the early 1750's the Cherokee were swept into numerous eighteenth-century European wars, culminating in a "Fourth and Final" conflict known as the French and Indian War, 1754-1763. It was the war which would decide if the future of North America would lie with the French or British. Both claimed the area between the Appalachians and the Mississippi; both had begun successful colonization of North America almost simultaneously—at Jamestown in 1607 and at Quebec in 1608. They had already engaged each other in three other colonial wars and now this "Fourth and Final" conflict was to start in 1754. The Cherokees were divided as to which side to support, but in reality it was a hopeless situation whichever side they chose.

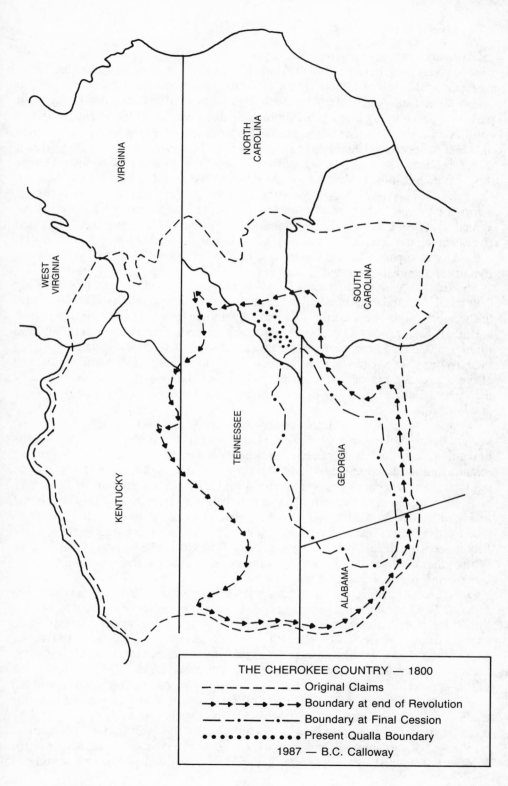

THE CHEROKEE COUNTRY — 1800

— — — — — — Original Claims

→—→—→—→—→ Boundary at end of Revolution

—·—·—·—·— Boundary at Final Cession

•••••••••••• Present Qualla Boundary

1987 — B.C. Calloway

For many years the most persuasive pro-English influence among the Cherokee was the vigorous personality of Attakullakulla, the nation's peace chief who succeeded Old Hop of Echota. Born at the turn of the eighteenth century he was called "The Little Carpenter" by the whites because of his uncanny ability to fit parts of a peace treaty into a good diplomatic document, artfully bringing various conflicting minds together in the political framework of his nation. This wizened old chief believed the Cherokee loyalty as well as their security lay with the British; therefore, he advised his people to turn deaf ears to the pleas of the French. During the French and Indian War, he agreed to send five hundred warriors to help the English, but only in exchange for arms and ammunition, and the construction of a fort for the protection of the Indian women, children, and aged. The British agreed, and Fort Loudoun was built at the union of the Little Tennessee and Tellico rivers among the Overhill Towns in 1757. It was the first garrisoned fort on Tanasi soil and was separated from the nearest British settlement by some 250 miles of Indian land, mostly forested mountains.

The English won the French and Indian War and that same year (1763), King George III declared the Appalachian mountain barrier as the boundary for settlement; the western lands, beyond the great eastern mountain chain were designated as an Indian reservation. This decree, however, did not keep settlers out. Within a three-year lapse of time, they poured down upon the mountains and valleys; hating the Crown, craving freedom and space. The Cherokee became extremely uneasy at the encroachment of the white people on their hunting grounds, but actually the loss of Indian lands had begun when Columbus accidentally discovered the New World.

Decades passed, with the influx of new immigrants increasing yearly. The coastal settlers began moving into Cherokee country near Indian towns along the foothills of the mountains. The newcomers, as settlements became crowded, pressed further inland, looking for unclaimed land. The constant encroachment by the colonists onto the Cherokee hunting grounds caused the Indians to become extremely uneasy and resentful. By the latter part of the eighteenth century, a trading post was being operated by two English fur traders, Pearis and Price, at their sacred island on the Holston, and at the Watauga River a large settlement was being formed; some fifty miles from the established boundary line. The Cherokee harbored a deep sense of rage that their sacred lands were being defiled, and that their hunting grounds were being pre-emptied of game.

Different nationalities had a somewhat diverse opinion concerning the Cherokee Indians. The Spaniards and French viewed them as a curiosity who posed no serious threat; the British and the colonists saw them as ignorant savages to be exploited; and the frontier settlers, as well as the early Americans, regarded the Indians as an uncivilized enemy to be pushed out of the way or destroyed. To the Europeans, land was a commodity to live from, an object of barter and trade. The vast wilderness of the Appalachian West offered rich farm land, plenty of trees for building cabins, and forests filled with wild game offering food for the larder as well as pelts for trade. To the white man, all of it seemed free for the taking.

The Cherokee, who felt they were superior to the whites, viewed them as weaklings with an unhealthy color. They were cowards who screamed when burned or otherwise punished; people who never kept their word; fools who would sell his worst enemy a gun with which he himself could be shot; people whose one ruling passion was to get money or own land.

The Cherokee believed the land had been given to them by the Great Spirit and it could not be sold, bartered, or owned by individuals. Their ownership of land stemmed from pre-historic ancestral traditions and customs. It was given to them to live on as custodians, to be shared with all living creatures, and held in trust for the generations yet to come. The Cherokee, at first, were willing to share the use of the land with the whites, receiving trade goods and supplies for its use. Later they were powerless to combat the legal methods employed by the land-hungry whites. Tribal ownership of land by whole societies had come down through many generations and early treaty agreements were based on ancient, Indian thinking and traditions. To them, no treaty was final or permanent. However, they were eventually controlled by the courts and laws established by the European colonists.

As readily seen, the customs, common laws, and accepted practices of the Europeans and the Cherokee were so entirely different it was inevitable that the cultures would clash. These differences became the basis of the many bloody conflicts that developed, leading finally to the total defeat—and near annihilation—of the Cherokee Nation.

TYPICAL CHEROKEE HOMESITE

Located in the fertile bottom lands along the mountain streams, each Cherokee homesite had its own vegetable garden, orchard, hog pens, poultry coops, and hot-house. In structure, the one-story log cabin was similar to that of the whites. They had dirt floors and were usually windowless. A mat or an animal skin covered the small doorway. Cherokee men were of medium height and muscular. They had bronze skin. Their heads were shaved except for a patch of hair dangling from the crown, decorated with beads, feathers, and porcupine quills. Cherokee women were usually tall and delicately built. Their skin was paler than that of the men. Their jet-black hair was worn long, decorated with beads and ribbons. Both sexes wore clothing made from buckskin, feathers, and furs.

46

V

THE FRONTIERSMEN

By 1763 the population of Colonial America was over two million. These maritime people inhabiting a long, narrow terrain of thirteen colonies of the Atlantic seaboard—whose natural bent had been to face eastward—were now beginning to turn westward. For nearly a hundred and fifty-eight years, like a small trickling stream, they had inched mile by mile and cabin by cabin from the sea to the seemingly insurmountable Appalachian mountains, an obstacle never before encountered. Beyond them was the wild country reserved for the Indians by the British king, a region extending westward to a distance no man yet knew.

There were three natural gateways through the mountain barrier; two already had been used by the British armies during the Indian wars. The Mohawk-Oswego route, offering water transportation via the Niagara portage to the western Great Lakes, led westward from the tidewater of the Hudson to Lake Ontario. The second route actually was two military roads, Braddock's and Forbes', leading across the Allegheny mountains to the forks of the Ohio connecting the settled portions of Virginia and Pennsylvania with that great river. Braddock's road, built in 1755 and 110 miles long, started at Fort Cumberland in Maryland, and Forbes road, built in 1758 and 197 miles long, started at Rayestown, Pennsylvania. Both led to the French Fort Du Quesne at the junction of the Allegheny and Mononqahela rivers, the present site of Pittsburgh, Pennsylvania. The third route, the mysterious Great Indian Warpath, or Warrior's Path, was further south, and went southward across Virginia, followed the towering eastern wall of the Appalachians to the deep gorge of Cave Gap (present Cumberland Gap), and then disappeared.

Most likely the first white man to cross Cave Gap was Gabriel Arthur in 1674. He and a party of Cherokees from Echota had been traveling for several months along ancient Indian war trails in search of game. As they were homeward bound in the Ohio Valley they were attacked by a band of Shawnee who wounded Arthur in the thigh and captured him. When the Indians discovered by his long blond hair that he was a white man, they returned his weapons, tended his wound, and treated him kindly. The Shawnee told Arthur they would let him return to Echota

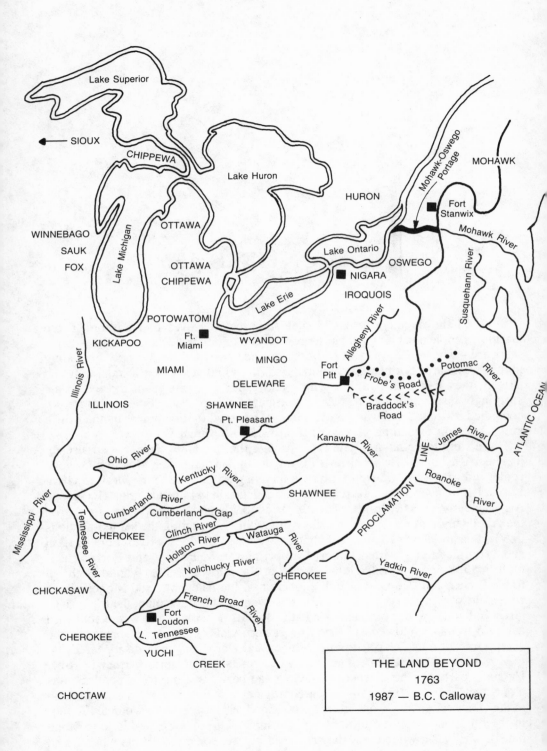

Lake Superior

SIOUX

CHIPPEWA

Lake Huron

HURON

Mohawk-Oswego Portage

MOHAWK

Fort Stanwix

Mohawk River

WINNEBAGO

SAUK

FOX

Lake Michigan

OTTAWA

OTTAWA

CHIPPEWA

Lake Ontario

Lake Erie

OSWEGO

NIGARA

IROQUOIS

Susquehann River

POTOWATOMI

Ft. Miami

WYANDOT

MINGO

ATLANTIC OCEAN

KICKAPOO

MIAMI

DELEWARE

Allegheny River

Fort Pitt

Frobe's Road

Potomac River

Braddock's Road

Illinois River

ILLINOIS

SHAWNEE

Pt. Pleasant

Kanawha River

LINE

James River

Roanoke

Ohio River

Kentucky River

SHAWNEE

River

Cumberland River

Cumberland Gap

PROCLAMATION

Mississippi River

CHEROKEE

Clinch River

Watauga River

Tennessee River

Holston River

Nolichucky River

CHEROKEE

Yadkin River

CHICKASAW

French Broad River

Fort Loudon

L. Tennessee

CHEROKEE

YUCHI

CREEK

CHOCTAW

THE LAND BEYOND
1763
1987 — B.C. Calloway

48

if he would promise to go back to the white men of the east coast to work up a trade arrangement between them and the Shawnee. Arthur agreed. Shawnee guides conducted him to a path leading southward across the meadow lands of **Ken-ta-ke** (present state of Kentucky) to the Great Gap in what is now the Cumberland mountains, and then on to the Cherokee capitol. The path was evidently well defined, and Arthur followed it to Echota. From here, the village chief and several of his braves took Arthur to Fort Henry in the Virginia colony. Unlettered as he was, he kept no written record; and it would be over seventy-five years more before the discovery of this natural gateway into Kentucky was recorded (Kincaid, 30).

Unknown by white men of the time was the fact that two other branches of this same path also led to Cave Gap. One ran from Sandusky, on Lake Erie, by a direct path to the mouth of Scioto (present-day Portsmouth, Ohio), and then across what is now Kentucky to the gap. The other branch ran from the Creek country in Georgia and present-day Alabama northward through the southern region of East Tennessee to the present Tennessee and Virginia border; there it turned west toward the gap. The path, called by the Indians the **Athawominee**, or the Path of the Armed Ones (Kincaid, 30), had been used for centuries by the northern and southern tribes traveling on long hunts, missions of peace, or raids of war. It was a major link in the trail system of the North American Indians long before Columbus discovered the Americas.

Dr. Thomas Walker is credited with recording the existence of this famous gateway leading into what is now Kentucky. Early in March of 1750, the Loyal Land Company of Virginia sent out a small, land-surveying expedition led by Dr. Walker. It was to explore and survey the new land grants the Virginia company had recently acquired in the west. A short time later, on a bright April morning, the expedition, having followed basically the same route as that of the Great Indian Warpath, walked through Cave Gap into present Kentucky. Dr. Walker, being the first explorer to record this gap, named the great river, the mountains beyond it, and the gap—all three—Cumberland, in honor of the Duke of Cumberland, son of King George II. Nonetheless, this natural gateway would not be used until the time of Daniel Boone. The travel of Dr. Walker's time continued solely down the east side of the Blue Ridge, along the flank of dark mountains which blocked the westward path. Later it would be known that this famous gateway connected the Valley of Virginia (Shenandoah) with that of the Ohio, clearing up any geographical mystery about this part of the western country.

At about the same time Dr. Walker was exploring the region of present-day Kentucky, Christopher Gist was surveying the lands in the Ohio Valley for the Ohio Land Company. These two major land companies, which pre-dated the French and Indian War, were rivals created to act as spear heads for speculators.

By 1750 the population of the British colonies, though basically Anglo-Saxon in stock and language, was mottled with sizable foreign groups. In its time, the cultural variation of Colonial America was perhaps the most mixed of anywhere in the world. For more than a century, many foreign groups left their native lands, fleeing economic oppression, religious persecution, and the ravages of war, and flocked to North American shores in large numbers. The largest segment of the population, 62%, was English and Welsh. The Scotch-Irish, who made up 7% of the population, were not Irish but Lowland Scots who had first been transplanted to Ireland. Because of severe economic oppression early in the 1700's, they pulled up stakes and came to the colonies. Germans, mainly in the backcounty of Pennsylvania, made up 6% of the total population. The largest non-English group was from Africa. This group was predominantly Negro slaves and comprised 20% of the colonial population. Other foreign groups, such as the Dutch, Irish, Swedes, Hebrews, Swiss, French Huguenots, and Scottish Highlanders, made up another five percent of the population (Bailey, 65-67). Whatever their national origin, excluding the Negroes, ninety percent of the colonists spoke English, and about ninety percent of the people lived in rural areas.

At the top rung of the social ladder were the aristocrats, a class in America made up of merchants, landed gentry, wealthy professional men, and clergy of the established churches. Below the aristocracy was the middle class—the backbone of the colonies. It consisted mainly of small yeoman farmers, skilled artisans, and smaller tradesmen. Below this rung were the propertyless poor whites and hired hands. Even lower were the indentured servants or "white slaves"; those souls who could not afford to pay passage across the Atlantic and in return for transportation had voluntarily agreed to work for a period of years (Bailey, 68-69). Huddled on this same social rung were the convicts and paupers who were involuntarily shipped over as indentured servants. At the very bottom of the social ladder were the Negro slaves who were concentrated in the warmer climate of the South.

As the colonists expanded from the sea deeper into the interior, and immersed themselves in the process of building a nation, they encroached upon Cherokee lands. The principal breeding ground for the succession of generations that settled the Southern Appalachian frontier was at the foot of the mountains in Virginia, Pennsylvania, and the Carolinas. During the decade from 1740 to 1750 there was a slow, steady progression of early settlers across the Appalachian divide, but the French and Indian War—soon to engulf the border—halted this advancement for more than a decade. According to Mooney, this invasion of Indian territory awakened a natural resentment of the native owners (39).

Following the French and Indian War and the Royal decree of 1763, a new chapter in the American-Cherokee drama was opened. It was the hour of history when one set of major actors quit the stage, and a powerful new group—the frontiersmen or backwoodsmen—rushed forward to take their place. All at once, land became vital to the drama. The Indian trade and relations involved complexities which neither the British officials nor the colonial backwoodsman understood or could control. The Indians did not fully comprehend the distant, international treaties involving their territory. Their main interest was in keeping the white man away from their lands, while maintaining relations with him that permitted the continuance of trade. With such a setting and problems the great westward movement across the Appalachians opened.

The early border people who crossed the Appalachian mountains were a multifaceted group, varying greatly in colonial, ethnic, and class origin. Usually they came plodding into the wilderness with only what they could carry on their backs, and lived in abandoned cabins, caves, or crudely built shelters. There, abandoning Old World habits and customs, the newcomers shucked off—if they had known them—the superficialities of older and better established societies. Class divisions were soon forgotten as families struggled with the land and joined with neighbors to assault the wilderness—and its owners, the Cherokee. In the Virginia records proof is found that the irresponsible borderers seldom let pass an opportunity to kill and plunder any stray Indian found in their neighborhood.

A true backwoodsman was a makeshift personality of the old-world living in a primitive stage of society. He was purely a regional character living by his own code, framed by the environment in which he lived. Therefore, the pioneer of the Appalachian Frontier was entirely different from the frontiersman of other regions whose problems were in contrast to his.

On the Appalachian border there was neither time nor place for amenities like those of the older, more settled coastal communities. Because of the constant struggle to face the necessities of life, backwoods life was lived at an elementary social level. In the backcountry of the Appalachian West, hard work was a pronounced characteristic, and the average backwoodsman's fortune was earned only by long and arduous labor. Hacking a clearing out of the wilderness demanded strong muscles, long hours, and great nerve. Human contacts were limited and differences in economic conditions remained undefined. In the backcountry, more often than not, one man or family was as socially acceptable as another. Isolation from the British colonies and the ever-present threat of Cherokee raids made neighborliness a necessity on the frontier. Neighbors were indispensable for making a clearing, raising cabins and other buildings, cultivating the newly-cleared land, and countless other chores essential to settlement.

All newcomers confronted the frontier, and all encountered the Cherokee Nation and its vast territory. The early frontiersmen were separated from help and supplies in the east by mountain ranges dividing the more advanced and more exposed homesteads from the older settlements. They were separated from each other by distances made longer by lack of roads. Each location was either held by one family or, at the most, by two. Its isolation made even the support of its equally weak and nearest neighbor too often too late.

The steady advancement of the settlements quickly produced an uneasiness among the Cherokee, who saw in it a serious threat to their way of life. One of the ironies of history is that the Scotch, Irish, English, and German pioneers of the Appalachian highlands were in many ways very similar to the Cherokees—yet they became the Indians' worst enemy. Before the end of the nineteenth century, they and other white men would destroy more than two-thirds of the settled Cherokee Nation (*At Home in The Smokies*, 43).

Although a few backwoodsmen were friendly with the Cherokee, the average one made little distinction among the Indians. To him an Indian was an Indian— all were his enemies to be shot on sight. A Cherokee scalp of either sex in Williamsburg was worth as much bounty—usually fifty to a hundred British pounds—as a Shawnee's, an Iroquois', or a Delaware's. Captured Indian children could be sold or traded. According to Caruso, racial prejudice prevented all but a few of the unmarried frontiersmen from taking Indians as their wives, though they seldom overlooked an opportunity to take them for their pleasure (217). The English could never hope to win the esteem of the Indian so long as they disdained to intermarry with them. Free of prejudice, Frenchmen encouraged intermarriage with the natives, and by this wise policy they strengthened their interest with the Indians.

Inevitably the movement of the pioneers toward the interior led to an invasion of lands claimed and defended by different Indian tribes who hunted and lived on them. Later, even the boundary line established by the British would not keep settlers out of Indian lands, and it was this constant encroachment which ultimately led to the long period of border wars from 1754 to 1794. Feeling there could never be peace as long as white settlers continued to claim more land, the Cherokees took to a wider warpath, and the whole frontier from Pennsylvania to North Carolina felt their fury.

The Cherokee's major purpose was to break the will of the frontier people to stand their ground. By terrorizing them and making their existence unbearable, they hoped to compel them to retreat back over the mountains. Cherokee military power was aided by their location and an inherent mountain fastness from which they could sally forth at will, and into which they could retire when pressed. As a result, their primary weapon was the Indian raid.

A Cherokee warrior regarded war as a supremely dangerous game in which he was able to demonstrate those qualities of courage and cunning which most became a man. Death in battle represented an irretrievable personal failure. The individual warrior sought first the opportunity to display his contempt for danger while proving his ability to terrify his enemies. The reward of returning to his own town with horses, trinkets, captives, and scalps as unmistakable tokens of his valor was prized far more highly when won at the expense of his most bitterly hated adversary—the white settlers.

A common raiding party consisted of twenty to forty warriors. Surprise was always an important element in making the raid successful. The typical raid started with a swift and secret approach to one of the settler's clearings, followed by a sudden, brief, incredibly violent eruption of death and devastation of the inhabitants, then ending with an equally swift and secret withdrawal from the scene of carnage.

Once the Cherokees surrounded a homestead, for a brief moment the wild, eerie howling heard as they burst from the forest cover gave warning, but in the next instant the inhabitants were literally paralyzed with fright by what they saw. To the families of the western frontier, an Indian painted for war momentarily glimpsed was indeed a very frightening sight, to say the least. With his tall, muscular, naked form painted red and black, with head shaved or a patch of hair dangling with feathers, grotesquely tattooed, perhaps with white and green circles about the eyes and mouth, with stretched ear-lobes and dangling earrings, and necklaces of claws or shells hung around the neck, holding a tomahawk or war club in one hand and a long spear in the other, howling short, but very loud war whoops, he appeared more to be a demon from the nether regions than a human antagonist. In the extreme excitement, the raiders appeared possessed by a satanic frenzy. The breasts and any unborn child of a woman was carved from her convulsing body and cast into the hearth fire. Some scalps were torn from the living, especially the aged. Men were disemboweled; their entrails cast about the cabin floor. Infants torn from their mother's arms were swung by the heels to crush their skulls against near cabin walls or trees. Small children were casually axed. Young children were shot with arrows or speared as they ran (Clark, 59). Older children and sometimes young women were taken captive. Mercifully for most, death was swift. The possessions of the white family were gone through and trinkets as well as any useful weapons, guns, or ammunition were taken; everything else was burned. The cabin, other out buildings, and fields were torched as the Indians disappeared back into the woods (Van Every, 119).

Usually, it would be days, weeks, or even months before some party of white men would stumble onto the carnage. With the forest reclaiming the land, the bodies of the dead—mutilated, burned, or decayed beyond recognition—with no identifying objects to be found would be laid to rest in a shallow grave. Sometimes there was only the burned-out cabin with no indication as to whether the family had been carried off, or had fled in time. Most often, there were no survivors to tell the tale (Van Every, 116). Van Every is correct in asserting that most of the raids remained unrecorded and the names of the men, women, and children who perished unknown (116).

The widely scattered western settlements were easy prey for the savage Cherokee. Through the depths of the wilderness surrounding every stockade or cabin, the Indians were able to approach with little chance of detection. Every family was required to live with the constant assumption that any hour might bring unspeakable disaster. No man could hoe his fields, no woman go to the spring, no child play in the dooryard without continually straightening and turning to peer and listen. The daily existence of every inhabitant of the Appalachian West was vexed by perpetual apprehension that at any moment there could be an Indian behind the woodpile, or perhaps a hundred Indians in the underbrush fringing the clearing. Sometimes the Cherokees, as well as other Indians, were known to hide in the woods near some homestead or settlement for days, waiting for the right chance to kill an unwary hunter, to capture an unsuspecting berry picker, to steal a child or a horse.

During the long period of the border wars, 1754-1794, the Cherokee and other Indians carried off hundreds of white captives. At their towns during the victory celebrations, many prisoners were burned or tortured to death for sport; some were forced to run the gauntlet or kept as slaves; several were sold in Detroit for a hundred pounds per prisoner or traded among the tribes; and others were adopted into the clan—literally becoming Indians. Surprisingly, when the Indians were forced by treaty to return white captives, most refused to go, or if taken against their will, ran away and returned to the Indian villages.

For the inhabitants of the Old West, the sky was always dark with low-hanging war clouds from which bolts of lightening regularly descended. There seemed to be no relief from the danger, no surcease from dread. For them a day that passed without an attack was only a day when an attack might be but an hour away.

This terror, however stark, became less so by repetition. Survival was more often than not a matter of chance. According to Van Every, when at war the Indians were never known to exhibit any tendency which could be identified as humane (120). However, the resolution with which the western frontier people clung to their clearings and stockades, year after year, against odds which appeared ever more helpless, frustrated the design of the Cherokee to force his white adversary back across the mountains.

By 1768, a steady stream of permanent settlers had begun moving into America's first western frontier, East Tennessee. Most came from Virginia in a natural progression because of the easy water access down the Holston forks and the tributaries of the Watauga. Accomplished woodsmen were of first importance in the early days of each new settlement. Their acquaintance with the country readily established them as guides and scouts; their hunting skills helped keep the community fed, and their wide-ranging served to warn against Indian threats.

Among families making the decision to cross the mountains it was common practice for the man of the family first to come alone in order to hunt and look around. The hunting always proved better than he was led to believe, and everything else about the new country appealed to him. Although soil qualities varied radically, some of the most fertile land and the most variable weather conditions were found in what is now present East Tennessee. Coming to a meadow, a spring, or a stand of trees which indicated the richness of the soil, the backwoodsman would pick out a section close by, stake out his claim, clear the land, build a cabin and plant a corn patch. Learning to utilize forest resources, he chose poplar or chestnut for his cabin as the wood would not decay, and shingled his roof with oak because it split straight and thin. Afterward, he went back to get his family.

The ever-present Indian menace made rapid building imperative; thus, "cabin raising" was shared by all, with neighbors coming on foot and by horseback to the newcomer's holding to help him clear the land and erect his new home. These log houses. generally speaking, gave protection against Indian attack. They resisted gun fire effectively, except where chance shots penetrated vulnerable cracks or when the doors were thrust open by surprise attacks. In structure the cabins varied from twelve to fifteen feet in height and were twenty to thirty feet in length. Fire was their greatest threat.

Most families lived in a one-room log cabin with a lean-to at the back. It was built of logs in the round with walls high enough to permit a crude second-story under the apex of the roof. The cracks between the walls were filled with blocks of wood and daubed with mud and grass; the spaces between the logs were chinked with clay and moss to seal out wind and rain. The roof was either thatched or made of broad split boards held in place by long poles fastened down by wooden pegs. The earth usually served as the floor, but in some instances logs cloven in two with the flat side up were used. There was a flagstone hearth for warmth and cooking, with a chimney made of either stone or mud and sticks. Cross poles overhead often supported a rough, second-story board floor, and a ladder of five rounds of pegs driven into the wall served as a stairway. Corners filled with cross-sticks served as storage shelves and racks. The door was thick and heavy; window panes were of paper treated with either hog fat or bear grease. A lean-to built across the back was used as either an extra bedroom or for storage space.

In dress, the frontiersmen were indebted to the Indian. Except for the coonskin cap with tail attached, there was no essential difference between the attire of the native and the pioneer. Deerskin, the most widely used peltry, was softened until it was as soft as velvet, and then made into shirts, dresses, men's leggings, jackets, boots and moccasins. A man's hunting shirt, made of coarse linen or dressed deerskin, was a loose frock reaching halfway down the thigh, and big enough to lap over about a foot in front when belted. This bosom served as a wallet for jerky and bread as well as tow for wiping out a gun barrel. In cold weather, mittens and the bullet bag were also carried there. A breechcloth was worn Indian-fashion about the lions, and if there was an undershirt, it was likely to be of linsey or soft deerskin. A wide sash, which was always tied behind, also served several purposes, e.g., holding a tomahawk or scalping knife. Moccasins cut from a single piece of deer or buffalo skin were worn on the feet, and leggings of similar material were the dress for the legs and thighs. A large cape, usually fringed with a raveling of cloth of a different color from the shirt, hung over the shoulders. Raccoon caps with tail attached, or hats of beaver, completed the frontiersmen's outfit.

Cloth was made from the prickly nettle plant. Nettles were gathered in late winter or early spring after wet weather had rotted the stalk. Their fibers made a very strong thread which, combined with buffalo-wool yarn, formed the warp of a very serviceable cloth. From this cloth were made drawers, undershirts, aprons, infant wear, and bed-clothing. Frontier dress was not significantly different between the woodsmen and farmers until the early nineteenth century.

According to Clark (13), the most effective combination of forces to attack the woods was a young man and a sturdy bride. Not only did they bring land under plow, but with their large families they added materially to the western population. As settlers combined their efforts to achieve a common purpose, cabins and cleared fields became more characteristic of the westward movement than anything else. At no time in American history has the physical man counted for more. With sound muscles he cleared the woods, built homes, plowed and planted fields. His only passport to esteem, according to Caruso (208) was his own merit. Physical courage, the capacity to amuse and instruct, innate civility—these were the qualities that decided a man's standing as a desirable neighbor. Without them he was friendless and unwanted. Women, though subjected to many hardships, were relied on for increasing the population, for manufacturing clothing, for laboring on the farm, for cooking for her large family, and for supplying the necessary element of domestic stability to frontier society (Clark, 14).

Sometimes the institution of marriage presented a dilemma for the back-country people whose settlements, more often than not, were far distant from communities where legal marriages could be performed. Usually this problem was solved by common-law matings, many of which were later legalized. When marriages did take place, they usually were early in life, with girls legally marriageable at fourteen, and boys at sixteen or seventeen. Families grew rapidly for a large family was helpful in the fields and about the house. Weddings were festive occasions involving quiltings, house-raisings, and house warmings. There was a wedding feast, a dance, and an infare (a day-after dinner served in the groom's house); all offered an excuse for social gathering and entertainment for the entire neighborhood.

The frontiersman and his wife made soap from ashes and fat, dyes from barks of trees, baskets from withers split from oak trees, and their own buckets and barrels. The grinding of corn into meal on the hand mill, or pounding it into hominy in the mortar, was the work of either or the joint labor of both.

The genuine frontiersman was more of a hunter than a farmer. Game supplied most of his food, with the furs and skins being more readily salable than whatever crops he could raise. His most prized possession was the Kentucky rifle, manufactured between 1728 to about 1760 by skilled German gunsmiths living around Lancaster, Pennsylvania. The rifle weighed from eight to twelve pounds and was usually either a .30 or .50 caliber. For accurate shooting the lead ball was loaded with a greased patch of cloth. In addition to hunting, the man cleared the land, planted, plowed, and gathered the crops. He erected the cabin or built the fort in which women and children were placed for safety and made the furnishings as well as most of the tools and utensils for the home or farm. All the furnishings and most of the utensils were handcrafted on the spot.

The frontier woman led a life of hardship. Working from sun-up to sun-down, she did as much work as any man. A few of her chores were cooking, milking, churning, sewing, washing, preserving food, and mixing medicines. In addition, she carried water, chopped wood, and hoed the fields—all the while caring for her children and husband.

Because there was almost no money in the backwoods settlements, early merchants, more often than not, exchanged their wares for produce and peltry; and when they carried their furs to market, they brought back merchandise rather than cash. Barter of beaver, buckskin, bear, wildcat, fox, coon, and mink was the common exchange. A ham of deer or buffalo could either be marketed or smoked for eating at home. Deerskin was dressed and cut into bridles, plow lines, and traces. Deer horns served for spoons and buttons, the antler for coat and rifle racks (Frome, 60). Little was bought. Nearly all tools, utensils, receptacles, household furnishing, and guns were homemade. The long-barreled, backwoods' rifle was a product of the early western frontier and became a standby throughout the Southern Appalachian mountains. The crescent-shaped butt (to avoid slipping) was made from hard maple or walnut, and its cradle of peeled hickory bark. To insure precise workmanship, the barrel was made from the softest iron available. It was forged at home on an anvil. The rifling of the barrel, or cutting the necessary twists into the bore, required an iron rod with steel cutters. All metal, including the double trigger, was blackened with a dulling stain or crushed leaf. The finished long-rifle weighed over six pounds, and its length—its trademark—was more than five feet. These home-crafted rifles were very accurate and were the companion of thousands of young men, husbands, and fathers.

The frontiersman planted a variety of crops, raised a small vegetable garden, and cultivated apple and peach trees. The forest supplemented his diet and supplied him with numerous medicinal herbs, roots, barks, and leaves. The first manufacturing enterprises on the frontier were sawmills, grist mills, and tanneries. Other manufactured articles such as glassware, iron, and powder had to be imported from long distances.

The average backwoodsman, ignorant though he was of many of the refined institutions and conventions of the older society, was never oblivious of the need for social and political order. At first, each small town or community had its own laws, but later the Appalachian West would develop its own rudimentary system of government.

Neither religion nor education could keep pace with the advances into the East Tennessee wilderness; therefore, the great majority of the early backcountry people got away from the influence of both. On the whole, the new civilization planted across the mountains was by men and women who were mostly uneducated and unreligious. Education to thousands of people simply meant the ability to write one's name, to cipher well enough to conduct a simple business, and to be able to spell out enough of a newspaper to keep track of main local news and political trends (Clark, 390). This elementary education was primarily for males; educating females was thought of as a waste of time.

By the latter 1700's there were a few schools, called "old field" schools, built on land no longer under cultivation. The school year, usually three to four months, was only when it wasn't "croptime." Most often just the three R's were taught: readin, ritin, and rithmetic (At Home in the Smokies, 84). Any higher education, such as the classics or foreign languages, was considered a frivolity of the wealthy.

Education was expensive and textbooks were scarce, and it would not be until later in the nineteenth century that free schools would begin to replace subscription schools. For many years there was no required education for teachers. Preachers, self-taught struggling lawyers, and even peddlers out of stock supplemented their meager incomes by keeping school during the week. According to Clark, the only requirement for "old field" teachers was the ability to raise a goose quill pen and switch with equal vigor (391). But by no means were all frontier teachers ignorant or bad; there were many good teachers who succeeded both in the classroom and at subsequent professions. Nevertheless, illiteracy was high for it was felt education was not becoming to men of virility. To these men it was more important to know the ways of the forest, to be the quickest shouldering the flint-lock, the most dexterous in wielding an axe, the quickest to lift a scalp, and the mightiest in a physical encounter (Abernathy, 161).

Nearly every boy entering his teens was given a rifle which he learned to shoot accurately by practicing on raccoons, squirrels, and turkeys. By constantly jumping over brambles and fallen timber he developed the agility necessary to escape from the Cherokees. He also learned to walk over fallen leaves without crushing one or breaking a twig, and to extricate himself from Indian ruses. By their late teens or early twenties, men had developed a remarkable sensitivity to sound and were able to detect the slightest inaccuracy in the imitation of an animal. They could tell by the crack of a rifle whether it belonged to a white man or to an Indian. The craft of imitating the songs of birds and the calling of animals was a necessary part of every frontier boy's education. This "forest speech" was the settlers' secret code of war—by it, in the woods, they kept track of each other and could trick an Indian into betraying himself.

Generally during the earliest years the backcountry people were too preoccupied with problems of safety and economics to establish church houses, but not all of the them were godless men, nor were they all without some church background. Because the early, western frontier movement had its beginning in the colonial period, its religious background reflected the conflicts which developed east of the mountains in the various revolts against the established churches (Clark, 227).

By the mid 1770's there were circuit riders in the Holston and Watauga river valleys, spreading the doctrine of the Methodist, Baptist, and Presbyterian faiths. Early circuit riders were ideally suited to sparse settlements where they worked with families and small community groups. The circuit rider lived on his horse; his house was his saddlebags. Rain or shine, he rode his circuit. Following the narrow trails he sometimes covered a territory of four or five hundred miles. Amid constant danger from Cherokee attack, he usually preached with his eyes constantly shifting from Bible to gun. Most often services were held in a cabin, on his horse, or under the branches of a tree. According to Caruso, highly educated preachers were regarded with suspicion by the backcountry people. They thought that ministers should come from the people and should support themselves by pursuing secular occupations. Uneducated preachers belonged economically to the same class as the majority of the settlers and fitted well into the social pattern of the Southern Appalachian frontier (224). Nevertheless, many backwoods preachers, using the Old Testament as a source for their sermons, were marvelous orators and great showmen. Itinerant preachers traveling along and through long stretches of woodlands had time to think out and organize oratories that literally smelled of sulphur. Much of their preaching was loud, picturesque, emotional, and full of fire and brimstone (Clark, 229-30).

Doctors were practically non-existent on the western frontier. Of those that were there, most never saw the inside of a medical school. They were educated by apprenticeship. Young apprentices ground powders, mixed pills, adjusted plasters, and learned to sew up wounds by watching the doctor at work. Some doctors learned from books alone. On the Appalachian frontier, anyone claiming to be a physician or surgeon could practice. There were also "yarb and root" doctors, white medicine men who had been captured as children by Indians and brought up in Indian villages. There were faith healers, and quacks who affected all their cures with secret remedies. Too, there were a few sheepskin doctors from an eastern college who learned much from these irregulars. Over sixty of the herbs used to cure sickness on the Appalachian frontier are now listed in the modern pharmacopoeia (Dunlop, 4-5).

Lice and fleas, as well as the itch, were common afflictions. Smallpox was the scourge of the frontier. Tuberculosis baffled the doctors; they could do nothing for any person stricken with it. Other prevailing diseases were typhoid fever, pneumonia, scurvy, rheumatism, and diarrhea. In addition, accidents, encounters with wild animals, and wounds inflicted by Indians all took their toll. Many aliments were caused by exposure, insufficient and improper food, and over exertion.

Early doctors on the Appalachian frontier, called saddlebag doctors, fought Indians, built cabins and roads, and searched the woods for leaves, herbs, barks, and roots. They often rode long distances, sometimes sixty to a hundred miles, to visit a patient, and had to rely upon the contents of their saddlebags to make cures. They made their own medicines—often improvised cures— and relied heavily on red pepper, flaxseed, mustard poultices, and herb teas. Whiskey was the only anesthetic and laudanum, when available, was used for pain. Saddlebag doctors learned to "make do" with available materials, improvising many necessary apparatuses.

If persons became ill, their life depended on whether their constitution could overcome not only the disease, but also the concoctions prescribed to cure it. Nearly all homes had their own store of medicines and most communities their granny-woman, a wizened, elderly woman who practiced mid-wifery and the art of doctoring. She was respected by many, but others considered her a witch. Her collection of drugs included roots, herbs, leaves, barks of various trees, cat-gut, bear grease, kerosene, spider webs, soot, animal dung, and occasionally, human urine (for the urea content). She often rode the same number of miles to visit her patients, deliver babies, and affect cures as any doctor.

Definitely these backcountry people were as much a blend of that which was coarse as fine. Their code was based on Biblical teachings with the "Laws of Moses" strictly adhered to. Marksmanship was their first line of defense and their principal theater was their own clearing. They detested a thief like the plague. As a rule they were hospitable and honest; yet they were capable of as much cruelty as kindness. They could scalp an Indian as expertly as the natives; behead an enemy and then eat out of the same sack in which the severed head was carried. They could gouge out an eye or bite off an ear in the process of fisticuffs, or devour rancid flesh—ignoring the stifling odor. These frontiersmen loved to fight and cuss, to shoot and gamble, and to drink and dance. They chewed tobacco and their women smoked pipes. A common custom among them, begun by the French and later adopted by the English and American traders, was to maintain an Indian family in the wilderness and a white one elsewhere. They were a hardy race. Men tilled their fields with a rifle by their sides; women churned with one hand and held an infant or weapon in the other; and children learned to rip off a scalp at an age when others were learning to read. To them the mountain rampart was no longer a barrier, but a challenge. The frontier people, having dared to cross the mountains, dared to stay. Warned by the Cherokee and by the Royal Governor of North Carolina, Alexander Cameron, to remove themselves, they refused; and remained where they were.

On the Southern Appalachian frontier the people had incensed the Indians, aggravated officers of the Crown, ignored decrees, and defied the British troops. They were producing a brood who would add, in a single lifetime, the span of a continent to the infant dominion of a new nation.

It was not courage the frontiersmen lacked, but an identity of themselves as a people. The western frontier did develop its own society which, in many ways, was peculiar to itself. It was affected by the geographical conditions under which it came into existence, by continual contact with the Indians, both as enemies and as friends, and by the older society of the eastern seaboard with which it maintained a limited intercourse. According to Clark, for the backwoodsman the future was a throbbing challenge of change, and change a manifestation of progress. They never looked upon either their own, or their country's, condition as it was, but as it would be (8). Having to adapt themselves to the western backwoods' environment, they had to solve social and economic problems in their own way in order to survive. Work became the habit of the backwoodsman, and throughout American history, it has remained a national virtue. The western frontier was not the birthplace of the common man, but in few regions of history has he thrived so well, or his opportunities for social advancement been so great. The more available and desirable the lands were, the more affluent were the social and economic patterns of individual settlers. It was the land speculator and squatter who focused lasting attention upon the western region of the Appalachian West.

All people in the western backwoods were squatters and violating the King's proclamation; therefore, troops were dispatched to enforce the decree and remove the squatters. The backcountry people, a term coined by the easterners, were harassed, threatened and driven bodily from one location to another; their cabins were burned, their livestock was seized, and the army told them that if they did not clear out, they would not be protected from the Cherokee. A few left, several returned to the ashes time after time, and many were killed.

The families of the first western frontier discovered that fear was a more deadly enemy than any Indian could be. The horrors the frontiersmen saw gave them the impulse to strike back. Time taught them they would not be saved by waiting on occasional marches of armies, acts of their government, or by the efforts of their neighbors—if they were to be saved, they must save themselves. Many, with their homes in ashes and their neighbors dead or fleeing, remained convinced that these events, though grievous, were but passing afflictions.

For the history of the United States, the timing of the crossing of the mountains by these backcountry people was important. If events had taken the orderly course envisioned by the framers of the Proclamation Line, if the gateways had been successfully guarded, or if the interlopers had postponed their venture until some future date, the story of America's first western frontier, of even America, would be very different. Then American independence, so gallantly fought and narrowly won, would have been an independence limited to the Atlantic seaboard. The interference of these uncontrollable, stubborn men came just in time. In a few short years the American Revolution would come and by that time a new breed of frontiersmen would arise in the Old West, one no longer easy prey for the Indians. They were men who had become accustomed to the forest and hardened by trail travel, who had for years proved they could venture widely and freely, men who knew that whatever turn of circumstance, they could come and go, live and try again. In bringing out their families this new breed had made a final and fateful decision. They had come to stay. Homesteads wrested from the western wilderness became places of birth, death, and burial; they were sites of struggles and accomplishments, of family ties, of frustration, and disappointments—they were newly—and permanently—owned.

On the East Tennessee frontier, racial differences and prejudices played a major role in the relationships of the backcountry people and the Cherokee. Their cultures were in direct conflict—one depending upon the woods, the other upon plowed fields and pastures; one exploiting natural resources for livelihood, the other relying upon cultivated crops. The Cherokees' occupation of the land was a barrier to the whites. Ill will between the Mother Country, the colonies, the new Appalachians, and the Cherokee Nation was growing. The search for an answer to the aggravating Indian problem became one of the basic themes of the first western frontier's story.

Typical Family Wagon

Grist Mill

TYPICAL "BACKWOODS" HOMESITE

Illegal squatters on land reserved for the Indians, the inhabitants of the Old West lived in constant danger from Indian attack. Most lived in a one-room log cabin with a lean-to at the back. The cabin was built of logs in the round and chinked with clay and moss. The chimney was made of either stone or of mud and sticks; sometimes it was half and half. Generally speaking, the cabin gave protection against Indian attack. Men and women married early and raised large families. They lived a life of hardship, working from sunup to sundown. Most men chewed tobacco and their women smoked pipes. Most women could shoot a rifle as well as their man. Cabin raisings, weddings, and quiltings were festive occasions that all neighbors participated in.

VI
THE EARLY SETTLEMENTS

The first ripple of the main tide of settlers toward the southern Appalachians fretted the outer edges of the central wilderness long before the first permanent settlements were made. By the mid 1700's the Scotch-Irish, German, and English had begun (in thousands) to move westward into the interior of Pennsylvania; and from there they went into the backcountry of Virginia and North Carolina, into the valleys of the Shenandoah, the Yadkin, and the Catawba.

These early settlers of the mountain valleys, called "the borderers," were a new and distinct kind of people, providing the frontal edge and outer defense line of the new Appalachian frontier. According to Frome, they were a breed who readily adapted themselves to the struggle for survival and who loved their roving room; room to breathe, to hunt, to wander at will. They were democratic by nature, resenting the implications of social superiority, and resisting interference in their affairs by any force (57). The borderers were a people long familiar with the dangers and demands of existence in the outer fringes of the wilderness. They had already experienced several years of the bloody border wars, and the horrors of the French and Indian War as well as Pontiac's War. They knew, as no one else could, the realities of the danger awaiting beyond the leap over the mountain barrier into the great western wilderness; yet they were the first to make it. Once the tide of migration began to flow into the Appalachian Southwest, there was no stopping it, not by Indians, not by wars, nor by the laws of England. With the defeat of the Cherokee in 1761 and the end of the French and Indian War two years later, this slow-moving current became a steady stream.

The bloody strife of the French and Indian War was particularly unfortunate for the Cherokee Nation. By the end of the war, the Cherokees were reduced to the greatest extremity. Many of their towns were in ashes; everything habitable destroyed, fields and orchards wasted. With many of their bravest warriors dead, the people were fugitives in the mountains, without cover, hiding in caves, living on grubs and roots, or eating their horses for food. To add to their woes, another attack of smallpox raged among them. Their population, estimated to be at least

63

5,000 braves before the war, was now reduced to less than one half that number. The miseries of starvation and the terrible scourge of smallpox combined to bring the reduced nation's morale low (Frome, 52-53).

Upon Old Hop's death in 1760, Standing Turkey became emperor, but the real ruler from then on was not the emperor but a war-lord, Oconostota. He and Attakullakulla, as principal chiefs of the nation, would rule through the end of the American Revolution.

In September of 1761, Attakullakulla and a delegation of chiefs traveled to Charles Town to meet with Governor William Bull of South Carolina, where a treaty of peace was made at Ashley Hall, or Ashley's Ferry. In November of that same year, the brother of Attakullakulla, as an ambassador from the emperor, accompanied by about four hundred warriors, came to the English fort at the Long Island of the Holston River, to treat for peace. This island, known as Great Island, Peace Island, or simply, Long Island of the Holston, was a place of refuge for the Cherokees, and a place of general rendezvous for whites and Indians (Williams, 66-67). Fort Robinson was located near the upper end and east of the Long Island, within a mile of the crossing place of the Holston River (present vicinity of Kingsport). The Cherokee branch of the Great Indian Warpath crossed the Holston over the island. A treaty was concluded here between the Cherokee and the Virginians in late November, independently of the one being signed in South Carolina. Following the signing of the treaty, the Cherokee chiefs urgently requested that an officer visit with their people for a short time to bind the new friendship; therefore, Lieutenant Henry Timberlake volunteered to return with the Cherokee warriors to their towns where he spent several months. At their leaving, the fort was evacuated, the colonial troops withdrew, and the fort was never again occupied by a military command (Williams, 67).

Following the Treaty of Paris and the Royal Proclamation of 1763 all of the Indian tribes across the Appalachian divide westward to the Mississippi came under the jurisdiction of Great Britain—or so the British contended. The tribes themselves were of a different opinion. The Cherokee were faced, as were all these tribes whether under British jurisdiction or not, with many postwar problems originated by the whites. Disputes over boundary lines, an increase in crimes committed by white men, further encroachment of whites on Indian lands, and the latter's unreasonable demand for more and more land harassed and angered the Cherokees and enflamed their animosity (Woodward, 82-83).

Perhaps no other royal proclamation to date caused such consternation in North America as did the Royal Proclamation of 1763. It was a complex document, formulated by men in London who had failed to see the actual situation in Colonial America. Its general principle rested upon a policy of reassuring the Indians that the British did not want to take their lands, but only to establish trade with them. It clearly recognized the Indians' rights to the western lands; however, the western boundaries of the Carolinas, Virginia, Georgia, and Pennsylvania had not definitely been determined (Clark, 86). This, of course, created a most confusing situation. Another factor to be dealt with was the old boundary and trade rivalry between these colonies. The British government refused to allow holders of grants from the Ohio or Loyal Land Companies to settle within the western lands. It was feared by the Crown that the vastness of Canada and the West would permit people to escape into the backwoods beyond the control of the government, but the British failed to initiate an effective military force on the frontier. Several colonies—especially Virginia, the Carolinas, Pennsylvania and Connecticut—had charters granting them lands west of the mountains, but these were ignored by the proclamation.

To lessen some of the pressure of the population pressing against the western line, Quebec province was created in the north, and the two new southern provinces of East and West Florida were formed, in the fallacious assumption that the westward movement could be diverted from its course (Clark, 84; Williams, 284). The new government of West Florida was commonly known as the Natchez country.

Although France's military forces had withdrawn from the western woods, French traders and stragglers remained and still had the willing ear of some of the Indian tribes. Thus, the French continued their trade with the Indians from New Orleans and their posts west to the Mississippi. They, as well as Anglo-Saxon hunters and land scouts, continued to roam the woods of the reserved region.

In October, 1763, the British Board of Trade assumed control over the Indians and trade with them, becoming the main obstacle in colonizing the newly won West. Two Indian Superintendents were appointed by the King to supervise and protect the Indian rights, from north to south. Sir William Johnson was placed in charge of Indian affairs north of the Ohio, and Captain John Stuart, a close friend of the Cherokee chief Attakullakulla, was appointed to supervise all tribes south of the Ohio River.

John Stuart, beloved and highly regarded by the Cherokee, was perhaps the most talented negotiator the British ever had in the South. Always mindful of his rescue from certain death by Attakullakulla at the seige of Fort Loudon in 1760, Superintendent Stuart kept in close touch with the Cherokees. To help with their postwar problems, he sent them two Deputy Commissioners of Indian Affairs, Alexander Cameron and John McDonald.

Cameron, called "Scotchie" by the Cherokee, arrived in their territory around 1766, took a Cherokee wife and settled on the Little River on land given to him by the tribe (present-day Abbeville County, South Carolina). John McDonald, a young man of nineteen and Stuart's second deputy sent by his Georgia employers to Fort Loudoun to trade with the Cherokees, arrived in the Overhill towns the same year. Here, he married Anne Shorey, the half-blood daughter of William Shorey, an early trader and interpreter among the Cherokee who died at sea in 1762. The McDonald's daughter, Molly, some years later, became the wife of Daniel Ross and the mother of Chief John Ross.

With Stuart, McDonald, and Cameron all in sympathy with them, the Cherokees turbulent affairs were kept well in hand for several years—at least until the outbreak of the Revolutionary War. During this period mixed-blood marriages or consortia of the Cherokee with Scots, Germans, English, and Irish were possibly more numerous than in previous years (Woodward, 80). Prior to the Revolution, John Adair, an eighteenth-century trader and historian who lived among the Cherokee for forty years, married a full-blood of the Deer Clan. John Stuart, named "Bushyhead" by the Cherokee because of his thick shock of red hair, married Susannah Emory, who was one quarter Cherokee—their mixed blood descendants took the surname Bushyhead, and it is an honored name today in Oklahoma. Nancy

Ward, Ghighau of the Cherokee Nation, married Bryant Ward. Nathaniel Gist's consortium with Wurteh, a niece of Attakullakulla, resulted in the birth of Sequoyah around 1760; he is the inventor of the Cherokee alphabet. The fur-trader George Lowery married a full-blood, Nannie, and their son George figured prominently in the affairs on the Nation until his death in the mid-nineteenth century. Lt. Henry Timberlake's consortium with a full-blood resulted in a son, Richard, and a grandson who later married a descendant of Nancy Ward. Presently numerous descendants of Timberlake are in Oklahoma (Williams, 273).

From these mixed-blood unions consummated during the Colonial period came many talented offspring—future leaders, saints, and sinners. Hundreds of other interracial marriages or consortia in the Colonial period strongly influenced the Cherokees, encouraging them to embrace western civilization, but the real steps toward that would not be taken until the nineteenth century by offspring of the Cherokee mixed-blood unions. Until that time, by choice, the majority of the Nation continued with their traditional culture (Woodward, 86).

The problem of controlling an expanding population was the main issue involved in the administration of the new western territory. Land and furs were very important to colonial economy, and both were to be had in abundance west of the mountains. According to Clark, no one could hold the backwoods trader in check, short of destroying him, without an elaborate inspection and police system, for he lived by the simple rule of going where the furs were to be had and paid little attention to formal rules. The same was true of the hunters and land scouts. There was also difficulty in making the land claimant, who moved from one backwoods cabin and corn patch to another, respect an intangible line on the ground (86).

As early as 1748, Colonel James Patton purchased from Virginia for $50 a grant of land comprising 200,000 acres in the upper Holston Valley (the original present-day Bristol tract). This area, known as Sapling Grove (eventually acquired by Evan Shelby) was first surveyed by John Tayloe, Jr. in 1749—the record is in the surveyor's book of Augusta County, Virginia. Stephen Holston (about 1746) had built a cabin thirty feet from the headspring of the Middle Fork of the Holston River, near the Warrior's Path (Lay, 4). Not long afterward, Dr. Thomas Walker and Christopher Gist surveyed the area. They found uninhabited Indian huts on land between the two forks of the Holston, and recorded reaching the camp of one Samuel Stalnaker on Reedy Creek (this creek passes through present-day Kingsport). Being a trader among the Overhill towns and thus familiar with the western regions, Dr. Walker offered to employ Stalnaker as a guide, but he refused, being too busy establishing a home of his own on the Warrior's Path, nine miles west of the headwaters of the Holston—the deepest penetration into the western wilderness by the advancing settlements of 1750. Dr. Walker helped Stalnaker in building his cabins before he and his party trekked on west of Reedy Creek and crossed to a branch of the north fork of the Holston, on their way to the far distant lands of what is now Kentucky. About 1751, Richard Pearis and Thomas Price set up a trading post in the vicinity of the Long Island of Holston, but it was soon abandoned. Another hunter/trader, John Honeycutt, had a small camp near the Sycamore Shoals, on one of the tributaries of the Watauga about this same time. In 1756, Edmund Pendleton obtained a land grant of 600 acres located on Island Road, along the banks of Reedy Creek at the junction of the two forks of

Holston from the Loyal Land Company. Island Road was one of two roads laid out by Fincastle (Virginia) Court leading from the Shenandoah Valley. From the Valley of Virginia, it went past the site of present-day Blountville to the Long Island of Holston. The other road was called "Watauga Road"; the two branched at the "Ford of Holston" (Williams, 379). Daniel Boone, who had crossed the Blue Ridge as early as 1760, had several hunting camps in the Watauga section. In that same year he carved the following boast deep into the bark of a large beech tree, on the Watauga stream which today bears his name: "D: Boon cilleDDA Bar on ThE Tree in YeAR 1760." In the spring of 1762, following the signing of a peace treaty between the Cherokees and the Virginians at Fort Robinson, Gilbert Christian, John Sevier, and others planted corn and built cabins on Reedy Creek, near the upper end of the Long Island, but abandoned their claims upon learning of the Pendleton Grant (Lay, 6). In due course, Eaton's Station (sometimes called "Heaton's Station") was established on a ridge above Island Flats (now Chestnut Ridge, in the vicinity of present-day Kingsport).

The slowly advancing settlement over the Appalachian divide from the Great Valley of Virginia was halted for more than a decade by the French and Indian War which engulfed the whole mountain border. Scattered families continued to live in the foothills, and after the war the Proclamation of 1763 was almost completely ignored by them, as they again inched toward the mountains. Numerous hunters and traders ranged in the hidden coves and the Holston, Clinch, and Powell valleys, following buffalo paths to big licks, wandering up and down tributary streams, crossing high mountains, and setting up temporary camps from which they operated. Friction increased daily in the field of Indian fur trade and land acquisition, as the Indians saw white settlements creeping closer to their hunting grounds.

About 1765 a migration had begun to the Natchez district of West Florida which was open to settlement by the proclamation of 1763. Many went by water down the Holston and Tennessee rivers, running the gauntlet of the Cherokees who murdered numerous emigrants. There was already a glacier-like migration down the Holston onto Indian lands and the Cherokee feared an avalanche.

By 1766, transient traders such as Andrew Greer and Caesar Dugger were trading among the forested Watauga hills, and for the next two or three years made frequent trips between their homes in Virginia and the Cherokee towns carrying furs and pelts one way and trading-goods and trinkets back for the furtherance of their trade. According to Clark, by 1768, in the South about five thousand families had moved across the mountains, over the Line, onto Cherokee lands. It was felt if these families were not protected, a general Indian war would ensue (90).

The Cherokee were more numerous than the other Indian tribes living north of the Ohio and, on the whole, were somewhat less warlike than the Shawnee and Iroquois. Their villages were more compact and they possessed a very effective rudimentary system of national government. It was into this Cherokee country, of the Appalachian frontier that the Europeans from the British colonies advanced during the second half of the eighteenth century with renewed vigor as the French and Spanish relinquished their North American claims.

The availability of so much unclaimed land became as a magnet drawing every dissatisfied colonist—especially from Virginia and the Carolinas—to the beautiful

Nolichucky River near Limestone

View from Eaton's Ridge

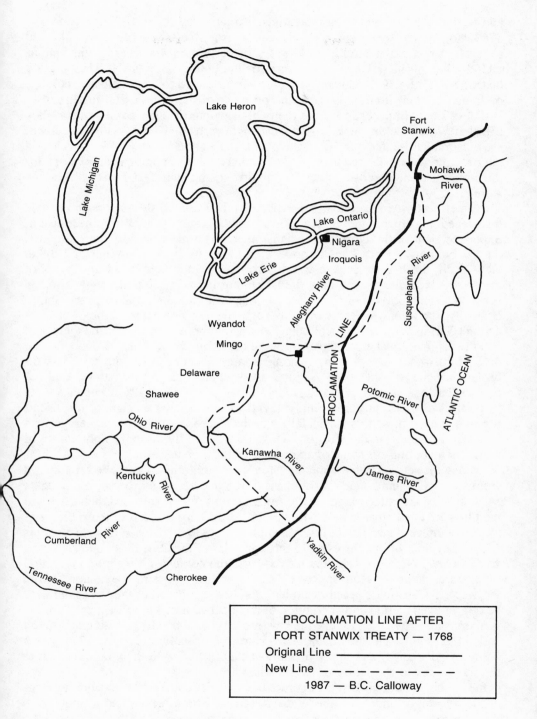

Lake Heron

Lake Michigan

Lake Ontario

Nigara

Iroquois

Lake Erie

Fort
Stanwix

Mohawk
River

Wyandot

Mingo

Delaware

Shawee

Ohio River

Kentucky

River

Cumberland River

Tennessee River

Cherokee

Kanawha River

Alleghany River

PROCLAMATION LINE

Susquehanna River

Potomic River

James River

Yadkin River

ATLANTIC OCEAN

PROCLAMATION LINE AFTER
FORT STANWIX TREATY — 1768
Original Line ——————————
New Line — — — — — — — —
1987 — B.C. Calloway

and fertile valleys beyond the mountains. Although by order of the manifesto of 1763, no private person could purchase land from the Indians, nor was allowed to legally settle in the central wilderness, the early pioneers regarded the land as a God-given heritage which was theirs for the taking (Dixon, 3). They argued that since all the wild land had not previously belonged to any company, colony, or Indian Nation, it could become the property of the first person to take, use, and develop it. In order to escape the overcrowding of older communities, they traveled west—seeking a cabin site and a farmstead. These avid woodsmen, speculators, hard-bitten hunters, fur trappers, Indian traders, and land scouts would later see the woods cleared away and eventually substitute their winter camps for the family fireside, their trap lines for the furrow, and their pack horses for a small store.

In an effort to stem the tide of migration, and because the speculators and traders threatened to breach the policy of the proclamation, Sir William Johnson, Superintendent of the Northern Indians, arranged a meeting with the Indians of the Six Nations at Fort Stanwix on Oneida Lake. In the late summer of 1768 at New York, the British Empire and the Iroquois Nation negotiated the Treaty of Fort Stanwix, affecting not only the whole northern line, but allowing it to run across a sizable portion of Cherokee and Shawnee hunting grounds in the South. Basically, the Kanawha River would become the new line between the Cherokees and the Virginians, with a local bulge westward about the forks of the Ohio, but still the original line held at the crest of the mountains. Johnson was overstepping his administrative authority by making an agreement with the northern Indians for land which lay in the South. Although the land procured in the south was claimed by the Shawnee as part of their ancient domain, it was actually occupied by the Cherokees as their hunting grounds; therefore, the Shawnees right to dispose of it was in question. At this particular time, the Cherokee were too concerned with white men already on the Holston to become excited by the future possibility of white men settling on more of their land in far Kentucky.

Among the settlers to the upper Holston were emigrants who moved southward from the Susquehanna and its tributaries, tramped across Forbes or Braddock's road, crossed unsettled ranges of the Appalachians to Fort Pitt, and then traversed the Ohio River to what is now Moundville, West Virginia. From there they zig-zagged southward through narrow mountain valleys to the Great Valley of Virginia where they bore off southwestward through parts of the Greenbrier and Kanawha river valleys. Numerous settlers moved from the colony of Virginia in a natural progression down the Holston River. Many early settlers were "regulators" from the western Carolinas, people who had revolted against what they considered to be oppressive taxation and corruption of the local courts. These western Carolina farmers had earlier tried to take the law into their own hands, resulting in a revolt called the Regulation Movement. The protest was finally crushed in 1771 by the battle of Alamance, and many of the Regulators fled with their families across the mountains to the Holston and its tributaries.

In October, of the same year, in order to legitimize some of the squatter holdings at the Sycamore Shoals on the Watauga River, Britain negotiated a treaty with the Cherokee at Hard Labor, an Indian village in upcountry South Carolina. John Stuart, His Majesty's Southern Indian Superintendent, drew a boundary line back of the Carolinas and Virginia—starting near the Blue Ridge at Fort Chiswell, on New River, running due north to the mouth of the Great Kanawha on the Ohio; beyond which whites were forbidden to settle. This line wasn't surveyed until the following year because the treaty was not signed until November, too late for surveying in the mountainous county. With these two treaties the British has acquired from the Indians a sizable block of land lying in the present states of Virginia, West Virginia, and western Pennsylvania.

After the afore said treaties between the Indians and whites concerning the King's western boundary, the border people assumed they were at liberty to make claims beyond the mountains in the western wilderness, and proceeded to do so. Before long streams of pioneers had pressed further than the Hard Labor cession. This land was claimed but not occupied by the Indians; therefore, the appearance of these individuals in the upper Holston Valley west of the line soon necessitated another agreement. Accordingly, in the fall of 1770 at Lochaber on the South Carolinian estate of Alexander Cameron, Stuart again negotiated a treaty with the Cherokee, wherein they ceded a triangle of territory west of the Hard Labor Line meant to legitimize the squatter claims in the upper Holston Valley. Like the treaty of two years before, the northern anchor of the line remained as the Ohio at the mouth of the Kanawha, but the southern end of the line was moved seventy miles west from Fort Chiswell to a new point six miles east of the Long Island of the Holston. Thus it happened that the early frontier people thought they were settling legally on lands which were a part of the Virginia colony.

Tennessee's first permanent settler of record, Captain William Bean of Virginia, arrived in 1768. He and his wife, Lydia, had already seen the paradise west of the Appalachians while on hunting expeditions with Daniel Boone and Andrew Greer. The Beans especially liked the Watauga section; therefore, in an area where he thought the hunting was good, Bean wisely chose as his homestead one of Boone's hunting camps, on a creek about one hundred yards from its junction with the Watauga River. Bean named the stream Boone's Creek, in honor of his friend Daniel Boone. In the same year he cleared the land, planted crops, and raised a cabin on the side of a ridge which hid the site from Indians who might pass by canoe along the river. The waterfall at the immediate mouth of the creek prevented the turning of a canoe out of the river onto the creek. The following year he brought his family to the lower Watauga, and it was here that his son, Russell, was born—the first white child born to permanent settlers on Tennessee soil. The family was soon joined by kith and kin from southern Virginia.

Two years later, early in the spring, a grimy traveler weary from the long and difficult journey across the mountains arrived in the Watauga Valley at the Sycamore Shoals on a tour of inspection of the country. The stranger was a man of modest means and limited education. He had left his home in Orange County, North Carolina, in the throes of the Regulation movement. His relationship to this movement is unknown, but no doubt he sympathized with it. The stranger's name was James Robertson, and he was destined not only to play a part in the history of America's first Western frontier, East Tennessee, but also in the early history of Middle Tennessee. He is honored, therefore, both as "The Father of Tennessee" and as "The Father of Middle Tennessee."

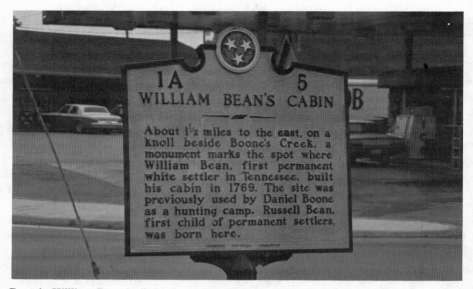

Captain William Bean built his log cabin (1768) on a knoll along Boones Creek, about one hundred yards from its junction with the Watauga River. In 1769, he moved his family to the new country and, in that same year his son Russell—the first white child born to permanent settlers on Tanasi soil—was born. The waters of Boone Lake cover the original site.

BOONES CREEK WATERFALL

According to legend, on one of Daniel Boone's frequent hunting trips in the area, he discovered Indians "dogging" his tracks. With nowhere else to hide, he took off at a fast trot to a nearby waterfall. There, he quickly hid under its concealing curtain of water until the Indians gave up their search and went away. The waterfall was then about four feet high. Today, due to erosion, it is much smaller. The waterfall is located about half a mile from Boones Creek Middle School.

Robertson, mounted on a good horse with a rifle in his hands, came to the Watauga alone, following one of Boone's trails across the mountains—the route which to the Indians was "The Great Trading and Warrior Path." Near the confluence of Roan Creek and Watauga River, Robertson accepted the hospitality of a hunter named John Honeycutt. The twenty-eight year old visitor was thrilled by all he saw, especially a few miles downstream where the Doe River joins the Watauga as it tumbles out of the mountains. Here, above the Sycamore Shoals, was a rich open valley—ancient Indian old fields which had been cleared and tilled by them in remote times. These "Watauga Old Fields" seemed to Robertson, as he said in later years, "the promised land."

There with the help of Honeycutt he cleared the land, planted a crop of Indian corn, and built a cabin and a corn crib. After the laying-by of his corn crop early in August, Robertson turned homeward through the mountains. A period of heavy rains set in and the sun was obscured for many days. Robertson soon lost his way. Upon reaching terrain his horse could not navigate due to the heavy covering of rhododendron and laurel thickets, he was compelled to abandon the animal. He tried blazing a trail only to discover that he was continuously re-crossing his former tracks. Drenched by the rain, Robertson was unable to keep his powder dry, rendering it useless for the shooting of any game for food. Lost and desperate, subsisting on what few berries and roots he could find, he might have died from starvation and exposure except for the chance encounter with two hunters out in the mountains looking for game who gave him food and a horse to ride. At last, after fourteen days of wandering, Robertson arrived home.

Enthralled by the colorful accounts he gave of the Watauga region, several relatives and friends agreed to accompany him and his family on the return journey. Late in September, a party of sixteen to twenty families headed west for the Sycamore Shoals. It is told that they settled in the vicinity of the "old field flats" on the Watauga, creating a small community in the forest wilderness well beyond civilization. Later it became a point of rendezvous for all those who followed the Beans and Robertsons.

In spite of the uncertainty about the land and the law, by 1772 there were approximately 75 to 85 farms along the banks of the Holston and Watauga rivers. The number of settlers in the upper valleys of the Holston, Clinch, and Powell rivers had swelled so rapidly that the new county of Fincastle was created to conduct that affairs of the Virginians living west of the New River. Later, this county would be expanded to include most of present Tennessee and practically all of present Kentucky.

In most locations the new settlers were strangers upon arrival, but they were obliged to quickly learn to work together. There were no clear boundaries, the King's proclamation was still in effect, and any titles to the western lands were entirely dependent upon Britain's action. Almost all permanent settlers believed they had settled in either Virginia or North Carolina.

As the frontier people gathered in the vicinity of the Long Island, it was realized that the old fort (Robinson) had fallen into disrepair. Later in 1776, a new one was built near the same location and called Fort Patrick Henry. It served not only as a bastion of protection, but as a supply depot to help destitute settlers and to aid outbound immigrants on their way into the more westerly lands. Wagoners supplied the fort.

In the same year that the Robertson party settled at the Sycamore Shoals, another settlement was made and a store established on the west side of the Holston River, a few miles below the junction of its two forks (near the site of present-day Rogersville). The store was set up by John Carter and his partner, Joseph Parker, to procure the Indian pelt trade. The vicinity has ever since borne the name "Carter's Valley," in honor of its first settler who was a member of the firm of Carter and Trent located across the James River in Virginia. The establishment at Carter's Valley was designed as a trading post to do business with the Cherokee as well as other Indians out on hunts or visiting from the Cherokee towns on the Little Tennessee, and to sell goods to migrants on their way down the Holston, Tennessee, Ohio, and Mississippi rivers to the Natchez country. The post became so popular with the Indians that other traders, living in the Overhill towns, griped about it hurting their own trade. Chiefs of the different villages warned Carter and Parker more than once to move out. These warnings were unheeded and in a short time the store was pillaged by the Indians. Carter then moved to the Watauga; Parker abandoned the store and returned to Virginia. Although the Carter's Valley settlements were not in anyway connected with the Watauga settlements, John Carter became an important figure in the affairs of the Watauga Association. Later, he would be appointed chairman of the authorized Washington District and Washington County, holding the position until his death in 1781.

Another noteworthy person to be briefly mentioned at this point is John Sevier. Although he founded no settlements, he was a very important figure in the early affairs of the Watauga. He and his brother, Valentine, visited the Watauga country several times, and in 1772 they, their father, and other brothers with their families settled on the north side of the Holston in the Keywood settlement. John, always searching for better land on which to build a better home for his growing family, moved to the Watauga in 1775 (where he played an important part in the Revolution), to the Nolichucky in 1778 (where he earned the title of "Nolichucky Jack" by being a great Indian fighter), and finally, to Marble Springs, near present-day Knoxville, in 1790 (where he was elected six times as governor of Tennessee and four times to the Congress of the United States).

The second mercantile establishment in the settlements was actually a combination trading post, way station, and stockade erected north of the Watauga by hard-drinking Evan Shelby, a Marylander, originally from Wales. This fort, known as Shelby's Station and covering over an acre and a half, was built on a hill above Beaver Creek (above the corner of present-day Seventh and Anderson streets in Bristol, Tennessee) as a bastion against the Indians. During the French and Indian War Shelby was a scout with Braddock and commanded a company with Forbes. Afterward, he became a fur trader among the Indians. During his travels in and out of the western wilderness, he heard about a tradesman named William Bean and a farmer, James Robertson, who had settled on the Watauga and the Sycamore Shoals, respectively. They had visited the upper East Tennessee region, surveying the lay of the land before deciding to move their families to the wild country, and after several months had returned to their old surroundings regaling everyone they met with tales of the golden land west of the Alleghenies. It was these and other tales which fascinated and inspired Shelby, a skilled and crafty woodsman, to go see this wonderland for himself.

He first appeared in what is now the East Tennessee country about the close of the year 1770 and was excited by all he saw. He wrote his sons of his satisfaction with the territory, telling them that the soldiers and officers of the French and Indian War would undoubtedly receive grants of land there, and for them to purchase as many of the grants as possible. They did as he suggested.

The following year, at the age of 51, Shelby moved his family to the Holston country and settled at a place called "Big Camp Meet" (now Bristol, Tennessee-Virginia). The place was a prehistoric Indian village named, according to legend, because numerous deer and buffalo met here to feast in the canebrakes. An Indian trail, which the early settlers would traverse, followed an old Buffalo path from what is now Bristol to present-day Blountville. Shelby renamed the site Sapling Grove (which would later be changed to King's Meadows, and still later to Bristol). Here, the Shelby family engaged in merchandising, farming, and cattle raising (Lay, 5).

The Sapling Grove tract, when surveyed and sold to Colonel James Patton in 1749 for fifty dollars, consisted of 1,946 acres. Later, the title was acquired by John Buchanan from executors of Patton's estate. About 1768 General Shelby and Isaac Baker bought the 1,946-acre Sapling Grove tract for three hundred and four pounds, each receiving 973 acres which was supposed to be in Virginia. However, when the boundary line was finally established, Shelby's estate became the site of what is now Bristol, Tennessee, and Baker's land became part of present-day Bristol, Virginia (Lay 5-6).

John, a brother of Shelby, followed him to the western frontier, settling near Shoat's ford (present-day Bluff City). The ford was located on an old Indian trail—later the Watauga Road—from Wolf Hills (present-day Abingdon, Virginia) to the Watauga settlement (present-day Elizabethton, Tennessee) over which thousands of emigrants would travel to settle along the bank of the upper Holston and Tennessee rivers. Around the two plantations of the Shelby brothers sprang up a small community supposedly in Virginia.

"Shelby's Station" (i.e., Sapling Grove) was an important trading post which soon became a rendezvous for migrants passing through the territory on their way farther west and for expeditions heading northward. Shelby's sons assisted him with the store and among their many customers were Daniel Boone, James Robertson and his brother Charles, John Cox, Valentine Sevier, father of General John Sevier, William Bean, and many other well known pioneers. Evan Shelby left many descendants, among whom was his son Isaac who became the first governor of Kentucky.

Sapling Grove had its nucleus at the Long Island of the Holston where another settlement evolved near the dual forks of the river. According to Lay, Gilbert Christian was one of those daring individuals who paid more attention to land he wanted than to boundary lines; therefore, he seized a portion of the Pendleton grant and staked a claim for two hundred and fifty acres at the mouth of Reedy Creek, opposite the Long Island. This claim was officially recorded in 1782 (6). Others, finding the area attractive, began to establish permanent homes near Christian's plantation, and by 1771 they had moved down the Island Road as far as Eaton's Station.

The area comprised by the Sapling Grove and Long Island of the Holston communities was called the "Fork Country," or North-of-the-Holston, by the Wataugans. It was a fast growing area governed as part of Virginia which later became part of the Watauga Association.

The Long Island of the Holston, also called Great Island or Peace Island, was the sacred sanctuary of the Cherokee Nation, a jealously guarded possession. The island is strategically located a short distance up-river from the junction of the north and south forks of the Holston River; it is four miles long and averages half a mile wide. Ancient Indian tribes used the island for villages, but the historic tribes during the Cherokee period used the island as neutral ground; a sacred place of refuge where nothing was killed. Its horizon had been lighted with the flames of many council fires as war and peace pacts were negotiated. It was here that the Cherokee met with chiefs of other tribes from the North, East, and West for talks, treaties, and to smoke the pipe of friendship; later they did the same with white men.

The Great Island was the "place of general rendezvous" for the Colonial and Revolutionary militias; the scene of momentous events during the early years of exploration and settlement of the first western expansion; the springboard for the initial settlement of Kentucky and Middle Tennessee—in 1775, Daniel Boone gathered his thirty axemen at the Long Island to open the famous Wilderness Road to Kentucky in order to settle land purchased from the Cherokees—and it was here that John Donelson and his group gathered before beginning their river journey to the Cumberland settlement.

There are probably two reasons why the pioneers did not move into the immediate vicinity of the island—one was that most of the fertile land for several miles up Reedy Creek had been included in the Pendleton grant; the other was the custom of the Indians to tarry on the island. The constant encroachment of whites on Cherokee land as well as their desecration of Peace Island gave the Indian even more cause for retaliation. The beloved Long Island was one of the last pieces of land ceded by the Cherokee.

Southeast of Sycamore Shoals, adjoining the Watauga, is the Nolichucky—which comes from the Cherokee word **Nula-tsu'gu-y** meaning "spruce tree place (another Indian name was rushing water). The river flows westward from the Blue Ridge divide into the Tennessee-Holston system. The first settler, though a temporary one, in the Nolichucky Valley was John Ryan, who was among one of the groups of Regulators which left North Carolina for the Southern Appalachian frontier in 1768. He sold, for eighty dollars and a wagon load of trade goods, his preemption claim to two large parcels of land on the Nolichucky to Jacob Brown sometime in the year 1771.

Jacob Brown was an itinerant merchant from South Carolina who had made previous trips with his pack horses into the Cherokee country, and was attracted by the rich, broad river bottoms along the Nolichucky which were similar to those of the Sycamore Shoals. Seeing the prospect of trade with the Cherokees, Brown— either by using the empty log structures left by Ryan or by building cabins of his own—opened a supply store and set up a blacksmith forge and gun repair shop on the north bank of the Nolichucky River just over the low ridge from Sinking Creek on the Watauga about midway between the present towns of Jonesborough and Erwin. With him he brought a group of Regulators and their families from North Carolina (Williams, 351). Here Brown, a blacksmith and a gunsmith as well as a small trader, found his services much in demand by the Indians who hunted in the area. The Cherokees were glad to have a man with these useful skills living nearby; therefore, he soon ingratiated himself with them. Before long Brown's smithy, gun repair shop, and storehouse became sort of an Indian and hunter hangout. Here, in the middle of their hunting grounds, the Cherokee could meet, obtain powder and lead, trade their pelts, have their guns mended, and obtain needed supplies.

Both the Watauga and Nolichucky settlements were more than fifty miles west of the British proclamation line of 1763. Neither were within the jurisdiction of either Virginia nor North Carolina. The settlers of the Nolichucky were several miles southwest of the Sycamore Shoals and, therefore, fifteen miles nearer the Overhill Cherokee towns than the Watauga settlers. Originally the Nolichucky settlements were not connected with the Watauga settlements nor the Watauga Association, but during the American Revolution they became closely identified with both.

Later in the year 1771 as the leaves began to fall John Donelson and Alexander Cameron, with Attakullakulla on hand, surveyed the boundary line formed by the Treaty of Lochaber, beginning at the Virginia-Carolina corner just southeast of Fort Chiswell. Before long it became apparent to the surveying party that all settlers at the Sycamore Shoals and most of those around Sapling Grove were on Cherokee land. The Wataugans had not settled in Virginia as they believed, but within the bounds of North Carolina. The Little Carpenter, feeling sorry for the settlers near the survey line, consented to have the line run down the south fork of the Holston River all the way to the Long Island corner formed by the Lochaber cession. Thus it was that the holdings of the Beans, Robertsons, and their neighbors were not legitimized, but the holdings of Shelby and his neighbors were. After the survey, Cameron advised the Wataugans that they were illegal squatters on Cherokee land— their presence was displeasing to the Indians and obnoxious to the King. He ordered them to remove themselves. This command did not apply to the Virginia-governed North of Holston settlement and he mentioned neither the Carter's Valley settlement nor that of the Nolichucky. Even so, Carter withdrew to the Sycamore Shoals and Brown to the Watauga. The Wataugans, feeling it was too inconvenient to move back across the mountains and unwilling to lose the labor bestowed on their farms, decided to remain where they were.

An equally grave matter for the inhabitants of the lower Holston was that of government protection. Falling within the bounds of North Carolina rather than Virginia, the Wataugans could not see any prospects of security or protection from that province. Too, fearing the Watauga settlement might become a haven for criminals and others eager to be beyond the reach of any law, and reflecting on the necessity of recording deeds, marriages, wills, and other public business, the Wataugans felt it was imperative to organize themselves. According to Van Every, their political self-sufficiency was to prove an enormously strengthening element in the total political fabric of the new nation of which they were in time to become a part (15).

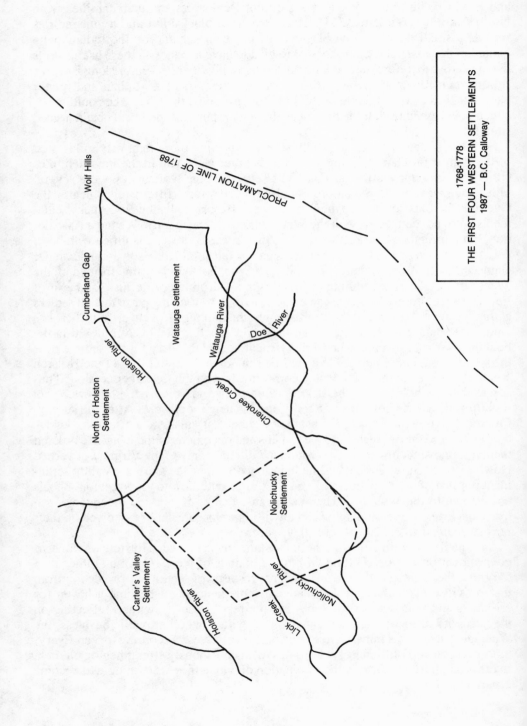

Wolf Hills

PROCLAMATION LINE OF 1768

Cumberland Gap

Watauga Settlement

Watauga River

Doe River

Holston River

North of Holston
Settlement

Cherokee Creek

Nolichucky
Settlement

Carter's Valley
Settlement

Holston River

Lick Creek

Nolichucky River

1768-1778
THE FIRST FOUR WESTERN SETTLEMENTS
1987 — B.C. Calloway

78

VII
THE WATAUGA COMMUNITY

To the thirteen British colonies along the Atlantic seaboard, the new transmountain settlements of the Watauga community had trifling significance. These colonists were more concerned with the numerous tax schemes the British were trying to enforce rather than what might be developing in the far forests across the Appalachians.

In 1774 in response to the many years of oppressive taxation and numerous acts imposed on the colonies by the British parliament, the First Continental Congress was summoned. It was a consultative rather than legislative body, a convention rather than a Congress. Representatives from all the colonies except Georgia deliberated at Carpenters' Hall, Philadelphia, for seven weeks from September 5th to October 26th. A document known as The Association was drawn up by the Congress and called for a complete boycott of British goods. It and all other petitions of the Continental Congress were rejected by the British parliament. As a result, many groups of colonials, known as the "Sons of Liberty," took the law into their own hands. They tarred and feathered tax officials, willfully destroyed tea cargoes, participated in smuggling, and encouraged open drilling of the colonial "Minute Men." Faced with the breakdown of law and order in the colonies and hoping to forestall further troubles, Britain started landing troops at different New England harbors. According to Bailey, many of the soldiers unfortunately were drunk and profane characters. For the colonists, the red-coated regiments only served to fan the existing flames of discontent. Resenting their presence, many liberty-loving colonials taunted the "lobster backs" unmercifully (92).

While events in the East were rapidly moving toward armed conflict, the people of the Appalachian frontier were pursuing their own struggle for survival and adaptation to the harsh and rugged wilderness. Far from the coast, the wilderness occupied by Indians, borderers, and wild beasts was thought of by the easterners as but another Crown colony—separated from the eastern frontier by a north-south line designated by the King. Commonly referred to, always disparagingly, as the "back country," it was known to be a haven for fugitives from justice, a place

79

where no civilized person—only a few, foolhardy "back woods men"—would live. This new transmountain frontier was separated from its neighbors to the east by two hundred miles of nearly impassable, forested mountains and was hemmed in on all sides by twenty-six Indian nations, who were in constant touch with each other and united in their fierce opposition to any further advancement of the whites.

Life on the Appalachian frontier was strange and crude, entirely different from the comfort and security of the East. The rugged conditions of the present and the hazards of an unknown future changed the pioneers' patterns of living and, consequently, their habits of thoughts. Those who could not adapt to the new surroundings perished. Unable to depend on the easterners for protection, the frontier people quickly learned to depend upon themselves. Hacking their way through the wilderness, living off the land, and relying on their own resourcefulness, they developed strength, individualism, self-confidence and a spirit of independence. That these scattered western settlements of the backcountry, settled by so-called "foolhardy back woods men," had already begun to shape the future of a new nation—and would continue to do so during the next one hundred years—was a development not yet evident to anyone.

In just three short years before the American Revolution (1772-1775), these frontier people would openly defy the British parliament, the King and his royal officials, acquire a land lease from the Cherokee, organize a frontier militia, and establish a government of their own. They would send delegates to the First Continental Congress, and on the eve of the Revolution they were in the process of establishing a new colony in the Kentucky region.

All the western settlements were illegal by English law. Separated by a great distance from the East, they were also separated from each other by miles made longer by lack of roads. Raids by Cherokees as well as other Indians were frequent. English armies were not the guardians of the settlements, but instead were their enemies. The inter-colonial conflict over the western territory aborted any attempt by the colonial government to provide frontier defense. Though the inhabitants had created their own laws and established homesites, their legal status was one of confusion. They did not know what province—if any—they resided in, or the laws of what government—if any—they should recognize, and they did not yet know how, when, or if ever, their land titles would be accepted as valid. The duty of the King's representatives west of the mountains was to deal with the traders and Indians, not with the settlers.

The extraordinary hardiness of the frontier people, forged in the fires of many wars, gave them their dominating and only common trait, self-reliance. Their past was criss-crossed with many bloodstained marches, cruises, and battles, and miraculously their prolonged suffering during twenty years of border wars had served not to crush them, but only to arouse them. Though not yet independent, they were very independent minded. So far their claims to the land had been denied by the British royal government, the eastern land companies, often by rival settlers, by one or more provinces, and by the Cherokee. Finally, they chose not to live outside the law, but to make their own laws.

Needless to say, there were many reasons for forming a government in the isolated, infant community at the Watauga River. They were outside the jurisdiction of Virginia, subjected to constant Indian raids geographically isolated from North

Carolina, had no visible means of defense, and were alienated from the East. However, the two reasons given by the Wataugans themselves were the want of a proper legislature and the necessity of recording deeds, wills, and other civic affairs.

The Wataugans realizing that neither North Carolina nor Virginia recognized their right to live within Indian country, and apprehensive that their community might become a shelter for criminals who had put the mountain wall between themselves and justice, wanted a legal way to maintain order and to do public business; so they decided to take matters into their own hands.

The making of the Watauga Compact and the leasing of Cherokee land were intimately related to each other. In May, 1772, a meeting of all freemen over the age of twenty-one was called. Using the Virginia laws as a guide, the men met to form an organization of government under "Written Articles of Association" (called the Watauga Association) for the infant, mountain colony in the backwaters. They agreed upon a court through which they could govern the community. This federation also gave them a unity by which they could raise a militia, sanctify marriages, manage land affairs, and facilitate other functions of government. According to Dixon, the political history of what was to become Tennessee began with this meeting (16).

The framers of the Watauga Association established a court of law with five magistrates—none of whom had any legal training—a clerk for recording procedures, and a sheriff. Its functions were numerous and frontier justice was harsh. There was a whipping post and pillory in the center of town; horse thieves had the letters H and T branded on each cheek, and hanging was the sentence for murder. A man who stole fresh-baked bread was nicknamed "Bread Rounds," a name that spread rapidly throughout the entire community. Each time the thief was seen in the community, or even nearby, the name "Bread Rounds" was shouted as well as his full name. This oral punishment was sufficient. Soon, shamed and unable to endure the stigma, the man left the town and its vicinity.

It is believed by most historians that the meeting of the Wataugans was held after the Cherokees agreed to lease, but before The Little Carpenter arrived in Watauga to work out the particulars. Unfortunately the original articles are lost; more is known about the lease than the compact, and very little is known about the connection between the two—but it was surely no coincidence that the Watauga Association was formed in 1772, the year the settlers leased their land from the Cherokee Nation.

As to the historical importance of the association, most historians agree that the articles were the first constitution west of the Appalachians, and one of the most thoroughly democratic instruments ever penned in the New World. There is no doubt it was the prototype for several other self-government resolutions on the southwestern frontier, such as the Boonesboro Resolutions of 1775, the Cumberland Compact of 1780, and the Franklin Constitution of 1785.

A number of historians refer to the articles as a "squatters' agreement" created simply to acquire land from the Indians and as a temporary means to deal with a security problem. The other line of attack by critics is the assertion that the Wataugans created a free and independent colony, "The Republic of Watauga"; again, there are those who support this notion, but most feel the case has been overstated, noting that the Articles of Association was a constitution, not a declaration of independence.

Although there was no formal declaration of Watauga independence from either Britain or North Carolina, nor any formal recognition of its self government by any colony, the Wataugans' de facto sovereignty was nonetheless real and impressive. They did not seek higher approval nor recognize any superior authority other than that vested in the five magistrates chosen by them. They freely adopted laws of Virginia, added their own local ordinances to them, and enforced both through courts of their own creation. Under such laws they functioned as an autonomous government, being virtually an independent colony for nearly five years.

As far as is known, the Watauga Constitution and the records of the Watauga government have perished; not a single copy has come down to us. When the association dissolved, the documents fell into private hands—whose, we do not know. We know of its existence through the Wataugans' own brief, collective testimony in 1776, the testimony of early historians of Tennessee who knew some of its principals, and excerpts from private papers, diaries, and family records of a few early Wataugans.

For approximately two years, following the land lease of 1772, the Watauga community lived in peace with their Cherokee landlords and substantial migration followed. During these quiet years they formed a frontier militia in which all males over the age of sixteen years were to serve, distributed the land they had leased, improved their roads, enforced laws, improved their buildings, enlarged their clearings, and went about their business of making a living on the Appalachian frontier. Life was primitive, but gradually there appeared a look of permanence in the valleys.

After the Donelson survey of 1771, the Southern Indian Deputy Commissioner, Alexander Cameron, advised the Wataugans that they were illegal squatters on Indian lands and ordered them to move. Faced with an immediate decision of whether to retreat or resist, they decided to follow the advice of Daniel Boone, who strongly urged them to stay. In order to gain more time, they asked if they might remain until spring to harvest the crops already in the ground. Cameron and the Indians agreed. Then a meeting of the heads of families was called to discuss the situation—all agreed to ignore the Indian agents and the royal governor of North Carolina, and since forbidden to buy the land outright from the Cherokee it was decided to see if they could procure a lease from the chiefs. James Robertson and John Been were deputed to treat with the Cherokees.

Robertson and Been journeyed the hundred and fifty miles through the perilous forests to the sacred town of the Overhill Cherokee, Echota, and there in a meeting of the Tribal Council, discovered that the Indians were not of one mind about what to do. Therefore, they sought out chiefs willing to lease the land; to them they presented their gifts, made proposals, and negotiated. A vote of the Council was taken and the matter was agreed upon. Chief Attakullakulla, "the Little Carpenter," was chosen to go to the Watauga settlement to work out the details of the lease and friendship pact. There the Wataugans agreed to the "Articles of Accommodation and Friendship" and a ten year lease of land. For $5-6,000 in merchandise and trade goods, plus some muskets, ammunition and household articles, the Cherokees granted to the Wataugans use of all the country on the waters of the Watauga.

Jacob Brown, who was then at the Sycamore Shoals, arranged a meeting with Oconostota and some other chiefs at his house in order to transact a separate lease with them. For an unknown amount of money and trade goods, he secured a similar lease from the Cherokee for a large section of the Nolichucky Valley on both sides of the river. The two leases acquired by these joint communities, which now numbered eighty heads of families, or eighty homesteads, were truly shrewd pieces of strategy; a real backwoods coup for the Watauga and Nolichucky settlements. The Cherokees were now their landlords and seemingly a decade of peace lay ahead. By the lease the tenantry gained a legal hold on the western land, one which might lead to possession. In any event, the tenancy was a key to the Wataugans' survival.

To celebrate their land leases and new understanding with the Cherokee, in the spring of 1774, a day of athletic games, horse racing, and other sports was planned at Sycamore Shoals. White people and hundreds of Cherokees gathered from all over the territory. All during the day, several ruffians from Wolf Hills had been lurking in the nearby environs, watching for an opportunity to start trouble. Among these rowdy men was one Isaac Crabtree, sole white survivor of the massacre the previous fall of the James Boone party near Cumberland Gap, who had vowed to kill any Indian who crossed his path—friend or foe. Late in the afternoon, during one of the racing matches between the Cherokee and Wataugans, before bystanders could prevent the action, Crabtree from the nearby woods deliberately fired upon and killed one of three Cherokees. The murdered Indian was named "Cherokee Billie, or Billey," kinsman of old Chief Ostenaco (called Judd's Friend or Mankiller, by the whites). The remaining Cherokees, greatly angered, but fortunately unarmed, silently gathered their goods together and with dark countenances, hastily withdrew to their homes. The Wataugans were greatly alarmed at this needless killing; it immediately endangered their quiescence with the Cherokee and exposed them to the Indians resentment and the real possibility of retaliation. They knew the whole community, as well as other settlements, would suffer if the warriors sought revenge. The Magistrates offered a reward of 50 English pounds for Crabtree's arrest; an additional reward of 100 English pounds was offered by Governor Dunmore of Virginia. Fearful of the consequences of this rash act, James Robertson volunteered to travel to Echota to try to make amends. He took the trader, William Faulin (Falling) along with him as companion and interpreter.

After the long and dangerous journey of one hundred-fifty miles, he and his friend arrived safely at their destination. Already in council was a big assembly of chiefs. The two emissaries requested and received permission to speak to the Council. Through his interpreter, Robertson apologized for the heinous crime committed by an outsider, explaining that his people were horrified at such a deed. He promised that the culprit would be severely punished when caught. The Cherokees were amused and pleased at the white man's loss of face; nevertheless, the young chiefs, hot-headed braves, and relatives of Billie's family demanded revenge. However, the older chiefs were pleased with the white's sentiments and the request for continued friendship. Wanting to keep peace, they accepted the apology and agreed to take no vengeance on their white brothers. For the time being the elders had averted a bad situation.

Although war had been adverted momentarily in East Tennessee, events were taking place on the Ohio frontier which would bring the Cherokee and whites once more into conflict. The Ohio Valley was not only claimed by both the Cherokee and the Shawnee, but two American colonies—Virginia and Pennsylvania—were arguing over ownership of the area.

The western frontier was advancing irrepressibly, defying every attempt by the British government to limit it to the territories outlined in its Indian treaties. The frontier people trespassed into the rich valleys of the Clinch and its tributaries, pushed on to far away Kentucky, and settled along the banks of the upper Ohio River. Even though this region was claimed by the Shawnee and Cherokee as their hunting grounds, the beckoning of the virgin lands was irresistible to the frontiersmen. As they had in what is now Tennessee, they first came to hunt, then to survey, and finally to settle. They cleared fresh lands and built new homes—knowing that so deep a thrust into Indian country would, without the slightest doubt, bring on an Indian war.

At the same time James Robertson and William Faulin were in Echota making amends and talking with chiefs Attakullakulla and Oconostota concerning the "Cherokee Billie" affair, the Raven and a small party of warriors were in the Ohio River Valley talking to Chief Cornstalk of the Shawnee. The Ohio tribes were seeking a Cherokee alliance to hold back the white advance across the Appalachians. The Shawnee could see no other solution short of war to the problems of these frontiersmen and surveyors who in 1773-74 were blanketing the upper Ohio. The Cherokee declined to support the Shawnee and, therefore, did not participate in Dunmore's War which was soon to follow.

The backwoodsmen of Virginia and Watauga felt justified in their invasion of the Ohio Valley by the treaty of Fort Stanwix. In it the Iroquois had ceded to the British lands south of the Ohio as far west as the Tennessee River; however, the tribes that lived there were of a different opinion. They said the land belonged to them. The great Shawnee chief, Cornstalk, favored peace with the whites. He, as well as chiefs of the other Ohio tribes, had given repeated warnings to the white men to stay out of the Ohio Valley, and had tried to ignore crimes committed by them. Still, indifferent to the resentment of the Ohio tribes, an insatiable appetite for bottom lands more fertile and extensive than their own drove the frontiersmen on.

At the beginning of 1774, Lt. Governor Dunmore took the region of Can-tuc-kee, what is now Kentucky, under the protection of Virginia. Before long, in addition to the hunters, traders, and surveyors already in the country, officers and soldiers who had obtained land grants from Lord Dunmore were traversing the Ohio searching for their lands. Upset and angry, the Shawnee decided to defend their hunting grounds.

Knowing war was probably inevitable, different Shawnee leaders met with other tribes in the area beseeching them to realize that the Shawnee cause against the white man was a common Indian cause. These tribes listened carefully to the Shawnee plea, hearing that the number of whites encroaching on the Indian hunting grounds and their harassment of the Shawnee in the Can-tuc-kee was increasing daily. They also were told of several white men masquerading as Indians who stole horses and other possessions from them as well as whites. These masqueraders murdered and scalped other whites so the blame would be placed on the Shawnees and other Indians. Though the Shawnee could fight their own battles against the white man, they alone could not guard the entire frontier against the invasion of the frontiersmen. There were rumors that the white leaders of the East were amassing armies to come against the Shawnee, and the Shawnee thought all the Ohio tribes should unite to try to stop the incursion of the whites. The other Ohio tribes, although feeling the complaints of the Shawnee were justified, ignored their plea and did not offer them any support.

In the late Spring of 1774, shortly after the murder of Cherokee Billie during the horse races on the Sycamore Shoals, another senseless killing took place; this time it was along the Ohio River. One afternoon in early May, a large canoe bearing Jacob Greathouse and three other border ruffians put ashore directly across from the mouth of Yellow Creek at the farm of Joseph Baker, called Baker's Bottom, on the south bank of the Ohio River two miles downstream from present-day Wellsville, Ohio. At this particular time a small party of Mingoes were camped at the mouth of the creek. When Greathouse and his men landed they were met by an unsavory character named Tomlinson and his motley crew of twenty-seven men. Within minutes these two leaders formulated a plan which they then discussed with the rest of the men. After full darkness, Greathouse and Tomlinson crossed the river to the Mingo camp where they were greeted by Shikellimus. Greathouse, fairly fluent in the Iroquoian language, told the old Indian that he and a party of six men were camped across the river and they would like the Mingoes to join them for some rum, and perhaps engage in a marksmanship contest. Shikellimus declined for he and the other Indians would be breaking camp the next morning and had a lot of work to do. However, not wanting to offend the white men, he agreed to send over five or six good marksmen to represent the Mingoes.

Among the Mingoes who went over to Baker's Bottom was a pregnant squaw, the sister of John Logan (also the daughter of Shikellimus), her husband, and her brother, Tay-la-nee. John Logan, or Tal-ga-yee-ta, was the Mingo chief of the Cayuga Indians, one of the five tribes grouped with the Iroquois. He was a friend of the white man and widely respected by both races. Logan's father, Shikellimus was a Frenchman who, as a youth, had been kidnaped and adopted by a tribe of northern Indians. He was a renowned friend of the whites along the shores of Cayuga Lake in New York, and was a close personal friend of James Logan, founder of the Loganian Library in Philadelphia. So intimate was this friendship that Shikellimus named his second son after him. Just as his father had been a friend and provider of the whites in New York, Chief Logan's home at Mingo Town along the shores of the Ohio River was one of warm hospitality and friendship to all. Chief Logan had refused to take part in the French and Indian War nineteen years earlier and Pontiac's War which followed. Instead, he was a notable peace maker during both wars.

These were the Indians and white men who sat together by the river drinking rum and engaging in some sharp shooting. Thus engrossed and talking while reloading, the Indians did not realize anything was amiss until Logan's sister suddenly screamed an alarm as she ran toward the river. Startled, the tipsy Mingoes looked around and were surprised to find themselves alone in the center of an arc of white men who had leaped from hiding. A volley of shots rang out, and all the Indians fell dead or dying. Knowing the remaining Mingoes across the river would come to investigate,the entire party of whites went to the river's edge where they hid until the canoes came within rifle range, then, thirty-two rifles roared at once, and most of the occupants of the boats were killed instantly. A few escaped by diving into the river and swimming for the Ohio shore, but Shikellimus was not among them. It was indeed a heinous and senseless crime which would change the heart of the mighty Mingo chief John Logan who had never raised his hand against the white man (Caruso, 126-127).

The next day as Chief Logan stood over the scalped and mutilated bodies of his kinsmen, he recalled the warning given him several nights before by a young Shawnee brave when recounting the killing of two companions by Michael Cresap's party. The brave had also overheard the men planning to destroy Logan's Yellow Creek Village, up-river from present-day Wheeling near Steubenville, Ohio. He thought that because he had ignored the warning, his family was dead. Logan did not know exactly who had committed the unprovoked and unjustifiable murders, but he blamed Captain Cresap and his men (Eckert, 82; Caruso, 127).

With great anger raging in him, Logan's soul thirsted for blood. Raising his tomahawk high, a cold, frightening fire must have burned in his eyes as he re-nounced his partiality for the white man and told the Mingoes with him that the peace had ended. He vowed that his hatchet would not again be grounded until he had taken ten lives for every one slain at Baker's Bottom (Eckert, 82).

Before long, the Mingo tribe was joined by a number of young Shawnee warriors who had become impatient with Cornstalk's inaction. The wrath of Chief John Logan was terrible; his vengeance fell with a horrible rage upon the unsuspecting settlers in the Shawnee country (Addington, 50).

In the middle of May, Cornstalk (Hokolesqua), the principal chief of the Shawnees, was invited to come to Fort Pitt to talk peace. He agreed to come, bringing only his brother and sister with him. Upon arrival at the fort, while being escorted to the quarters of the post commander, Colonel Croghan, the three Shawnees were attacked by an angry mob of frontiersmen. Hearing the commotion, Croghan rushed to the scene, fired his pistol into the air, and demanded that the mob fall back. They did so. In a wide circle of frontiersmen Cornstalk and his sister, Non-hel-e-ma (known to the whites as the Grenadier squaw), were back-to-back with a knife in one hand and a tomahawk in the other. Their brother, Silverheels, lay on his back sorely wounded. The profuse apologies by the white men were not enough. That the principal chief of the Shawnee should be invited to talk peace and be thus treated was unforgivable. All hope of peace was shattered (Eckert, 83-84). Now, in addition to Logan's blood-thirsty group, there were angry bands of Shawnee, Delaware, and Senecas harassing the frontier people in the Ohio Valley and Kentucky.

At the outbreak of hostilities the whites began fleeing, and by midsummer not a white man was left in Kentucky. It was feared that the Cherokee might enter the war to appease their wrath for the murder of Cherokee Billie, even though their chiefs were strongly opposed to war with the whites at this time.

In late July, Logan's coterie of Mingo and Shawnee braves visited with the Cherokees in order to induce their warriors to join them on the warpath. However,

Oconostota and the Little Carpenter, the principal chiefs of the Cherokee Nation, told Logan they had given their word to the Wataugans not to seek retaliation for the murder at Sycamore Shoals. At this particular time they were against war with the whites. The Cherokee Nation would remain neutral. Still, there is little doubt that a few of the friends and relatives of Cherokee Billie seeking revenge may have secretly joined Logan's expedition, despite the advice of their chiefs.

Disappointed at the refusal of the Cherokee's chiefs to assist him, Logan and his associates turned their footsteps toward the Clinch and Holson rivers, glutting their vengeance by stealing, burning, scalping, and ravaging the frontier settlements and the thin line of forts along these rivers and adjacent creeks. At each place they attacked, a war club was left behind as a threat and challenge. According to Addington, one of the war clubs left at Moore's Fort (near present-day Castlewood, Virginia) was different from the others. Daniel Boone, who was in general command of the fort, identified it as belonging to the Cherokee (56). From Moore's Fort, Logan's band trekked through Moccasin Gap to the neighborhood of King's Mill on Reedy Creek (near the present-day site of Kingsport, Tennessee). There they brutally murdered and scalped the James Roberts family (Kincaid, 86). At the Roberts' cabin, Logan left a note addressed to Captain Cresap—the man he wrongly blamed for the death of his family on Yellow Creek—written in gunpowder ink and tied to a war club. A few days later, about the last week of September, having finally satiated their thirst for vengeance, Logan and his warriors withdrew to the northern mountains as swiftly and silently as they had come (Caruso, 127).

In the same month (July) that Logan visited the Cherokee, Virginia's military commander, Lord Dunmore, sent out a call for volunteers and ordered out the militia in the Shenandoah and Holston valleys. He decided to divide his army into two wings. The southern wing would be under Colonel Andrew Lewis and composed exclusively of mountain men from the western counties; the northern wing, which he himself would command, would be made up of mostly northern frontiersmen who were already gathering at Fort Pitt. The home front was to be under the command of Alexander Campbell, a major in the Augusta County militia (Kincaid, 85). Campbell was to organize the home guard at scattered forts along the Clinch River and the edge of the settled areas of the Holston and Watauga rivers.

Dunmore's initial plan was for Lewis to meet officers of the western counties of Virginia with their troops at Camp Union (the present-day site of Lewisburg, West Virginia); from there he was to march down to the mouth of the Great Kanawha River at Point Pleasant on the Ohio, build a fort, and unite with Dunmore for a combined assault of the Shawnee villages along the Scioto River near the Pickaway Plains.

In late August the Watauga militia met with the Southern commander Andrew Lewis and his mountainmen at Shelby's Fort. There, under the command of Captain Evan Shelby, they set off on the two hundred mile march to Camp Union on the Ohio River. By the first week of September, Lewis had assembled his men and began the march to Point Pleasant, reaching there on October 9th. There he received orders from Lord Dunmore not to wait for his division, but instead for him and his men to cross the Ohio and attack the Scioto villages. Before Lewis could carry out the orders he was forestalled.

Cornstalk's spies, who had been watching both wings of the army, reported to their chief about the first week of October that Dunmore was still far up the Ohio at Wheeling, and that it would take many days for them to reach the much smaller army of Lewis near the Great Kanawha. Cornstalk immediately summoned the Shawnee and their allies—the Mingo, Delaware, and Wyandot—to arms; they came by the hundreds, eager for war. On the afternoon of October 9, 1774, the Indians began their march to Point Pleasant. Approaching the Ohio, they halted in a dense forest three miles above the mouth of the Great Kanawha near the present town of Addison in Gallia County, Ohio. After dark, using rafts, they quietly began crossing the Ohio, landing about three miles from Point Pleasant. Under the cover of darkness, swiftly and silently they passed through the wilderness toward the whitemen's camp, arriving just before dawn. Then, yelling and screaming they attacked the soldiers. From dawn to dusk the Indians and whites were engaged in a bloody, hand-to-hand brutal fight. Toward sunset, with both sides nearly exhausted, Cornstalk got word that another division of Lewis' army was approaching from the rear. As the sun sank, the Indians began disappearing into the woods behind them, taking their wounded and dead. Lewis did not pursue them. The battle had ended in a draw, but the Shawnee and their allies were defeated. Weary, they withdrew across the river and returned to their villages on the Pickaway Plains. There, Cornstalk called a council and it was unanimously decided to make peace. Runners were sent with the decision to Lord Dunmore who was on his way to Point Pleasant, about fifteen miles away. Arriving several days after the battle, Dunmore established a camp about six miles from Cornstalk's village on the Scippo Creek, which bisected the Pickaway Plains. He named the camp Charlotte in honor of the Queen. There, on October 18th he and Cornstalk negotiated for peace. By the Treaty of Camp Charlotte, Cornstalk agreed to give up his white prisoners, stolen Negroes, horses, and other valuables and to cease hunting or visiting on the south side of the Ohio, a promise the Shawnee never kept.

Lord Dunmore's War between the frontier militias and the Shawnees was one provoked by frontiersmen, waged by frontiersmen, and won by frontiersmen for the sole benefit of frontiersmen. By this first war on the frontier, the western people had won a new land, made possible the settlement of Kentucky, and opened their own way west. The war had scarcely been won before those settlers who had hurried away were hurrying back again. According to Kincaid, without Lord Dunmore's War more than likely when the Colonies finally gained their freedom, their western boundary would have been fixed at the Allegheny mountains (38).

Another land company, in addition to those of Virginia, was also interested in Kentucky. A North Carolina lawyer, Richard Henderson, and his Transylvania Company had learned from its agent, Daniel Boone, that the Cherokees might be willing to dispose of their lands in western Kentucky—if the price was right. After the war with the Shawnees in 1774, Henderson reorganized his company, added new stockholders, and with ten thousand pounds in cash and merchandise for bait, he hoped to lure the Cherokee into selling the title to their ancient hunting grounds between the Kentucky, Cumberland, and Tennessee rivers. He made no attempt to obtain approval from the Crown.

Late in 1774, he traveled to the Overhill towns where he made his proposal and arranged for a delegation, which included the Little Carpenter and his squaw,

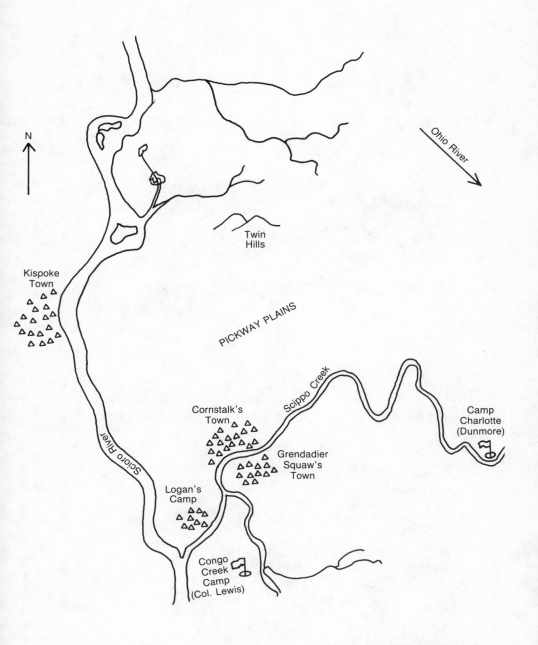

N

Ohio River

Twin
Hills

Kispoke
Town

PICKWAY PLAINS

Scippo Creek

Camp
Charlotte
(Dunmore)

Cornstalk's
Town

Grendadier
Squaw's
Town

Scioto River

Logan's
Camp

Congo
Creek
Camp
(Col. Lewis)

CAMP CHARLOTTE TREATY
1774
END OF LORD DUNMORE'S CAMPAIGN

89

DRAGGING CANOE'S PROPHECY

Dragging Canoe bitterly opposed selling the Cherokee hunting grounds of "Kaintuckee" (1775) to the whites. During negotiations on the treaty grounds at the Sycamore Shoals, he rose to his feet to protest. Pointing a finger toward Kentucky, he stamped angrily and said, "A cloud hangs over the land you buy. Its settlement will be dark and bloody." Then in haughty grandeur he stalked from the council. He would never take part in any other treaty with the whites.

to visit North Carolina to view the goods amassed for payment. They did, and were impressed with the cabinful of presents. Returning home, Attakullakulla began summoning his people for "treaty talks" on the Watauga.

Late in January, 1775, Henderson had the merchandise loaded on six wagons and taken to Sycamore Shoals where it was stored in huts built for that purpose. Shortly afterward, a large number of Indians and settlers began to gather on the flats at the Shoals.

On March 14th, after several days of festivities and talks, the real negotiations began with Henderson's proposal: outright purchase of the whole Cumberland Valley and southern half of the Kentucky valley for ten thousand pounds of English money—two in cash, eight in merchandise. The audience was astounded. This land had already been sold by the Iroquois at Fort Stanwix in 1768 and had from the earliest times been claimed by Virginians. To pay the Cherokees for land already relinquished by the Iroquois fit precisely with that tribe's own recent plan to steer the whites away from their country, off to the west. Still, the Cherokees continued to hesitate, but only because of their reluctance to include in the purchase a right of access which would impinge upon land near their towns.

Chief Oconostota felt the white men had already taken too much of his people's hunting grounds and that they would not be satisfied until they occupied all of the Cherokee land; he exhorted his people to resist any further encroachment. Then a tall young chief, Tsugunsini, better known as Dragging Canoe, jumped angrily to his feet, telling his elders they were paving the way for the ultimate extinction of their race—the whites would not be satisfied with the purchase but only want more land and eventually even the homes of the Cherokee.

For a time the Indians conferred among themselves and finally the 80 year old Attakullakulla, who was still dominate at Cherokee councils, persuaded the elder chiefs to comply with the desires of the white men. His son, Dragging Canoe, was bitterly opposed. Rising, he declared that he, for one, would never yield another foot of native soil. Then he pointed toward Kentucky and told the buyers that a dark cloud hung over that land, and its settlement would be bloody; the words proved prophetic. He then stalked away from the council and went home. In the coming years, his name would be dreaded along the frontier more than any other.

On March 17th, the older chiefs again prevailed and Henderson's purchase was achieved. By the Treaty of Sycamore Shoals, sometimes known as the Treaty of Watauga, the frontier people had acquired almost all the state of "Kaintuckee," an immense tract of "Tanasi"—comprising the entire Cumberland River watershed; some twenty million acres for ten thousand English pounds in cash and merchandise. It was the biggest private or corporate land deal in American history. And this was not all; for additional goods Henderson and the Transylvania Company secured a "Path Deed" between Kentucky and the Holston settlements. This deed included Carter's Valley, which Henderson transferred to John Carter for two thousand pounds worth of leather goods.

Leaders of the Watauga community, taking their cue from the judge, now came forward to seize the opportunity to buy the land on which they lived, and which they had leased. Therefore, two other deals were made at Sycamore Shoals.

On March 19th, two days after the Sycamore Shoals treaty was signed, Oconostota and the other chiefs sold to the Wataugans the land they had leased earlier, plus more. For two thousand pounds, the Cherokees sold them all the land on the Wataugan waters, land below the South Holston and the Virginia line, and the headwaters of the New River, consisting of a large portion of present-day southwestern North Carolina; in all, a total of two thousand square miles. Thus, this was the "Watauga Country" of the 1770's.

Jacob Brown negotiated separately his own purchase of lands on the Nolichucky. He secured land adjoining the Watauga on both sides of the Nolichucky River, from Camp Creek on the south to the Alleghenies on the east. For seventeen hundred Virginia pounds and forgiveness of debts totaling fifteen hundred pounds, Brown acquired a small principality of his own.

Daniel Boone was not present at the signing of the Treaty of Watauga. He and a party of forty axemen had started a week before, from the Long Island of the Holston, to explore the Kentucky River region where a settlement was to be established. Innumerable thickets of laurel, bramble, cane, and rhododendron stood in their way and the deep streams, mountains, and Indians posed a constant threat. Boone and the mountainmen, chopping and slashing their way, would traverse more than two hundred miles, blazing the Wilderness Trail. From the Long Island the axemen went northward to Moccasin Gap, turned westward and crossed the Clinch River, Powell Mountain and the Powell River. From Powell Valley they would enter the Cumberland Gap, file through it, pick up and pursue the Warrior's Path into the blue grasses of what is now the state of Kentucky, where Henderson had promised each of the road cutters a tract of land for his services.

When word of the transactions at the Sycamore Shoals reached the Virginia governor, Earl of Dunmore, he was furious. He immediately issued a proclamation for Henderson to leave the land at once—if he refused, he was to be fined and imprisoned. He reminded the Indians that King George III would not permit them to sell any land to private persons and, therefore, the Cherokee should rescind any contract made with Henderson or any other persons. Also, he sent word to the Watauga community informing them that no group of citizens had the right to take possession of Crown lands without a charter and that their purchases were illegal. Unconcerned by this uproar in official circles, Henderson spent two or three days at the Watauga making final arrangements. He left the treaty grounds at the Sycamore Shoals on March 20th, going to the Long Island, and from there, following the trail blazed by Boone's men, to Kentucky.

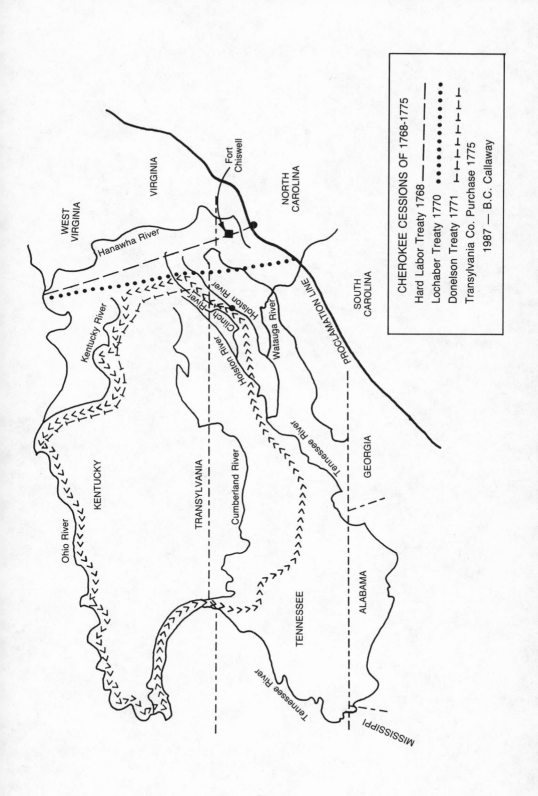

CHEROKEE CESSIONS OF 1768-1775

Hard Labor Treaty 1768 — — —
Lochaber Treaty 1770 ● ● ● ●
Donelson Treaty 1771 ⊢⊢⊢⊢
Transylvania Co. Purchase 1775 ⊢⊢⊢⊢
1987 — B.C. Callaway

VIRGINIA

WEST VIRGINIA

Hanawha River

Fort Chiswell

NORTH CAROLINA

SOUTH CAROLINA

PROCLAMATION LINE

Kentucky River

Clinch River

Holston River

Holston River

Watauga River

Tennessee River

Cumberland River

Ohio River

KENTUCKY

TRANSYLVANIA

GEORGIA

ALABAMA

TENNESSEE

Tennessee River

MISSISSIPPI

VIII
CHEROKEE WAR:
AMERICAN REVOLUTION

Hostilities had broken out in the East igniting the fire of independence which had been smoldering in the embers. Heavy smoke from this fire wafted across the Appalachians; its fumes occasionally tickling the nostrils of the western inhabitants. The skirmishes at Lexington and Concord came one month to the day after the Wataugans signed the land treaties, but it would take several weeks before the news reached them. To those souls in near isolation behind the rampart of two mountain ranges, such events were of little significance; their immediate concern continued to be their relations with the Indians. The recent land purchases had given the settlers a sense of security, and for the moment there was a lull in the settlements and the relationship of the Appalachian frontiersmen and the Overhill Cherokee was satisfactory.

In April of 1775, Henderson with the first settlers following in the wake of Boone started construction of Boonesboro, on the Kentucky River. Others soon followed and by year's end, over three hundred settlers were in the "dark and bloody land." The judge was still a wanted man, but before long Cameron and the proclaimers would be too busy fighting the spreading flames of independence—and later, trying to save themselves—to follow up their threats.

Late in the fall of 1776, Virginia, as had other colonies, declared herself a free and independent state and immediately began exercising sovereignty over her claims in the West. One of her first acts was to divide the enormous county of Fincastle, which extended some three hundred miles in length, into Washington, Montgomery, and Kentucky counties. Thus ended Colonel Henderson's dream of an empire in the Appalachian West. All was not lost, however, for in 1778 Virginia, denying the legitimacy of the purchase of land within its jurisdiction, compensated the Transylvania Company with two hundred thousand acres on the Green River in the new Kentucky county. In 1783, North Carolina, also denying legitimacy, put up an equal amount of land—ten thousand acres—for John Carter and his new partner Robert Lucas in the Clinch River Valley to compensate for their losses, and tendered the remaining 190,000 acres to Henderson and his associates in the nearby Powell River Valley.

The climax of the drama between the Cherokee and whites on the Appalachian frontier was drawing near. Gathering storm clouds had again darkened, lending to an uncanny calm similar to that just before an electrical storm. War, like rain, could be smelled in the air. The events of 1775 and early 1776 were heard like one tremendous uninterrupted roll of thunder. The curtain was about to fall on the scenes of colonial and frontier times and to raise on the period of the American Revolution and the Cherokee War.

In June, with the news of Bunker Hill and the appointment of George Washington as commander of the Continental Army, war became a certainty. On July 12th, the American Indian Department was created with Northern, Middle, and Southern sections to deal respectively with the Indians of New York, the Ohio, and the region south of Virginia. In separate meetings, a temporary truce with the Americans and a half-hearted pledge to the British Army was all that could be gained. In August, King George III declared a "state of rebellion."

With these events and others shaping up to a full-scale conflict, the Wataugans were forced to assess their situation. They feared the strong British influence over the Indians would turn them against the border settlements and that Dragging Canoe might see the situation as a way of regaining the Cherokee lands. Among themselves there was the question of loyalty to the British. Many of the frontier people, particularly in the Nolichucky valley, were Tory rather than Whig in their sympathies.

The colonials who opposed the King called themselves "Whigs," a name taken from the Liberal Party of England. This group had long opposed the conservative Tory element, or Party, in Great Britain. In the colonies and on the western frontier, the Patriots who adopted this name became known as the party who supported the American revolt. Those who supported the King's cause were called "Tories" — the name was taken from the Conservative Party of England. In the colonies, these Loyalist comprised about one-third of the population, and felt England would soon subdue the Rebels. The worst of the lot was the group of Tories, existing in every community on both sides of the Appalachian divide, who made the very name hated. Their whole effort in the war was for selfish personal gain, visualizing rich rewards for their faithfulness to the Crown. Loyalist whites and Loyalist Indians meant trouble ahead. In the fight against the Rebellion the British would use the Tories as well as the Indians for their own purposes. When through with them after the war, England would forsake these allies and leave them homeless, friendless, and without help.

A prime factor in determining which course of action would be taken by the Wataugans in 1775 was the fact that King George's Proclamation of 1763 continued to make their land purchases illegal. A conflict with Britain would provide a welcome opportunity to be rid of John Stuart and Alexander Cameron as well as a way to terminate the Earl of Granville's ownership of the northern third of North Carolina on which many of the frontiersmen were located.

On January 20, 1775, the North-of-Holston settlers met with the Freeholders of Fincastle County, Virginia, to form a revolutionary Committee of Safety with Evan Shelby as chairman. They designated themselves as the "Pendleton District," in honor of the Virginia patriot and statesman Edmund Pendleton who owned a large tract of land in the vicinity of the Long Island of the Holston. About mid-year, the inhabitants of the Watauga and the Nolichucky met in a joint convention to appoint a Committee of Safety with John Carter as chairman, and to designate themselves as the "Washington District"—named in honor of the new commander of the United Patriot Forces; the first territorial or civic division in the new country to receive the name. Late in the fall, the pioneers west of Donelson's line in Carter's Valley proceeded to organize their own Committee of Safety.

The Cherokees returning home from the Sycamore Shoals in March, 1775, were almost immediately caught up in the fervor of the beginnings of the Revolution. Although finding it incredulous that the whites should be at war with each other, that reality was realized when shortly their supply of shot and powder was cut short. That summer they began preparing for war—their ominous drumbeat could be heard softly throbbing throughout all the tumult occurring on both sides of the Appalachian mountains.

Before leaving the year 1775, one other event should be mentioned—at the time seemingly minor but later proving to be of major importance. Late that fall in Attakullakulla's village of Tuskegee, an Indian child was born to his niece Wurteh, sister of Corn Tassel (Onitositah) called Old Tassel by the whites, who had succeeded "Groundhog Sausage" as chief. The infant's father was Nathaniel Gist, a trader from Virginia and a favorite among the Cherokee. The boy was given the English name of George, but is better known by his Indian name, Sequoyah.

Crippled in a hunting accident in his youth, the young man became a skilled silversmith who although illiterate was very intrigued by the "talking leaves" used by the white man. This ability to "talk on paper" inspired Sequoyah to develop an alphabet for his own people. This would be the first time in history that a single person developed an alphabet for an entire nation—quite an accomplishment for a man who could neither read nor write.

By January of 1776 there was no longer any doubt as to where the loyalties of the Indians lay. In that month a large party of Cherokees arrived at St. Augustine to request supplies from John Stuart. They assured him of their loyalty to the British and complained about the whites on their land. Stuart, acting on orders from General Gage, made preparations to have his younger brother, Henry, go to Echota with a caravan of sixty pack horses, loaded with ammunition and the requested supplies. The caravan arrived in the Overhill capitol in April. There, Henry Stuart met with Deputy Cameron who was visiting in the village. Cameron informed Stuart that their problem would not be one of gaining active Cherokee support and aid for the British, but would be in restraining the young braves from making an immediate attack on the settlers.

In May, a Great Council meeting was held at Echota with over seven hundred Indians, their chiefs, and a few whites. The Indians asked Stuart and Cameron to write a letter to the inhabitants of the Watauga and Nolichucky, telling them they were on Indian lands without consent and their land purchases were illegal, and if the settlers did not move, they would be attacked and driven out by the Cherokees. Deputies Stuart and Cameron sent the letter giving the frontiersmen twenty days to remove themselves to British Florida or some other English possession where they could legally claim British protection.

The settlers were greatly alarmed, especially when the white courier, trader Isaac Thomas, told them that he thought the young warriors would attack the settlements whether or not the elders gave their approval.

Chairman Carter of the Washington District Committee, stalling for time, responded with an affirmation of loyalty to the Crown and asked for twenty extra days. The Cherokee agreed. But John Carter did not mean what he said, either about being loyal or about moving in forty days. Already, with the knowledge that Henry Stuart was among the Indians with arms and ammunition, the Wataugan Committee had appealed to nearby Fincastle County, Virginia, for help. But Virginia wanted no part of an Indian war; instead they suggested the Wataugans get off Indian land and retreat behind British lines. After this disappointing but emphatic no, the committee petitioned North Carolina requesting annexation, but were turned down as that colony also felt compelled to recognize the Cherokee claims to the land.

At this point faced with the threat of imminent Indian attack, the Wataugans speeded up preparations for defense. They purchased arms, lead, and powder through the Fincastle Committee—other weapons were repaired and new ones made; medicinal and food stuff was gathered, prepared, and laid by; clothing was mended and new footwear made. In addition, a number of forts were strengthened and constructed, some small and rather inadequate, others of fair size and stockaded. The backwoods log fort was perhaps the most common type of fortification on the Appalachian frontier. Whenever possible they were constructed on the highest point of elevation and near a river or stream. Although they varied in size and shape, they were much alike in their organization and purpose. Picket walls made of upright, pointed stakes with tops sharpened so as to impale anyone attempting to scale them, were embedded deeply enough into the ground to prevent their being pried out of place. The palisades were held in place by long, horizontal stringers fastened with wooden pegs near the top. At each corner were heavy log blockhouses with overhanging second stories from which to guard the walls. The area inside was about one acre. Rows of small log cabins separated from each other by log partitions, arranged around one or more walls, provided living quarters. The cabins sometimes had two rooms with puncheon floors, but more often were one room with dirt floors. The roofs were of clapboards, held in place by weights of rock or wood. The structures—either stockades, blockhouses, or bastions—and their cabin walls were loopholed and fashioned with small portholes at proper heights and distances. Usually the courtyard served as a stockpen, but sometimes there was a kind of lean-to, of which a wall of the fort formed one side. This small enclosure, located at the north end of the fort, sheltered the horses and cattle at night. A large, heavy folding gate made of thick log slabs hung on the wall facing the river or creek. If one side of the fort was built on the edge of a river bank (such as Fort Patrick Henry or Fort Nashboro), the gate was placed on the far, opposite wall. In times of danger or at night, it was securely fastened by a strong, heavy bar. Outside, the perimeter of the fort was cleared of trees and undergrowth to approximately three hundred feet, more or less. A short distance from the stockade, usually to the east, was a burial ground with most of its graves being those of frontier people who had lost their lives during Indian raids on the fort.

A blockhouse, or small station, was nothing more than a primitive loghouse with somewhat thicker walls. They, like the forts, were also built on a hill and near water. Less formal in their structure, they had one room with a projecting upper story. The walls of both stories had the usual loopholes and other openings peculiar to such buildings. Primarily strongholds, the heavily barred door and second story vantage points made them efficient barriers against small Indian war parties. Fire was perhaps the most effective weapon that could be used against these structures. When not being used as a gathering place for the frontier people against Indian attack, they were used as a kind of way station where weary travelers could get supplies, rest and eat a meal.

One small fort already built—circa 1775—called "Old Watauga Fort" was located at Boone's Creek about three miles west of the William Bean cabin. Because this fort was inadequate in size, a larger structure with a stockade was constructed on the Watauga, near Sycamore Shoals; it was named "Fort Caswell" (later called Fort Watauga) in honor of the Governor-elect of North Carolina, Richard Caswell. The farthest one was located on the Nolichucky frontier built down river from Brown's store on Big Limestone Creek. Originally named "Fort Lee" in honor of General Charles Lee, then in charge of the American forces in the South, it was later called "Gillespie's Station." A crude and inadequate fort was located at Amos Eaton's Station—sometimes called "Heaton's Station"—across the north fork of the Holston on Reedy Creek, and another was at the mouth of Big Creek in Carter's Valley. Then there was Shelby's Fort at Sapling Grove, Fort Robinson on the north bank of the Holston River, and one at Jacob Womack's, two miles east of the village of Chote's or Shoate's Ford (present-day Bluff City, Tennessee).

In May of 1776, the Americans had scattered a nest of Tories on the Nolichucky, and shortly afterward answered a Macedonian call for aid from North Carolina to help in her defense of Charleston against the redcoats.

While these events were in progress, adding new fuel to the blaze of war there had turned up in the Overhill Towns, in mid-June, a delegation of Indians from the Northern tribes: Mohawks, Delawares, Ottawas, Nancutas, Mingoes, Shawnees, and others of the Iroquois Confederation. They came painted black in an all-out effort to draw the Cherokee and other Indian Nations into the British Campaign against the Americans. The plan was for the British to attack the colonists from the sea side and the Indians to fight the frontiersmen from the rear.

Meanwhile, the allotted forty days had come and gone. Henry Stuart, realizing the futility of trying to dissuade the Cherokees or to restrain them, urged Dragging Canoe to refrain from killing Loyalists and their families, and then left to return to his brother John in Mobile. The Northern delegation departed for their long journey home. And in the Cherokee villages, women began preparations to put things in readiness for the march, and the men began their customary war rituals.

The Cherokee plan was for Chief Old Abram to take about 400 warriors and attack the Nolichucky and Watauga people. Chief Dragging Canoe would take another like number, march into the Long Island of Holston country, attack there, and then join The Raven going on into Virginia. Chief The Raven with a smaller force was to move into the Carter's Valley section, destroy the small settlement there, and move on into Wolf Hills, killing and burning.

Nancy Ward, knowing war would be disastrous for her people and would bring needless death and grief to her white friends, decided to warn the settlers. This had to be done in secret and by means of the four white traders in the village.

Old Watauga Fort in Boones Creek
Built over stream so those inside could have fresh water. Although the fort has been weatherboarded, the original portholes (for rifles) can be seen inside.

First battle of the American Revolution fought west of the Appalachian Mountains. Dragging Canoe and his band were defeated by the frontiersmen who lived on Eaton's Ridge. Dragging Canoe and the surviving Indians went on to Carter's Valley—looting and raiding.

She outlined the plan of attack to Isaac Thomas and then arranged for him and the other traders to escape from the Indian towns.

The traders left on the night of July 8, 1776 and arrived at the first border settlement on the Nolichucky by the morning of the 11th. The inhabitants immediately took alarm and fled, carrying off livestock and provisions. Therefore, a still incomplete but perhaps defensible Fort Lee was abandoned and its garrison fell back on Fort Caswell. John Sevier, who was in charge of construction, wrote a note for Thomas to carry on to the other forts. Couriers rushed out in all directions to warn the scattered and isolated settlers to gather inside the forts.

The Indians moved quietly but quickly up the Nolichucky, and in the pre-dawn hours of July 20, 1776, Cherokee war parties, with some Creek and Tory support, attacked the whole arc of the white frontier extending from southern Virginia across the western Carolinas to northern Georgia. The Cherokee War had begun; the blow falling as heavily on Tory settlers as on their Patriot neighbors.

Upon reaching the Nolichucky settlements, the Indians found most of the cabins deserted, and in their haste to catch up with the fleeing settlers, they did not bother any growing crops or animals left behind. Finding the unfinished and abandoned Fort Lee, they burned it. The group made another division of the remaining force here. The Raven had deflected from the main body near the bend of the Nolichucky to follow the Great War Trail across the Holston. Now, Dragging Canoe would lead his party on toward the settlements north of the Holston, while Old Abram continued to advance in the direction of Fort Caswell on the Watauga.

The pioneer force at Eaton's Station fearing the Indians might bypass the fort and in the rear destroy homes, crops, and livestock decided to meet them in the open. The two groups, about equal in number, met on Island Flats, five or six miles below the junction of the dual forks of Holston. In a fierce, close-quarter fray lasting about an hour, the Indians were defeated. Thirteen warriors were killed and many more wounded, among them Dragging Canoe with a broken thigh. Seeing this the warriors fled in confusion, carrying their wounded from the field.

The Battle of Long Island Flats was the first battle of the Revolution west of the mountains. Its success heartened the whites, giving them confidence in their ability to meet the Indian on equal terms and to hold their own in a fight. To the Cherokee, the day when the frontiersmen could be considered easy prey had ended. The braves lost faith in their prowess against the whites. The depressed Indians, from that time forward, gradually lost their old-time confidence in their own valor.

The western settlement in Carter's Valley was wholly inadequate to its own defense. As The Raven and his warriors approached, the inhabitants fled in terror; most of the men hurrying to Eaton's, while women and children were conducted towards Virginia. Finding little or no resistance, the Cherokees moved rapidly; burning cabins, destroying crops, and killing livestock as they proceeded. Dispersing in small bands, the Indians moved in a fan shape, scouring the nearly abandoned valley. With their western flank harassing settlers in the forts on the Clinch River in southwest Virginia (e.g., Blackmore's, Rye Cove, Martin's and Castle's Wood), others forayed the settlements near the Wolf Hills.

From their temporary camp on the Nolichucky, the division of warriors under Old Abram of Chilhowie continued its trek along the foot of Cherokee Mountain toward Fort Caswell. Periodically sending small squads out on scouting trips to pick up any whites as might be found, they discovered that most had already reached the security of the forts.

The next day in the pre-dawn hours on July 21st, Old Abram's war party reached the vicinity of Fort Caswell. At daybreak, a few of the garrison's women were outside milking when in the gray light they saw the swiftly approaching naked and painted warriors. Their screams while running for the gates alerted the defenders who quickly manned the walls and began firing on the Indians, giving the women time to enter the fort. During the confusion the gates were closed and the way blocked by braves before one of the females could get inside. The young woman was Catherine (Bonnie Kate) Sherrill, a tall athletic girl, about whom it was said could outride, outshoot, and outrun almost any man in the settlement. Seeing that the warriors had blocked her way to the gates, still running, she turned toward the nearest side determined to scale the fort wall. The shower of arrows and lead balls were coming like hail; it was now leap or die. As she made ready to spring to the top, a man leaning down from the fire step, stretched forth his hand and shouted: "Jump for me Kate." She did. The strong hand which pulled Bonnie Kate Sherrill to safety belonged to a man who would four years later marry her and who would become the first governor of Tennessee, John Sevier.

The Cherokees laid siege to Fort Caswell for about two weeks, occasionally harassing the defenders of the fort while small parties made raids in other directions; foraging the countryside, attacking the smaller forts, pillaging cabins, and killing some settlers while capturing others.

Another heroine during the siege was Ann Robertson, sister of James. During one attack on the fort, the Indians were making a desperate effort to burn the stockade at a section where rifle bullets could not reach them. It was wash-day in the fort; Ann, making a hasty decision, grabbed a bucket of boiling water, scaled the inner parapet amid a shower of bullets, and poured the scalding stream down on them. Though wounded, with the other women supplying more hot water, she continued to pour bucket after bucket until the burned Indians fled.

After hearing of Dragging Canoe's defeat at Island Flats, the warriors lost their taste for war. Discouraged and stunned by the loss, Old Abram lifted the siege; he and his braves left for home. Their departure was hastened by news that a Virginia relief force was marching to the aid of the Wataugans.

Among the captives taken back to the Overhill towns was a teenager named Tom Moore. He and a friend, James Cooper, had gone out from the fort one day to get boards to repair a roof. They were surprised by stray Indians at Gap Creek. Cooper jumped in the creek to escape the arrows and bullets, but was killed and scalped before he could swim away. Those in the fort could hear his dying screams and pleas of mercy. Moore was taken to the village of Tuskegee where he was cruelly tortured for days, and then burned at the stake.

Another prisoner was Mrs. William Bean, wife of Tanasi's first permanent settler, who had been intercepted as she was hurrying on horseback from her home on Boone's Creek to the safety of Fort Caswell. Taken to Old Abram's temporary camp on the Nolichucky, she was threatened with death and questioned about the forts in the area; how many there were, the number of soldiers in each, about food supplies and ammunition. She was kept at the Nolichucky camp-site throughout the siege. Afterward, she was taken to the Overhill village of Toqua where after further intense questioning she was condemned to be burned to death. Lydia, when her turn came, was taken to a mound where an upright log pole was buried near its center. There she was tied to the stake with leather throngs; then buffalo chips and wood were piled high around her, and a lit torch was thrown onto the heap. Suddenly, Nancy Ward broke through the watching crowd, rushed to the mound and with her own hands threw aside the burning fagots, kicked away the smoldering cane and stamped out the embers around the victim. After untying Mrs. Bean, this "Pocahontas of the West," in harsh words told the stunned warriors that it sickened her soul that they would stoop so low as to torture a squaw in this manner. Nancy led Mrs. Bean away from the crowd of glaring warriors, and took her to her home in Echota, the Town of Sanctuary. As Ghighau, she sentenced Lydia to teach the Cherokee women how to make butter and cheese; later, when it was safe, she was returned to her home unharmed.

Dragging Canoe, greatly humiliated at his defeat by the white frontiersmen at Island Flats, realized he could not return home as a defeated leader. He had nothing to show from the battle. Therefore, from his temporary camp on Limestone Creek (not far from its junction with the Nolichucky River) the young War Chief, unable to travel, sent several small war parties into scattered areas of the Powell, Clinch, and Holston valleys with instructions to raid, kill, and scalp. These warriors returned with some loot, several white scalps, and a few horses. Thus, the Canoe felt he had turned his defeat into a sort of victory.

About this same time, small groups of marauding Indians from the Upper, Middle, and Lower Cherokee towns were raiding and harassing the Georgia and Carolina frontiers. Also, larger raiding parties—of Tories, Cherokees, and dissident Creeks—were ravaging the white border settlements located in the western sections of the two Carolinas and North Georgia, returning with many white scalps of men, women, and children.

This ruthless period of Indian raids on the southern Appalachian frontiers did more to unite the frontier people against the British and their Indian and Tory allies than any fear of the King's detested red-coated troops could have possibly done.

Feeling the Cherokee Nation should be treated as at war in aid of the British, the military response to their attack that summer of 1776 was overwhelming and devastating. It was not a response of disorganized settlers who for the most part were confined in forts, but of the organized militia of four states in campaigns approved by the Continental Congress. A bounty of 75 pounds was offered for each enemy Indian scalp taken, be it warrior, squaw, or child. In addition, a hundred pounds was to be paid for every live prisoner delivered to the military.

In late July, Major Samuel Jack with two hundred Georgians marched against the towns on the upper Chattahoochee, Tugaloo, and Savannah rivers. A thorough destruction of villages and crops was accomplished. Few Cherokees were killed as most had managed to escape into the hills. In mid-August, Colonel Andrew Williamson of South Carolina, set out with 1,200 militiamen to punish the Lower Towns—destroying Alexander Cameron's home at Lochaber on the way. Every dwelling, food-patch, and orchard was burned; any livestock found was run off or killed. Then in September, General Griffith Rutherford led 2,400 North Carolinians down toward the French Broad where they joined Williamson in destroying all the Middle Towns and valley settlements, i.e., thirty-six Cherokee towns in all. All homes, out-buildings, crops, vegetable gardens, and fruit trees were reduced to ashes. Most Cherokee families had retreated before the vastly superior white armies, but any Indians sighted were killed as were their animals.

Appalled by the unforseen magnitude of the Americans' reactions and their retaliation against them, many Indians sought refuge in the more remote Overhill Towns, but sanctuary was not to be found there. During the first week of October, Colonel William Christian with 1,800 Virginians, 300 North Carolinians, and a light horse company of Wataugans left the new Fort Patrick Henry at Long Island bent on destruction of the entire Cherokee Nation. Marching through the Indian country, Christian met little or no opposition and after destroying Tuskegee, where young Tom Moore had been burned alive, the village of Togua, where Mrs. Bean has been held captive, and after sacking three other towns loyal to Dragging Canoe, he pressed on through the ashes of the Middle Towns across to the Little Tennessee to some of the Lower Towns, destroying everything in his path. The only Cherokee town spared was Echota, capital of the Nation—Town of Refuge—home of Attakullakulla and his niece, Nancy Ward. Perhaps this was because of the Little Carpenter's long friendship with the Nolichucky-Holston-Watauga settlements or maybe because of Nancy Ward's warning sent to the settlers before the July attacks. Whatever the reason, Christian's compassion for the Overhill Cherokee was very different from the attitude he displayed toward the inhabitants of the Middle, Valley, and Lower Towns during the Carolina-Georgia campaigns.

On the march back Colonel Christian's army halted at Great Island Town on the Little Tennessee River. There, on October 19th at Dragging Canoe's abandoned home village, Christian set up his camp headquarters. The next day messengers were sent to the Overhill chiefs to inform them of Colonel Christian's whereabouts, that he was tendering peace terms; offering them an ultimatum: a treaty or total destruction.

At Echota, delivery of Christian's message set off a fierce debate in the Cherokee Tribal Council. The Raven and elder chiefs were for appeasement, but Dragging Canoe who was still recovering from his wound was strongly opposed to any treaty; Cameron stood with him. Thus, the Council was sharply divided into two groups; those for peace and those for continuing the war. Finally, after much debate, a Council vote was taken. The elder chiefs and others desiring peace won. Nathaniel Gist, a white trader and friend of the Old Chiefs, was sent to report to Christian, telling him that a preliminary treaty of truce was agreed to, that the Cherokee would harbor no whites, particularly Alexander Cameron, and that the Indians agreed to attend a treaty-signing conference at the Long Island in the spring.

Completing preliminary plans for the June treaty meet, Colonel Christian posted rewards of 100 pounds each for the capture of Alexander Cameron and Dragging Canoe, dead or alive. Afterward, he and his army began the long march to Fort Patrick Henry.

Leaving Echota, Alexander Cameron fled to Alabama. Defeated and angry, Dragging Canoe made a drastic decision; he and his followers with their families would leave the Overhill country, move farther south, establish new towns, and fight on. He and the unruly Chiefs decided to move to an area near the Chickamauga Creek and Tennessee River, where an ancient village of the Creek Indians had been. The great exodus took place during the winter of 1776- 1777. Many families walked; others went by horse or dugout canoe. The sites chosen for the new villages were around the foot of Lookout Mountain (present city of Chattanooga). Dragging Canoe settled on the creek; his brother, Little Owl, settled further upstream, near Georgia; and others chose homesites on the river. Here, they were joined by Tory refugees, outlaws from other Indian tribes, renegade whites, escaped Negroes, and fugitives from justice in such large numbers that they soon became numerically stronger than the Cherokee proper. In due course, because of the Chickamaugan Creek name and an old Indian town site by the same name, these people were called Chickamaugans.

For the Cherokee Nation, the four state invasion was a blow from which they never fully recovered. Whole towns were destroyed and never occupied again, their homes and corn fields were burned, orchards cut down, and most of their livestock killed. This crushing defeat was the first step toward the decline which would end two generations later with the infamous Trail of Tears.

After his promotion to Colonel in January, Nathaniel Gist was sent by General George Washington to the Long Island for the scheduled conference with the Cherokees. He arrived on March 27, 1777, and immediately sent runners to the chiefs inviting them to a council with the whites. Many came; among them Old Tassel, Oconostota, and Attakullakulla, as well as five or six hundred warriors. Dragging Canoe, who had a price on his head, refused to attend. Instead, he continued his raiding and scalping in the Long Island vicinity.

Negotiations began about mid-April and the Great Island Treaty was signed on June 20th. The Cherokee agreed to return all white captives, stolen horses, and any Negroes or cattle they had taken. They ceded to North Carolina all the land which the Wataugans and Jacob Brown had purchased two years before — plus more, but reserved their beloved ''Peace Island'' for the use of Sequoyah's father, Nathaniel Gist. Gist in the meantime, had chosen to join Washington's army so did not use the island. Instead, Joseph Martin—newly appointed Indian agent—established a trading post on it and lived there with his wife Betsy, a daughter of Nancy Ward, for over a decade.

Earlier, on May 20th, at Dewitts Corners, South Carolina, another treaty had been signed. This peace treaty was negotiated between the Commissioners of Georgia and South Carolina, and Chiefs of the Middle and Lower Towns. In it, the Cherokee ceded to Georgia, large sections of their land on the Tugaloo, Savannah, and Saluda rivers. Also, to South Carolina, all of their land in that state except for a small strip along the western boundary. Thus, the Cherokee War of 1776, instigated by Cameron and Dragging Canoe, cost the Cherokee Nation over five million acres of land.

The Cherokees refused to take up the hatchet against Britain, but promised to be neutral; however, they could not speak for Dragging Canoe who had sworn never to surrender. Since he and his followers had moved away from the Overhill Towns and set up their own government at Chickamauga, the Overhill chiefs refused to be responsible for them or their actions.

At treaty's close, Washington District (later to be Washington County) was taken under the government of North Carolina. The North of Holston settlements or Pendleton District (present-day Sullivan county) were still considered under the jurisdiction of Virginia. New boundary lines were discussed. And North Carolina

105

commissioners appointed James Robertson as Indian agent to the Overhill Cherokee, and those of Virginia chose Joseph Martin to serve that state in the same office.

The first fourth of July celebration on Tanasi soil and in all the West was held at Fort Patrick Henry during the conference; among those present were troops from Virginia, Georgia, and the Carolinas; various companies of militia from the Nolichucky-Watauga-Holston settlements; at least twenty chiefs and approximately six hundred Cherokee warriors. It was a gala affair with uniformed troops in review, feasting, speech making, gun salutes, and to close the entertainment a dance was given by the Indians in their dress costumes. Thus it was that the very Indians whom the British had tried to incite against the colonist joined in a celebration of America's declaration of freedom from English rule.

On the surface, this event appears to be a fitting climax to the western Appalachian drama, but it is not. As the curtain fell on the exuberant colonist, free at last from the yoke of English rule, it rose on the final hours of the mighty Cherokee Nation.

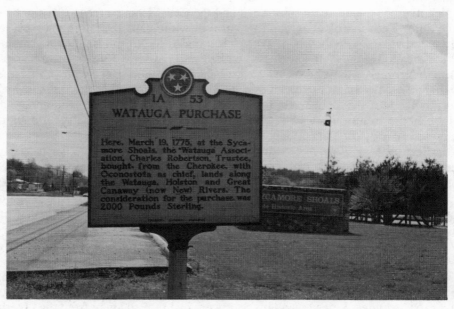

Rendezvous place of the Wataugans to lease lands from the Cherokee.

IX
ROAD TO STATEHOOD

Unfortunately all the war clouds had not been dispelled by the signing of the Great Island Treaty of 1777; the Cherokee War had not ended but only begun. For the next eighteen years the Cherokees continuously would dispatch roving bands of raiders throughout the territory—burning, looting, killing, and scalping. Going on almost without interruption from 1776 to 1794, the war was relentless, savage, and marked by many outrages by both antagonists.

While the treaty talks were yet in process at the Long Island, a party of Shawnee, dissident Cherokees, and Creeks were making attacks on the forts along the Clinch River in Southwest Virginia and against the settlements of Kentucky. At this time, only three stations in Kentucky remained inhabited: Boonesboro, Harrodsburg, and St. Asaph (Logan's Fort). The other six or eight settlements had been deserted at the outbreak of hostilities in 1776. Some settlers had moved to the afore mentioned communities, but the majority had fled back across the mountains to the safety of the East. These raids were primarily being made by stray bands of young, hot-headed warriors as an expression of their general aversion to white settlers, but were without sanction from their individual tribes.

Although the British, with Indian and Tory support, were engaged in serious battles on the New York frontier, around the lower Great Lakes, and on the upper Ohio, the leaders of the Indian nations nearest the critical Ohio-Kentucky-Holston frontiers continued their neutrality and restrained their braves. However, late in the autumn of that same year, a regrettable incident happened which shattered the peace so avidly sought by both the frontiersmen and the Indians.

Early in November, Chief Cornstalk, determined to remain neutral and to hold his Shawnee warriors out of the war, visited Fort Randolph (built upon the site where he and Lord Dunmore's armies had fought three years before) to renew his neutrality and peaceful intentions. Upon arrival, he and his two attendants were taken hostage by the commander of the Fort, Captain Matthew Arbuckle. A few days later, one of Cornstalk's sons, Elinisico, came to inquire about his father. He, too, was taken hostage. Then on November 10th, while outside the walls on a hunt, a member of the garrison was shot from ambush by an Indian assumed to be Shawnee, though some days later the killer was identified as a Mingo. Infuriated and determined to take retribution, the irate militiamen, over Arbuckle's protest, broke into the cabin where the Indian hostages were being held, brutally murdering the old Shawnee Chief, his son, and two attendants. This time, all regrets, apologies, and appeals for continued peace were useless. To the Shawnee Nation, the murder of Cornstalk only served to convince them of the folly of further restraint.

Usually the Indians refrained from warfare during the winter, but this time they did not wait. During a midwinter snowstorm on February 7, 1778, the Shawnee—painted and fully armed for war, led by their new chief Blackfish—invaded Kentucky. With the Shawnee were several Cherokee, Seneca, and Delaware Indians as well as a few Frenchmen and renegade whites. This invading force of over a hundred warriors surprised and captured Daniel Boone and twenty-six salt makers at their temporary camp some miles from Boonesboro. The prisoners were taken to the Shawnee capital of Chillicothe on the Little Miami River. Here, after running the gauntlet, sixteen of the captives were adopted into the tribe; the other ten as well as Boone were taken to Detroit. There the British lieutenant governor of Canada and the Northwest Territory, Henry Hamilton, had promised to pay Blackfish twenty British pounds for every prisoner he delivered. Returning to Chillicothe, Daniel Boone became the adopted son of Blackfish and was given the Indian name of Sheltowee or "Big Turtle."

In March, a large number of Shawnee, which included Cherokee, Wyandots, and Mingoes, laid siege to the three surviving Kentucky forts. In June, Boone finally managed to escape from the Indians, traveling over 160 miles from Chillicothe to the safety of Boonesboro. Here, Captain Boone realized that the settlers of the overcrowded and fetid stockades, weakened by hunger and disease, could not hold out much longer. Therefore, couriers were sent to the Holston seeking assistance. Although the Holston and Watauga settlements themselves were engaged in fighting off forays being made by the Chickamaugans, they accepted the responsibility for helping their fellow Virginians and Carolinians in far-off Kentucky. During the first week of August, two companies of militia arrived at Harrodsburg, and in September another body of mounted riflemen arrived at Boonesboro. Though small, this reinforcement was enough to make a substantial difference, and by late fall the Indian pressures on Kentucky began to relax. Still, for the next seventeen years the Shawnee would remain one of the most aggressive of all Indian enemies on the frontier.

Further North, Hamilton continued to stir up the Indians in that region. General Hamilton was trying to gain the support of all eastern tribes, north to south, in order to be ready to attack the backside of the colonies when another British coastal attack occurred. Hamilton—known as the "hair buying general"—held many conferences with allied Chiefs including Dragging Canoe, whose prowess as a warrior had spread among the northern tribes. When the time was right, Hamilton wanted to use the Chickamaugan braves in an attack on the southern colonies. In the South, however, the Cherokee chiefs' devotion to peace remained unshaken as did their resolution to having no control over the marauding Chickamaugans, led by Dragging Canoe.

The same year, Whiteyes, the pacific chief of the Delawares was assassinated while discussing plans for a new peace conference between his people and the Americans. For a time the white authorities were able to conceal the circumstances of his death by announcing that he had died of smallpox. The scheduled meeting was held, and the deceived Delawares renewed their pledges of peace and neutrality.

In the eastern Tanasi country during the years 1777-1778, another western migration occurred as a surge of newcomers moved farther down the Holston ignoring Indian boundary lines, and staked their claims many miles nearer the center of the Cherokee country. This greedy push of white men onto Indian lands only increased the Indian's resentment. Not only the Chickamaugans, but also the Creeks and even the Chickasaws considered the new settlers as trespassers who must at any cost be expelled. Alexander Cameron, who was old in both age and service to the British Crown, continued to prod Dragging Canoe and other tribal chiefs in their frequent raids on the whites.

During this period of relative quiet between the Wataugans and Overhill Cherokees, James Robertson, Superintendent of Indian Affairs for North Carolina, moved his residence from the Sycamore Shoals to the mouth of Big Creek, near present-day Rogersville, where he built a small stockade. Robertson, after spending over a year among the Cherokees, resigned his post in December of 1778. The following spring, he would lead a party of settlers to the French Lick on the Cumberland River.

Joseph Martin, Virginia's Indian Agent to the Overhill Cherokee, established his trading post at the famous rendezvous of the territory, the Long Island of the Holston, during November of 1777. He lived there with his Indian wife, Betsy Ward (daughter of the famous Cherokee chieftainess, Nancy Ward), for over a decade.

Adding further confusion to the British and Indian menace was the Tory problem. At the outbreak of the Revolution in April of 1775, thousands of Tories (those colonials who supported the King's cause) had abandoned their homes, either fleeing to seaport cities held by the British or taking refuge in the Bahamas, the Floridas, or Nova Scotia. Others escaped to Canada where they joined British armies. But many more, fled west to the frontier where they engaged in conspiracies, aroused suspicions among neighbors, organized militias (Tory rangers), and established relations with the British and the Indians.

Throughout America's struggle for independence, there was a "War of the Revolution in the West" which would continue until the bloody forays of the Northwest Indians was finally squelched on August 20, 1794 by General ("Mad Anthony") Wayne at Fallen Timbers in present-day Ohio; eleven years after the war in the East had ended. The Indian onslaught, British aggression, and refugee influx brought near anarchy to the Nolichucky-Watauga-Holston frontiers in 1778. Everybody was suspicious of everybody. Among the frontier people in the Appalachian West public excitement became intense, bordering on panic.

While British agents in the northwest and southwest territories were busy inciting the Indians to attack the frontier settlements of what is now Kentucky and Tennessee, the Virginia-Carolina officials were planning a campaign to move against Dragging Canoe as soon as possible. In January of 1779, Governor Patrick Henry of Virginia sent orders for the Wataugans to raise a militia, go at once to Chickamauga, and totally destroy that town and every other village near it in which the offending Indians resided. Colonel Evan Shelby was chosen as leader of the expedition, and it was decided to travel by water. The various companies of militia were to rendezvous during the first week of April at James Robertson's fort at the mouth of Big Creek on the Holston.

Before the pre-arranged meeting, two significant events occurred. On February 23rd, Hamilton the scalp buyer was captured by Colonel George Rogers Clark during his campaign in the Northwest. Hamilton and other British prisoners were marched hundreds of miles southeastward through the frontier wilderness and over the mountains to Virginia where they were incarcerated until 1781. Without Clark's conquest of the Northwest, the Canadian line might have been at the Ohio River rather than the Great Lakes. The companies of Watauga-Holston militiamen who had fought with Clark during the Northwest Campaign returned home after their northern tour of duty and joined Shelby's expedition.

At about the same time the frontiersmen were mustering on the Holston, news was received that John Stuart had died on March 26th in Pensacola, Florida. Deputy Alexander Cameron now became the Superintendent of Southern Indian Affairs. His deputies were Henry Stuart, the brother of John, and James Colbert who resided in Pensacola at the new British supply base, and John McDonald (also a deputy under John Stuart) who lived in an area near the foot of Lookout Mountain where the Chickamaugans had located.

By April, Evan Shelby had assembled about nine hundred volunteers at Robertson's fort, including a Virginia battalion under Colonel John Montgomery and a North Carolina contingent under Major Charles Robertson. Runners were sent to warn friendly Cherokees of the impending hostilities. On April 10th Shelby's flotilla began its one hundred and twenty mile trip from Big Creek to the mouth of Chickamauga Creek. Early spring rains had flushed the rivers, so the rapid current made for a fast trip down the Holston and Tennessee and the frontier force reached its destination in about five days. This totally unexpected, silent and swift approach by water caught the Chickamaugans off guard. The Indians resisted only long enough for their women and children to escape before retreating into the hills and forests themselves. The militia volunteers spent about two weeks at the Chickamaugan settlements. As ordered, all eleven towns were pillaged and burned to the ground. As there were no crops in the ground, there was none to destroy. A three-hundred pack horse load of supplies from the English base in Pensacola which was stored at John McDonald's for use against the northeast Tennessee settlers was confiscated. Also taken was a considerable booty of horses and a large cache of furs. Its mission successfully completed, Shelby's frontier force headed back. Some went upriver in dugout canoes; others went overland on foot or upon captured horses.

Although the destruction of the Chickamaugan towns and the loss of supplies were a severe blow to Dragging Canoe, it was only a temporary set-back. Following this surprise attack by water, this fearless war chief and his followers moved farther down the Tennessee, establishing five new towns alongside and below the breaks where the suck (also called boiling pot or whirl) of this mighty river made navigation difficult. This was good strategy on the part of the Chickamaugans for now a surprise attack by water was impossible. Before long, the ex-Cherokees had planted their crops, received a new shipment of supplies from Pensacola, and resumed their raids.

About this same time another event was taking place which would strain relationships between Cherokees and whites. Richard Henderson, who was yet undaunted by his failure to establish his colony "beyond the woods," Transylvania, was determined to repeat on North Carolina soil the venture which Virginia had denied him in the Kentucky lands. He wrongly thought that the Cumberland Territory when purchased from the Cherokees in 1775 was within the limits of North Carolina; therefore, he planned to locate the settlement of his new project in the region about the southern bend of the Cumberland River, commonly referred to as the French Lick, or sometimes called "The Bend" or the "Big Salt Lick." He persuaded James Robertson and John Donelson to be the leaders of his new enterprise. The expedition to the Cumberland country was to made in two parties. James Robertson and a group of single men, older male children, and skilled hunters with their livestock, brood mares, and packhorses would go by land; John Donelson, with women, younger children, small farm animals, and household furnishings, would go by water. Robertson and his men started first. Leaving his home at the mouth of Big Creek on the Holston in the fall of 1779, they took the Wilderness Road through Cumberland Gap, followed it for some distance, and then blazed a trail of their own as they progressed slowly in the deep snow and bitter cold for 395 miles. Donelson's fleet of boats with their families, slaves, and some older men left the Long Island in December of that year going down the Holston and Tennessee rivers, up the Ohio and Cumberland rivers. But because of extreme cold and ice, the thirty flatboats only floated downriver for about three miles before the party was forced to tie up along the banks of the Holston until mid-February. Robertson and his caravan reached the Cumberland River across from the French Lick around Christmas of 1779; some historians say January 1, 1780. There they drove their horses and cattle across the curving avenue of solid ice which was frozen so thick it supported both men and animals. Above the banks of the Cumberland at a place called Cedar Bluff, they built a fort and began clearing land and erecting cabins close by. Donelson's group reached the first new settlement on the north side of the river at the French Lick, present-day Nashville, on April 24th. Here they were met by Robertson and his men in a happy reunion. The perilous journey of 985 miles on ice-encrusted waters was the most courageous river voyage of frontier history. By the end of April, there were eight settlements scattered on both sides of the Cumberland hidden from each other by great stretches of cane which covered the ground. On a limestone bluff covered by cedars was the stockaded village of Nashboro, which became the center of the community. It was named in honor of General Francis Nash of Hillsboro, North Carolina, who had been a good friend of Colonel Richard Henderson.

On May 1, 1780 the male settlers age sixteen and above met to formulate the Cumberland Compact; a type of government similar to the Wataugans'. Although the new settlement was a part of Washington County, it was isolated from the county seat of Jonesboro by over 300 miles of wilderness. The new settlers of the Cumberland Basin were determined to handle their own affairs rather than referring them to the far-distant court at Jonesboro. The Cumberland Association was patterned after the Watauga Association formulated in East Tennessee in 1772.

Site where John Donelson and his flotilla of flatboats began their journey down the Holston River to the Cumberland Country.

Site on the Holston River which Donelson and his flotilla passed shortly before coming to the shoals at the mouth of Reedy Creek.

It has been suggested that the Cumberland Compact was jointly composed and written by James Robertson and Judge Henderson, and phrased to aid the Transylvania Company in selling its land grants to the settlers. But by this agreement the citizens of the Cumberland Valley, considering themselves citizens of North Carolina, acknowledged legal jurisdiction of North Carolina over the region. This meant that the Cumberland Court with its twelve judges was to refrain from sentencing persons to death, and that persons who committed crimes dangerous to the state were to stand trial in the courts of North Carolina. The Compact was adopted by the settlers on May 13th and two hundred fifty-six men signed it. Almost immediately after the pact was signed, massacres began by the Chickasaws, Shawnee, Creeks and Chickamaugans. They raided separately, and at times together.

Although the Cherokees and Chickasaws had driven the Shawnee out of the region several years earlier, in 1769 the Cherokees themselves were defeated by the Chickasaws and they now claimed the territory by right of conquest. Too, unknown to the new settlers who had felt secure from Indian attacks because they were supposedly on unclaimed land, the Cumberland Basin was used by many tribes and nations as a common hunting ground. The Indians greatly resented the whites trespassing upon their lands, and were determined to chase them out. The massacres at this time ignited a period of warfare which would last nearly fifteen years.

In Washington County, meanwhile, the Watauga frontier had become a refuge for Patriots rather than Loyalists. Later it would become a place for sequestering Loyalist prisoners. The Indian attacks, Tory harassment, and unwelcome refugees brought chaos to the Watauga-Holston frontier in 1778-79. The major cause of the problems was the British who were encouraging the Tories while supplying the Indians. Nevertheless amidst these scenes of civil disorder and violence the spiritual and educational life of the Appalachian frontier people were gaining in importance. Circuit preachers, many times being both an instructor of religion and a teacher of the 3-R's, were making their rounds fairly regularly by the mid-1700's. By 1773 the first building erected for religious services was built some four miles west of present-day Blountville. The log structure, called Taylor's Meeting House, was a place of worship for all denominations because the settlements were as yet too sparse for the organization of any single denomination. The building was also used as a fort and school. Single denominational churches soon followed. Buffalo Ridge Baptist Church, at present-day Gray Station, is accepted by historians as the first organized church body on Tanasi soil. Tidence Lane, who moved to Watauga in 1776 from North Carolina, established the church on Buffalo Ridge and was its first pastor. Salem Church, located near Jonesboro and organized by Dr. Samuel Doak of the Presbyterian faith, was the first presbytery in Tennessee. Ebenezer Methodist Church was the first methodist society in the area. It was organized in 1790 about one and half miles from present-day Chuckey. The Sinking Creek Baptist Church, first called the Watauga River Church, was built in 1783 near Sycamore Shoals and is the oldest church in Tennessee occupying its original location and foundation. Although there is doubt as to when its first church body was organized, it is known that Joshua Kelley served as pastor from about 1780-1785.

First building erected for religious services on Tennessee soil in 1773.
Place of worship for all denominations, the log cabin was also used as a fort and a school.

Oldest grave in Buffalo Ridge Cemetery (1789). Buffalo Ridge Church
has been moved from its original site to Gray Station; only the cemetery remains.

Sinking Creek Baptist Church
Oldest church in Tennessee still standing on its original foundation.

Sinking Creek Baptist Church—first called Watauga River Church
The congregation of Watauga River Church (later Sinking Creek) was meeting infrequently in different homes of their neighbors a few years before the log church building was erected.

115

Education for the settlers mostly was limited to home instruction and training, but a few of the wealthy relied on the educational opportunities back on the eastern coast. In 1780, one of three long buildings erected by Samuel Doak in Jonesboro was used by him as a private school and became the first educational institution established west of the Appalachian mountains. It was affectionately called "Doak's Log College" by the frontier people. In 1783 the North Carolina legislature granted Doak a charter for the school, and it was named Martin Academy, in honor of Governor Alexander Martin of North Carolina who was a close friend of Doak. Both men had graduated from West Nottingham Academy in Maryland. In 1785 the school was again chartered as Martin Academy by the State of Franklin. Then in 1795 it was chartered and given its present name of Washington College by the legislature of the Territory of the United States South of the River Ohio.

Early in 1779, a three-cornered rivalry evolved among Bean's lower-Watauga settlements, the Sycamore Shoals community, and the Nolichucky citizenry as to the location of a permanent court-house site. Eventually they agreed to a compromise location between the three of them. That spring, the North Carolina assembly passed a bill which authorized the building of a courthouse and the laying out of a town on the low ridge between the Watauga and Nolichucky waters. The new county seat, Jonesboro, was named after Willie (pronounced Wylie) Jones of Halifax, North Carolina, a man of prominence and wealth. This new seat of justice in Washington county became the first town established in the Tanasi country and the oldest town west of the Appalachian mountains.

That fall the North Carolina assembly met again, passing a bill to form a new county to be carved from Washington and to embody much of the Holston settlements. The new county was named Sullivan in honor of General John Sullivan of the Continental Army. The first session of Sullivan county's court was held in the cabin home of Moses Looney, near Eaton's Station. Later, in 1792, the village of Blountville became the permanent county seat.

Meanwhile, Britain had turned her attention to the South where she expected, and received, considerable Tory support. After several successful campaigns, the British invaded the Carolinas close to the frontier border. Thereafter, the vigilance and efforts of the Western pioneers were not confined to their own protection and defense, but also to that of their kin and countrymen east of the mountains. Throughout the war not only were the frontiersmen busy fighting Cherokees, they were also engaged in guarding the back door of the colonies and sending men to fight on the coast. Therefore, when the exigencies of Carolina called aloud for every absent son to return to her rescue and defense, the call was promptly obeyed. Always when there was a call for volunteers, more men than asked for from the Tanasi answered. Because of this, eventually the territory would become nicknamed the "Volunteer State."

Late in the summer of 1780, Major Patrick Ferguson, encamped at Gilbert Town, North Carolina, penned a threatening message to the Overmountain People: if the rebels continued to abstain from taking the oath of loyalty to His Majesty, Ferguson and his troops would invade the country, destroy their homes, and hang their leaders. Upon delivery of this warning at Sapling Grove, Isaac Shelby straightway rode to the Nolichucky settlement, where John Sevier now lived and where he and Kate Sherrill were celebrating their marriage with a barbecue. After two or three days,

Shelby and Sevier decided that a surprise attack against Ferguson would be the best plan of action.

The valley soon rang with the call to arms, and mountainmen began pouring into Sycamore Shoals from every direction. At daybreak on September 27, 1780, a long column of nearly one-thousand, buckskin-clad riflemen began its trek across the mountains. A few days later it was learned that Ferguson was in retreat toward the South Carolina border to join the safety of Lord Cornwallis' army. The Overmountain Men who had been joined by remnants of local militia and whose strength now was approximately 1,800, began a fast, forced march in pursuit. On October 6th, for reasons unknown, Ferguson decided to stand and give battle. He led his troops to the top of King's Mountain where he felt assured of an easy victory, but it was not to be.

The pursuing militia arrived on October 7th, and after tethering their horses and priming their Deckhard rifles, they charged up the mountain. The ensuing battle, fought with desperate ferocity by both sides, lasted just over an hour; afterwards, Ferguson was dead and over eight hundred prisoners were taken.

The victory at King's Mountain was the turning point of the American Revolution in the South. It forced the British forces to withdraw from the Carolinas and broke the Tory spirit in the whole backcountry. It heartened the frontier people and restored Patriots' morale. The victors, concerned about possible Cherokee attacks at home, did not linger. They left the next day with over 800 prisoners and what booty they could carry. The prisoners were left in Burke county where they were dispatched under guard to Hillsborough. From here, the Wataugan volunteers hastened home. The settlers of America's first Western frontier were sure now they had a country, and that they were a part of it. After King's Mountain, the Wataugans fought both British and Indians to the war's end in 1783. Against the British they participated on call from the East, though only for brief periods of service because of the continuing Indian menace at home. Against the Indians, their skirmishes would continue many years beyond the British surrender at Yorktown.

By the end of the Revolution, there was a temporary halt to the Chickamaugan-Cherokee attacks against the Washington and Sullivan county residents, but not against those of the Cumberland settlements. Much had changed in the Watauga west. Many familiar names and faces were gone. James Robertson, one of the first settlers and a founder of the Watauga Association, had moved away; John Carter, chairman and colonel of Watauga, had died in 1781; William Bean, the first settler, had long since moved some fifty miles below the Long Island, settling a place which became known as Bean's Station and in the 1780's was a stop-over point for Kentucky-bound immigrants. Among the Cherokee, the Little Carpenter, Attakullahkullah, had died in 1780 a few days after King's Mountain at an age above ninety years. And two years later, the grim reaper's sickle struck down another great chief, Oconostota, more familiar to us as "Old Hop."

As to other changes, Washington County had been divided twice—Sullivan County was created in 1779 and in 1783 Greene County, which included a large portion of western North Carolina, was created. That same year, the North Carolina government legislated the Cumberland settlements into a civil body, thus creating Davidson County. The county, named for General William Lee Davidson of North Carolina, embodied nearly 12,000 square miles and covered three-fourths of present-day Middle Tennessee. The following year, Nashboro was given the status of a town and its name changed to Nashville.

Over 18,000 persons now inhabited America's first, Western frontier—East Tennessee. And collectively they were unhappy with their relationship with the East, particularly North Carolina. Although the border settlements had been under her protection since 1777, the legislature still had not created any local superior court nor a separate military district across the mountains. In addition, after the Revolution, North Carolina had set aside great stretches of western land for military veterans and now she had begun to exhibit a willingness to sell out the settlers in the interest of peace with the Indians. But the frontier people refused to be discouraged as they continued their thrust into the wilderness and their march on the road to statehood. This move toward a separate and distinct state was initiated by the Overmountain People of the Watauga-Holston-Nolichucky settlements in East Tennessee. The far-removed community of Davidson County took no part in the movement. The residents there sought their own separate statehood.

At this particular time, the Confederation Congress (so called because it was operating under the Articles of Confederation) was weak and lacking in prestige. Although it was the only governmental body in which all thirteen states were represented, it had to deal with the new states individually rather than as a whole. After the Revolutionary War, each state had its own taxes, money and laws. Congress could only collect for the nation's heavy war debt by asking the individual states to contribute their share of money on a voluntary basis. It could not command, enforce, or coerce. All the states were jealous of each other, quarreling over boundary disputes and squabbling over taxes and commerce. Six of the states had no western lands, and the other seven were reluctant to relinquish the claims to their territories in the West. In 1784, the Confederation Congress had asked that the states with claims to territories in the West cede them to the central government in order that their use could be beneficial to all. Eventually all seven states would comply.

At the end of the American War of Independence, North Carolina was virtually bankrupt and thousands of her people had moved west of the Appalachians. Her western borders, specified in the old Crown charters, extended due west to the Mississippi River, and the state still claimed these lands as her own. Therefore, North Carolina's legislature began to include the land across the mountains in its bills and to levy taxes in the western districts. The fiercely independent mountain people of the West paid no attention to the directives, and refused to pay taxes to a state that had offered them no military protection, established neither courts nor schools, and had built no roads for them.

The Overmountain People had learned long ago that they could depend upon themselves in dealing with the hazards of the wilderness. They neither wanted nor expected aid from an outsider. An unfortunate by-product of this decision was the settlers ruthless treatment of the Indians. North Carolina's many treaties with the Cherokee Nation, as well as those made with the Choctaw and Chickasaw tribes, were ignored. The Indian lands were occupied or marked for future settlement. The warriors of these three tribes, feeling they had no other choice, began another campaign of savage attacks upon the whites in an attempt to drive the settlers from their lands. This in turn led to more than ninety white expeditions against the Indians in the decade beginning in 1780.

Finally, in April of 1784, North Carolina ceded her western lands to the Confederation Congress. Among the Overmountain People, news of this cession spread quickly by word of mouth from settlement to isolated cabin. The Wataugans and their neighbors met in Jonesboro in June to discuss the formation of a separate, fourteenth state. The Cumberland District, wanting to pursue its own goal for statehood, did not send representatives. Later, their leaders would petition Congress requesting that the Cumberland be separated from North Carolina and be allowed to form a state of its own. On August 23rd the men of Watauga, as well as others from the settlements in northeast Tennessee, met again at Jonesboro. This time, the three western counties of Washington, Sullivan, and Greene were declared independent of North Carolina. They formed a committee to discuss resolutions and guidelines for the goal of statehood.

When newspapers told the citizens of North Carolina about the Jonesboro convention in August, they were outraged at the rash actions of the "western rebels." To teach them a lesson, at a meeting of the state's legislature in October the Cession Act was rescinded. A third meeting opened at Jonesboro on December 14 without the District having yet received word of the repeal by the North Carolina Assembly. The decision was now made to form a separate state, independent of North Carolina. The delegates drew up a formal declaration of independence and a provisional constitution. A letter was written to America's venerable elder statesman, Benjamin Franklin, requesting permission to name the new state after him. At the close of meeting, commissioners were selected to petition the Confederation Congress in Philadelphia for recognition of their separate status. At this time, Congress had no choice but to turn the separatists request down because North Carolina had already rescinded her Act of Cession.

Disregarding this move by the North Carolina Legislature, in February of 1785 individual towns and districts of northeast Tennessee elected their representatives to the new state assembly who were to meet in Jonesboro in early March. In the meantime, a two-story, clapboard structure (called a statehouse) was being built in Jonesboro as a meeting place for the newly elected members. A letter from Dr. Franklin had been received, giving permission to use his name for the new state.

In March, 1785, the First General Assembly of Franklin met in its new statehouse in Jonesboro. Here, the Overmountain country of the Holston, Watauga, and Nolichucky settlements became the new "State of Franklin"; John Sevier was named governor and John Carter's son, Landon, as secretary of state. A few of those assembled attempted to name the new state "Frankland, "State of the Free," but it drew little support. The name selected and used on all documents was Franklin, in honor of the great statesman Benjamin Franklin. Then, the Assembly proceeded to conduct state business such as the provision of a militia, forming new counties, levying taxes, and so forth.

North Carolina having repealed its Act of Cession, refused to recognize the new state. Instead, its legislature offered pardons to the separatists and provided for the appointment of civil and military officers for the territory. Nevertheless, the Franklin assembly continued to meet and finally appealed again to the Continental Congress to be recognized as a separate state. This time Congress felt it could not act favorably on the Franklin legislature's memorial for recognition without North Carolina's approval and denied the motion. This was by a narrow margin, however. North Carolina, being an interested party, could not vote, and the delegates from Massachusetts and Delaware were not present. Needing a two-third's majority, the eight to two vote for statehood was not enough.

The people of Franklin were much divided and the proffered pardons only widened the division. Governor Sevier and his many friends were as determined to maintain Franklin's independence as the North Carolina Senator John Tipton and his small coterie were to see the region returned to the allegiance of that state. This rivalry resulted in two governments with two courts, two tax laws, and two sets of state officials functioning in the same country over the same people. With this inner strife, in addition to the many outside conflicts, the road to statehood seemed blocked at every turn. The government of Franklin gradually fell apart. The last fifteen months of its existence are shrouded in mystery as there are few surviving fragments of its records. Those which did survive are confusing and contradictory. But, there is no doubt that it disappeared forever in 1789.

The proposed Constitution of the United States, drafted in 1787, had been officially adopted on June 21, 1788, and the old Confederation Congress went out of existence. The following year the new federal congress met in Philadelphia; George Washington was elected President of the United States, and the hamlet of New York was chosen as a temporary capital of the new nation. In the same year, North Carolina finally decided to cede to Congress her western lands across the Appalachians.

Politically, this land was referred to as "The Territory of the United States of America South of the River Ohio," but this was misleading for Virginia claimed Kentucky County (which would be admitted as a state in 1792), and Georgia claimed the region which became Alabama and Mississippi, territory she would not cede until 1802. This left an area roughly within the present boundaries of Tennessee as "The Southwest Territory," which it was universally called. The country had two districts. One was the Washington District consisting of Sullivan, Washington, Greene and Hawkins counties, and the other was the Mero District, consisting of Davidson, Tennessee, and Sumner counties. The other regions were occupied by the Cherokees. In August William Blount was appointed by President Washington as Governor of the new territory and Superintendent of Indian Affairs in the South. He served in both posts from 1790 to 1796. Blount arrived in the Watauga community on October 10th. There, the forty-one year old governor chose as his official residence and headquarters the home of William Cobb, Rocky Mount, which stood at the fork of the Holston and Watauga rivers, near where the first permanent settlement of Tennessee was planted. For eighteen months, Rocky Mount near present-day Johnson City, was the capitol of the first recognized English-speaking government west of the Appalachian Mountains. Given instructions by Secretary Knox to solve the conflicts between the Cherokees and the white settlers, Governor Blount's position was difficult and required unusual tact. On one hand he was obligated to make attempts to satisfy discontented settlers who would not, or could not, understand the Indians' point of view; on the other he was pressured by the federal government to satisfy the grievances of the resentful Indians. In the interest of unity, Blount chose for his county officials many adherents of the old Franklin government. John Sevier and James Robertson were appointed brigadier generals of the Washington and Mero districts, and Daniel Smith was named Territorial Secretary. In addition, three judges, a clerk, and several minor military and civil officers were appointed.

In 1792, Blount chose the hamlet known as White's Fort as the new capitol of the Territory. He commissioned its founder, General James White, to lay out the streets for a town which he renamed Knoxville for General Henry Knox, Washington's Secretary of War, and he built "Blount's Mansion," the first frame house west of the mountains, as his official residence on a knoll near the Holston River.

Tennessee's first newspaper, the "Knoxville Gazett," was published in 1791 by George Roulston who had set up his press at Rogersville in Hawkins county. The following year the paper was moved to a permanent residence at Knoxville. Roulston set up his print-shop in a log cabin on a street now called Gay. This newspaper was a gold mine of information for almost every aspect of pioneer life in Tanasi and was used extensively by both the whites and Indians.

By 1794, twenty years of frontier bloodshed was drawing to a close. Two years earlier, one bright flame among the Indians had been quelled. This fiery adversary of the whites and staunch leader of the Cherokee had consistently refused to sign treaty deeds or barter the land of his people. Dragging Canoe, having fought his last battle, drank his last draft of whiskey, and danced to exhaustion at his last victory celebration, was dead at the age of 60 years. His successor was the half-breed John Watts, a grandson of Old Tassel. This new War Chief of the Chickamaugans, sometimes called Young Tassel, was not as hostile toward the whites, and eventually would agree to peace terms with them.

At the time of Dragging Canoe's death, Watts was in Echota talking with Governor Blount. Efforts were being made to win back the friendship of the ex-Cherokees in the Chickamaugan towns. At the same time, Dragging Canoe had been visiting the neighboring tribes to revive the war spirits of the southern Indians in their fight for survival against the frontier Americans. On the day before his death, the War Chief and his warriors were attending a victory celebration at Lookout Mountain town, present-day Chattanooga. Their frenzied war and scalp dancing, as well as the festive drinking, lasted all night. The next morning, March 1, 1792, the great Cherokee-Chickamaugan War Chief was dead. Runners were sent to Echota to inform Watts of the Canoe's death and to let him know that the Chickamaugan Council of Chiefs had chosen him as the new War Chief.

That year he asked Governor Blount for a parley. A big conference between the Cherokees and the whites was planned in November at the Tellico blockhouse just below Knoxville. At the Tellico treaty talks in November all the chieftains of the Cherokee nations were present, as were about two thousand Indians and most all the officials of the Territorial Government. The Creeks still waged war. Among the items of peace agreed upon was a $1,000 annuity to be paid to the Cherokees in compensation for their land cessions. Later this would be raised to $5,000 with a $50 deduction for each horse they stole and failed to return within three months. All land the Indians claimed was guaranteed to them for life. The next year, in council with the Creeks and the Chickamaugans at the military post of Colerain in the Cumberland region, the Tellico proposals of peace were ratified, and both tribes signed peace treaties. At long last the fierce and bloody Cherokee War was finally over—at least temporarily—and the country enjoyed peace for the first time in many years.

The Indians had learned well the forked-tongue way of talking from the whites, and this "Tomahawk Diplomacy" became their mode of procedure during treaty talks—i.e., "cover your tomahawk and knife with a blanket while you parley for peace." The Cherokee still owned vast regions of Tennessee, North Carolina, and Georgia and no matter what they agreed to or signed, they still wanted every white off their land. They knew that before long—like so many times before—the land hungry Americans and new immigrants would ignore treaty and boundary lines, clear the land, and erect cabins in Indian territory. Once more, there was no army to patrol boundaries or to protect the Indians rights. Thus, unable to get satisfactory results from the two-faced white officials, the Cherokee would follow their own code rather than the white man's law. Feeling they had a right to steal and kill, once again they would retaliate by burning, murdering, capturing, stealing, and scalping.

With the days of the Territorial Government drawing to a close, in October of 1795, the second Territorial Assembly met in order to take a census. Blount County was carved from Knox, and the towns of Blountville in Sullivan County, Sevierville in Sevier County, Greeneville in Greene County, and Clarksville in Montgomery County were chartered; towns which were and are the officials seats of the county governments. The census revealed a population of 77,262 of which 10,613 were slaves; slightly over the 60,000 required to apply for statehood. Daniel Smith, Secretary of the Southwest Territory, submitted Tennessee as the name for the new state. The Cumberland County by that name relinquished it and became Montgomery and Robertson counties.

A General Assembly met at Knoxville in January of 1796 to draw up a state constitution. This convention was attended by two old Wataugans: General James Robertson, now of Davidson County, and General John Sevier, lately of Franklin. Also present was young Andrew Jackson, a Jonesboro attorney now living in Nashville. This time when the state petition was presented to the Federal Government in Philadelphia it was not turned down. Tennessee was admitted as the sixteenth state to the Union of States by Congress on May 31, 1796. At this time there were eight counties in East Tennessee and three in Middle Tennessee; the western part of the state was still claimed by the Cherokee and Chickasaw tribes. John Sevier was elected Governor, with William Blount and Samuel Cocke as the first Senators, and Andrew Jackson as the first Congressman.

When Tennessee framed her constitution and was admitted to statehood, the fate of the Cherokee Nation was sealed.

DONELSON'S FLOTILLA

John Donelson's fleet of flatboats left the Long Island of the Holston in late December, 1779. It would take the expedition—comprised mostly of women, older males, slaves and children with their noisy farm animals—nearly four months to reach the safety of Cedar Bluff. Due to heavy snow and ice, the first day they floated only three miles, to the mouth of Reedy Creek. There, they encamped for a month. Finally in February, 1780, the thawing ice allowed them to continue the journey to the Cumberland region. Of the 200 people, at least 30 died from drowning, disease, and Indian attacks.

X

SURVIVAL OF THE SPECIES

Although the grayish-blue smoke from its many fires could still occasionally be seen, the intense heat of two long decades of savage frontier wars had finally cooled. The ashes had been scattered, and by all outward appearances the fire was extinguished; but underneath the warm residue the spark of the Cherokee race still flickered, struggling for air, and refusing to die. Much of the far-flung ash clung to the bosom of its mountain mother, the sanctuary of all forms of life. Here, this noble savage of the primeval forest knew he would be safe to kindle the spark and nourish the species. The mighty Cherokee Nation did not want to die; it wanted to live as do all natural species.

The near annihilation of the tribe and its survival is the story of the first forty years of the nineteenth century in Tennessee. It provides an important key to understanding the Cherokee down to the present day. Many volumes have been written about the period, but this story is designed only to relate the principal events leading to the end of the drama of the Cherokee and white man in America's first western frontier.

The grand state of Tennessee had been born. The year was 1796. It had been a long, difficult labor and a delivery with many complications. The state's parents were notorious: Watauga, the obstreperous child of Virginia and North Carolina, who was claimed by neither, and Franklin, the rebellious grandchild of North Carolina. But from these two were gleaned the child's strong will to survive, its fierce spirit of independence, and its voluntary self-aid.

These people of the new state of Tennessee did not think the Cherokee—who still claimed large sections of land in Tennessee, Georgia, and North Carolina by right of the Tellico treaty—should be regarded as a separate nation, but instead thought they should be under the control of the state. This bright, intelligent race were considered as strangers, interlopers as it were, in the path of national destiny. During the first ten years of statehood one of the main goals of frontier politicians was to gain control of Indian territories. During this time, the Cherokees were forced to give up most of their land in the new state. More than twenty new

Tennessee counties were formed; thus control of the land shifted from the Indian to the American.

Thomas Jefferson was inaugurated as President in the swampy village of Washington—the new national capital—in 1801. Colonel Return Jonathan Meigs, called "White Path" by the Indians, was appointed Federal Indian Agent to the Cherokees and Agent of the Federal War Department in Tennessee in May of that same year; posts he held until his death in 1823. Meigs' main duties were to arrange treaty conferences, direct "civilizing" programs for the Cherokee, encourage the Indians to move to the vacant West, and to serve as liaison officer between the two races.

In 1803 through the Louisiana Purchase the United States acquired an enormous region west of the Mississippi River. Early that year, while the American Minister Livingston was in Paris negotiating for the purchase of New Orleans, Napoleon I had suddenly decided to sell all of Louisiana. This immense area, whose boundaries were then only vaguely defined, was basically the same size as when La Salle first claimed it for France in 1682. After about a week of haggling, treaties were signed in April and the extensive Louisiana wilderness, including the vital New Orleans port, was sold to the United States by France for $15,000,000. This unknown country included land between the Mississippi River and the Rocky mountains, from the Canadian border to the Gulf of Mexico; 828,000 square miles were acquired for about three cents an acre. The vast territory more than doubled the existing United States. Its lower region was called the Louisiana Territory while the area about the Arkansas River became known as the Arkansas Territory because of an Indian tribe by that name which lived there. The upper section about the Missouri River was designated as the Missouri Territory.

Under increasing pressure from the states bordering the Cherokee Nation, President Jefferson suggested to Congress the desirability of moving all Southeastern Indian tribes to the newly acquired land west of the Mississippi River far away from settlers where it would be easier for them to preserve their culture. Residents of Georgia, Tennessee, and the Carolinas wanted to be rid of the Indians as soon as possible. Each state had already, on different dates, addressed memorials to Congress asking that Indian titles in the states be extinguished at the earliest possible moment and insisted that the Federal Government move both the Cherokees and Creeks off state lands. Therefore, the Secretary of War instructed Agent Meigs to use his influence to get the Indians to move. A few hundred families were persuaded to move to a new home in the vacant West (present-day western Arkansas). The Indians did this at their own expense, for as yet the federal government had not appropriated any money for this purpose.

Still not satisfied, and their appetites seemingly never satiated, land-hungry Americans continued to gnaw at Cherokee as well as other tribal lands. Between 1804-1807, Agent Meigs, working with Federal appointed commissioners, helped arrange several Cherokee cessions involving over 8,000 square miles of Indian territory which included a small tract in Georgia called the Wafford Settlement, lands in Kentucky and Middle Tennessee, and the beloved Long Island on the Holston (vicinity of present-day Kingsport).

In 1805, the biggest land treaty ever was negotiated at Tellico where 4.5 million acres of Cherokee land was ceded to Tennessee. The federal government had built the Tellico Blockhouse near the village of Echota on the Tellico River while Blount was Governor of the Southwest Territory (near present McGhee in Monroe County). Several early treaties with the Cherokees were signed here. In the First Treaty of Tellico, 1798, the Cherokee allowed new settlers to remain in the area about the Little Tennessee River by surrendering a portion of their tribal lands between the Clinch River and the Cumberland Plateau. In return, the federal government had pledged that it would guarantee the remainder of Cherokee Territory to them forever. The expanse of "forever" proved to be a short span as evidenced by the second and third treaties of Tellico in 1804 and 1805. In the large land transfer negotiated by the Third Treaty of Tellico, the Cherokees sold to the United States all the land north of Duck River and west of the Tennessee for $11,000, which united the settlements of East and Middle Tennessee. At the same time the Chickasaws sold 355,000 acres south of the Duck River for $22,000. The prehistoric hunting grounds of the Cherokee and their claims of land were quickly shrinking. These treaty cessions of 1804 and 1807 were not official transactions made by the Cherokee National Council, but deals arranged by Meigs and some federal officials by bribery and silent considerations to several prominent Cherokee chiefs who were in favor of moving their people west. Chief Doublehead was the main culprit who signed the illegal land deals, and under orders by the Council he was assassinated by a few, angry Cherokees for betraying his people. Within a year or so, others of the chiefs who had signed the treaties were also killed; the rest fled West for safety. The Principal Chief of the Cherokee, Little Turkey, and members of the Cherokee Council went to Washington to protest the treaties as illegal, but Congress ratified them in spite of the Cherokees' objections.

Most people in Tennessee believed that the Indians had lost any claim or title to their lands by helping Great Britain in the Revolutionary War, and they thought the vast land they held should be open to settlement. The federal government did not agree, however, and the United States Supreme Court ruled that the Indians were under federal rather than state control. Federal troops were sent to remove squatters from Indian lands, and perhaps Indian history would have been somewhat different if America and Britain had not fought the War of 1812.

When the United States declared war on Great Britain in 1812, many Indians, believing their rights would be better protected under the British government than the new American one, went on the warpath in support of the British cause. There was good reason not to trust the new Americans. In the first decade of the nineteenth century in the Ohio Valley alone the Indians had been cajoled into making treaties ceding more than one hundred million acres of their land to the United States. In addition, westerners seeking more land, were continually driving the Indians farther and farther west away from their ancient hunting lands.

Determined to save the country west of the Ohio River and preserve their homelands from further white invasion, the Shawnee Chief Tecumseh and his brother, known as "The Prophet," had managed to unite the tribes east of the Mississippi against further encroachments by the whites. Together, they had organized an efficient Indian Confederacy supported by warriors who believed that the Indians must return to their tribalism in order to preserve their existence. As terror spread along the frontier, the two brothers traveled south to bid for the support of the Creeks and Cherokees. At first both tribes responded with enthusiasm.

127

The Upper Creeks accepted Tecumseh as the leader who would restore the old life, but the Cherokee—after being warned by Agent Meigs and other progressives that to join the attacking Creeks, Shawnee and other northern tribes would invite destruction of their Nation by the United States—instead gave valuable support to the Americans during the War of 1812. At the bloody Battle of Horseshoe Bend, March 27, 1814, on the banks of the Tallapossa River in what later became the state of Alabama, they sent hundreds of warriors into the field behind Jackson against the Creeks, and were credited with turning the tide of that battle.

Defeated, the Creeks were forced to give up much of their richest lands in the Mississippi Territory. The year before, 1813, the Shawnee as well as members of other northern tribes had been defeated at the Battle of Thames near Detroit in Canada. Here, the great Chief Tecumseh, now a brigadier general in the British Army, was killed; with his death the Indian Confederacy collapsed and Indian military power east of the Mississippi was finally destroyed. The Cherokees, in return for their help and efforts at peace, returned home to find their towns ravaged and despoiled by white troops, new roads built across their lands, and five new treaties forced on them by 1820. Despite local encroachment and abuse, the Cherokee continued to place their trust in the federal government; a government which was anxious to be rid of them forever and which pressed them to move beyond the Mississippi, even though most Indians wanted to remain in their ancient homeland.

By 1817, the two thousand or more Cherokees who had moved West to the Arkansas Territory were having complications and hostile conflicts had developed. The Osage Tribe, who claimed the land north of the Arkansas River, and the Quapaws, who claimed the land to the south, both greatly resented the intrusion of the emigrating Indian families. Thus, the Cherokee complained to Congress, asking for more western land. They were told by federal commissioners that they could not have any additional tracts until an equivalent acreage was ceded in the East. The situation led to further illegal transactions by western chiefs who signed land cession papers by proxy and by some eastern chiefs who signed because of bribes. One such deal occurred in 1819 wherein the government offered the Western Cherokees four million acres of land along the Arkansas and White rivers in exchange for three large tracts in southeast Tennessee: the Hiwassee District, Sequatchie Valley, and a mountain area in Blount county. The treaty was signed at the Indian agency in present-day Calhoun, Tennessee. At a separate cession, the Cherokee were persuaded to give up their claim to the heart of the Smoky Mountains. By an odd circumstance, attached to the treaty, Chief Yonaguska—Ya'nu-gun'ski—who was better known to the whites as Drowning Bear, was allowed to stay. He and a few braves stayed on 640 square acres just a short distance above present-day Bryson City in western North Carolina, near the junction of the Tuckasegee and Oconaluftee rivers on the site of the ancient village of Kituhwa. This parcel of land was the size of an individual tract as arranged by Meigs and the federal government within ceded territory which was available only to a few "civilized" Indians. The Cherokees, in the process of obtaining western "civilization" and to prove they were indeed worthy of remaining in the East, had yielded by these two deals nearly 6,000 square miles, or one fourth of the land that still remained to them.

The previous year another land cession, known as the Jackson Purchase, had been negotiated between the Chicksasws and the United States in the Cumberland Region. James Robinson and federal commissioners met with the Chickasaws at Old Town in what later (that same year) became the state of Alabama. Here, the tribe gave up its claim to all of West Tennessee, for which they were paid $300,000 over a fifteen year period. Later that year, Hardin and Shelby counties were created, becoming the first counties of West Tennessee.

Being outnumbered and divided, with arrows being no match for lead bullets, the Indians had no power to enforce their claims nor to defend their homes. Their survival had become a perpetual struggle against more powerful forces. But the unending pressures for survival evoked the genius of the natural species. Not only did they gradually adapt to the white man's culture and form of government, but they also produced their own written language, an invention made more remarkable by the character of the inventor, Sequoyah, who never abandoned the old Cherokee mores or native religion. He was one of the Cherokees who never learned to speak, read, or write English. He invented the "talking leaves" not as a means of civilizing the Indian to white ways, but rather as the means of saving Indian beliefs. Sequoyah's syllabary was accepted by the Cherokee National Council in 1821, and within months almost all the Cherokees became literate.

At the beginning of the new decade, 1820, there were twenty-three states in the Union. The United States possessions included the Arkansas Territory, Missouri Territory (to become a state in 1821), and a huge, unorganized Mid-Northwest Territory—part of the Louisiana Purchase—whose northern boundary was vaguely defined as the 49th parallel, zigzagging along the Rocky mountains to the 42nd parallel. The untamed Oregon Country in the far Northwest was jointly occupied by the United States and Great Britain as per the Treaty of Ghent in 1818. Spanish possessions lay in the extreme Southwest bordering the Pacific Coast and territories of the western United States from the 42nd parallel line southward. Spain had ceded both East and West Florida to the United States in 1819 in exchange for the Texas country, which had been claimed by the government under the blanket of the Louisiana Purchase.

The decade of 1820-30 was an "Era of Good Feelings" for the white inhabitants of the Union of States who were beginning to regard themselves first as Americans and then, secondarily, as citizens of their respective states. A vibrant new Nationalistic spirit was emerging. Congress was no longer weak and a new national capitol (the old one was burned by the British in 1814) was arising from the ashes of Washington. The Second Bank of the United States had been established and it would contribute greatly to the economic life of the country. Americans were writing and painting for Americans; they were using American scenes and themes. New schools, churches, homes, roads, and industries were being built.

For a time this "Era of Good Feelings" was reflected by the Cherokee Nation who still trusted the federal goverment. How feverishly the American natives worked! Believing it was not their fate to perish, the Cherokees placed their trust in the government and gradually began taking over the white man's culture, trusting that acceptance of white civilization might insure their survival as a nation. The ancient capital of Echota was moved to northern Georgia to a site called, with hope, New Echota. The Indians foresook the warpath and their aboriginal hunting

129

ARKANSAS

TENNESSEE

NORTH
CAROLINA

CHICKASAW

CHEROKEE

SOUTH
CAROLINA

CHOCTAW

Mississippi River

CREEK

GEORGIA

MISSISSIPPI

ALABAMA

FLORIDA

LOUISIANA

SEMINOLE

**THE FIVE CIVILIZED TRIBES
BEFORE REMOVAL**

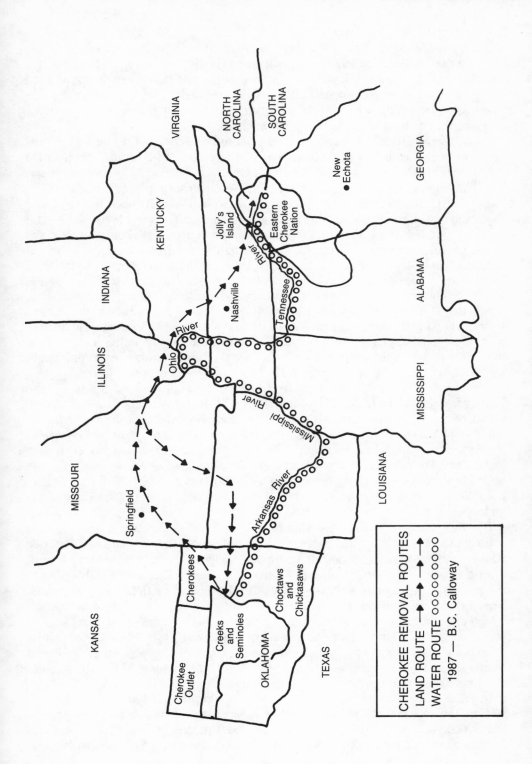

CHEROKEE REMOVAL ROUTES
LAND ROUTE 🡒🡒🡒🡒
WATER ROUTE ○○○○○○○○
1987 — B.C. Calloway

ways. They left the forests for the farm, wore the frontier costume, owned slaves, and sent their children to school. Many learned English and accepted Christianity. The National Council abolished the primeval custom of clan revenge, suppressed polygamy, and stressed temperance. They enacted strict laws regulating the sale of whiskey, which the whites craftily evaded. Yet, even by becoming "civilized" they would not be able to save their homeland.

As their mainstream of events became centered in Georgia, the Cherokees proceeded with great forward strides. In 1820, they adopted a republican form of government with a President or "Principal Chief" to be elected every four years. The Nation was divided into eight districts, each to be represented in the new bicameral legislature: the upper house or National Council made the laws and stipulated that all males above 18 years of age could vote; the lower house or General Council established a system of district and circuit courts. Both houses were composed of delegates from all the villages. A half-breed, John Ross, was elected President and Major Ridge was elected speaker of the lower house. John Ross, from Ross's Landing, Chattanooga, would become the greatest figure of the Cherokee Nation in the nineteenth century, but Major Ridge, though a great leader, would die a traitor to his people. The sovereignty of the Cherokees was recognized by the United States government. The Cherokee Nation was a separate and distinct community, occupying its own territory in which laws of the individual states of the Union had no right to enter without the assent of the Cherokee or in conformity with treaties and acts of Congress. This victory would be short-lived.

It was indeed a time of transition from red to white culture, and for awhile the Nation flourished. In 1822, a National Superior Court, later called the "Supreme Court of the Cherokee Nation" was established. Negotiating the sale of Indian lands to whites without consent of the National Council was the most serious crime; it was treason, punishable by death. The small republic had its own police system and collected its own taxes for roads and schools. Strict laws were enacted to regulate trade, and white people doing business in the Nation were required to have a license issued by the National Council. The Cherokees were successful on their farms and other small enterprises.

By 1827, the center of the new Cherokee culture had shifted to northern Georgia although there were still tribal remnants in the hills of North Carolina and Tennessee who were isolated from the outside world and clung to the old beliefs. In the future, after the destruction of the official Cherokee nation in the South, only there in the primitive Appalachian mountains would the Cherokee find the spark which would kindle their natural instincts for cultural survival. But in 1827 the new republic adopted a constitution, similar to the one of the United States; John Ross was its principal author. The document was poorly received by the Cherokees' white neighbors in the surrounding southland who felt the civilizing process promulgated by the federal government had finally gone too far. Undaunted by their attitude, the Cherokees continued their steadfast progression.

In 1828, just seven short years after Sequoya had presented his syllabary to the Nation, the tribe established a national newspaper, the Cherokee Phoenix, printed in both English and Cherokee, at New Echota. Unfortunately it was created just in time to record catastrophe, and it breathed its last in 1835. It is possible that no other nation ever made more sizable forward strides in so brief a span of time as did the Cherokee.

Since they were so far advanced, the United States government decided to allot to every Cherokee family 160 acres of land (one square mile) and made the proposal that they should be accorded the "full rights of citizenship," but the states of North Carolina, Tennessee, and Georgia responded with vehemence—no Indian was welcome to live within their boundaries under any circumstances. There were those who felt the Cherokees in their improved state were even more obnoxious than when "savages."

The election of Andrew Jackson to the Presidency in 1828 marked the beginning of the end for the Cherokee Nation in its hour of finest promise. He was the first president who did not come from a well-established American family, and the first to embody the American success story, from log cabin to the White House. At the time of his election, however, he was not a crude and simple frontiersman, but instead had entered the ranks of the gentry of the Southwest. Jackson, dubbed "Old Hickory" by the military troops he had commanded because of his toughness, was a folk-hero, greatly respected by the common man. His victory accelerated the transfer of national power from the shippers to the farmers, from East to West. For the Cherokee, however, he was the worst possible choice to be president. He strongly supported the removal of all Indians to the West, and immediately put through Congress the Indian Removal Act to transfer all Indian tribes west of the Mississippi River as soon as possible. The Cherokee were to receive more than seven million acres of land in the West in what would later be part of the state of Oklahoma, be given cash, and $200,000 for their schools. Once there they were told there would be no further encroachment by the whites. As a result, the western Cherokees left their villages in the Arkansas Territory for the western plains. This permanent frontier would only last about fifteen years as the whites continued their push further westward.

Sometime that same year, 1828, gold was discovered in the hills of Georgia, a discovery that sealed the Eastern Cherokees doom. Jackson, agreeing with his friends rather than Congress, advocated that all the Indians had to obey the laws of the states in which they resided. Georgia promptly passed an act confiscating all Cherokee lands, declaring all laws of the Cherokee to be null and void, decreeing no Indian could be a witness in any suit involving a white man, and forbade the Indians to hold councils or assemble for any public purpose. Their lands were distributed to white men by lottery. This unleased a bloody reign of terror by armed bands who brought plunder, torch, and murder. From the White House, "Old Hickory," who favored annihilation of the tribe, cheered the proceedings.

By 1830 the population of the United States numbered nearly 13,000,000—more than three times that of 1790. Most all Union lands east of the Mississippi had been admitted as states. The Indians who previously occupied the country had been pushed back little by little either by war, treaty, or purchase until they were huddled together only on small islands of their original lands, and even these meager portions were coveted by whites. President Jackson, being a veteran Indian fighter and having little sympathy for the plight of the race, signed into law a bill calling for the removal of all eastern Indian tribes, in one body, to the open plains west of the Mississippi River even though most did not want to move and many had already adopted the ways of the white culture. Among the tribes of the Southeast the Cherokee, Choctaw, Chickasaw, Creek, and Seminole were known as the Five Civilized Tribes because of their high degree of cultural development. Unlike other southeastern Indina tribes each of these had a written code of laws, an educational system, and a legislature. Nevertheless, more than 100,000 of these and other Indians were uprooted during the 1830's. In protest, Chief John Ross went to Washington to talk with the President, but Jackson refused to see him.

In subsequent years, after the removal bill, scores of treaties were negotiated with the Eastern Indians; many times they were coerced into signing the agreements. In some cases, Indians who refused to move were literally driven from their homelands by military force. Only a few put up any organized resistance. In 1832, over one thousand Sac and Fox Indians of the Illinois and the Wisconsin territories, lead by Chief Black Hawk, rose in rebellion. Their fray was crushed by militiamen and army regulars who drove them across the Mississippi River. Even though this so-called Black Hawk War was little more than a skirmish, a resistance by the Seminoles of Florida created a war which would last off and on for twenty-three years. In 1835 the Seminole led by Chief Osceola, supported by scores of runaway Negro slaves and numerous renegade Creeks, ambushed a company of army troops about seven miles north of the Withlacoochee River, near the Great Wahoo Swamp. The soliders were attempting to round up the Indians for enforced removal. Afterward, the Seminoles fled into the saw grass and sloughs of the Everglade and Big Cypress swamps where for several years they engaged in bloody, guerrilla fighting with the United States Army. In 1837 they were dealt a great blow when their half-breed leader, Osceola, was seized under a flag of truce at St. Augustine. The following year another great leader, Wild Cat, became chief and the Seminoles continued their warfare.

The highly civilized Cherokees of Georgia fought their resistance through legal action. In 1831 John Ross and a delegation of Cherokees took their case to the Supreme Court. In a renowned decision, the court ruled that because the Cherokee Nation had been formally recognized as a separate republic by the government of the United States, the state of Georgia had no jurisdiction over it and no claim to its lands. However, Georgia officials as well as her citizens simply ignored the judgement, and President Jackson refused to enforce it. The Cherokees also would be forced to leave their homelands.

A small minority of Cherokees influenced by Major Ridge felt they should move, and this led to the infamous Treaty of New Echota in December of 1835. New Echota had been moved from Georgia to Red Clay, Tennessee, that summer. The treaty confirmed the Cherokees title to seven million acres of land at a place which later became Oklahoma, and the tribe could buy more acres at an additional price. The land was to belong to the Cherokee Nation forever and could not become part of any state. They were to receive five million dollars for their land in the East. The treaty, signed by Major Ridge and three other minor chiefs but supported by less that ten percent of the tribe, caused a division among the Cherokees. The majority, led by Chief John Ross, were determined to fight for their homes and national existence. Early in 1836 he presented a petition, signed by over 15,000 Cherokees, to Congress indicating the illegality of the Treaty of New Echota. However, after one of the most bitter debates of its time, the Senate ratified the treaty by only one vote. On May 23th the Cherokee Nation was give two years in which to remove itself and resettle in the western land. Yet they clung to their trust in the federal government and hoped up to the very end that some favorable action might come from Washington.

At this time there were a few Cherokees, shut in from the outside world living in the hills of East Tennessee and western North Carolina, who clung to the old beliefs, and only here in the primitive mountains would the Cherokees eventually find the spark for their own survival. The Sequoyan print was secretly used here by the old order as a means of preserving ancient rituals, genealogy, folklore, secret formulas of the shamans, sagas of heroic warriors, and the ancient to present history of the tribe, heretofore passed only by word of mouth. Chief Yonaguska, or Drowning Bear, was a key figure in the Smoky Mountain story and a principal influence in holding his people to the mountains and to the old religion. He felt the Cherokee could only be happy in the country where nature had planted him.

Two years had passed and the Cherokee were still on their land while in Congress a few white men fought for their right to remain. By May of 1838, only about 2,000 of the 17,000 Indians had moved. Those remaining did not want to go in spite of the pressures brought against them and were hard to budge despite the new wave of brutality directed against them, e.g., public floggings with cowhides, hickories, and clubs. Women as well as men were publicly stripped and whipped without law or mercy, and the Indians were driven from their homesites by white men who scourged the men, raped the women, and murdered the children. Councils were held in protest throughout the Nation.

That summer, federal troops were sent to round up the Five Civilized Tribes of the Southeast; the round-up of the Cherokees was under General Winfield Scott. A chain of twelve stockaded concentration camps were erected throughout the Cherokee country: five in North Carolina, five in Georgia, one in Tennessee, and one in Alabama. General Scott was dispatched to force their eviction from the land with infantry, cavalry, artillery, and eager local volunteers, totalling 7,000 in number. Cherokee men, women, and children were seized at bayonet point wherever found and without notice, were removed to the camps where they were crowded together like cattle. Hundreds died. Their vacated houses and crops were burned; their farm implements, livestock, and household goods were distributed among the camp followers; and family graves were dug up for any valuables they might contain.

One day during this brutal round-up—perhaps by accident, or chance, or maybe by fate—soldiers came to the cabin of an old man named Tsali, or "Cherokee Charley," credited by many as the saver of the mountain Cherokees. At the time, he was just a simple man living with his aging wife, his brother, three sons, and their families on a hillside farm in the Smoky Mountains. All were seized and told they must come with the soldiers to the stockade at Bushnell near Fort Cass, Tennessee. Tsali had no way of knowing he had been chosen for martyrdom nor would he have understood it. Along the way Tsali's wife stumbled and was prodded by a bayonet to quicken her pace. Exasperated and furious, the fire in Tsali's old body flamed; the soldier had committed an unpardonable sin. Speaking in Cherokee, a language the soldiers did not understand, he urged the other men to join him in a dash for freedom. At the appointed place, each man sprang upon the soldier nearest him and in the scuffle, one soldier tripped and as he fell, his gun exploded, ripping a hole in the side of his head; the other soldiers escaped into the woods. Frightened, not intending bloodshed, Tsali and his family fled back to the mountains where unbeknown to them, hundreds of other Indians were hiding. These Cherokee had banded together under a noted leader named U'tsala, or Euchella, called "Lichen." Later in official documents these Indians were referred to as "Oochella's band" (Frome, 117). They stayed hidden in the mountains, but elsewhere in the Cherokee Nation the first of the exiles had started on their tragic march to the West.

During that fateful summer of 1838, 5,000 Cherokees journeyed down the Tennessee and Ohio rivers to the Mississippi where they disembarked and began their long trek across the Arkansas Territory. It was extremely hot; many sickened and died and their leaders asked and were given permission to wait until cooler weather to continue the march. By fall, most of the Overhill Cherokees had been taken to Rattlesnake Springs in the northern section of Bradley County in southeast Tennessee. From there they would be forced to march on a long, lonely trail which passed near the present cities of McMinnville, Murfreesboro, and Nashville, leaving the state through Montgomery county in Middle Tennessee. From there the Indians would continue their journey by walking through western Kentucky, southern Illinois, Missouri, and Arkansas to finally reach present-day eastern Oklahoma. In October the main procession of exile began; 14,000 Indians with 600 wagons bid adieu to their ancestral land and began their walk across the icy rivers in the dead of winter. Averaging ten miles a day over the frozen earth, amidst driving sleet and snow, they stopped only to bury their dead. This trail of exiles became a trail of death—all told more than 4,000 died of disease, exposure, starvation, and exhaustion. And even as this army of strangers advanced over the infamous "Trail of Tears," the new President, Martin Van Buren, advised Congress that all had gone well, the Indians had moved reluctantly, and the whole movement was having the happiest effects.

Not all Cherokees had allowed themselves to be driven West. Hundreds had eluded the soldiers during the round-up, or escaped the camps, or fled the trail of tears—defying every effort at capture, suffering starvation and exposure, enduring as fugitives and aliens—hiding themselves in different pockets of safety in their homeland. The main group of these fugitives was the mountain Cherokees, drawn to the bosom of the mountains from whence they came. Natural men returning to their warm, generous mountain Mother, a shrine and sanctuary to all natural species—a haven where they could nurture the spark of their race.

In late fall, after the last Cherokee who could be found had been sent out West, the soldiers turned their attention to the task of rounding up the fugitives in the mountains. Realizing the impossibility of tracking all of them down, General Scott, rather than pulling troops out of Florida who were rounding up stray Seminoles, seized upon the Tsali incident as an opportunity for compromise. He sent word to Oochella's band by Will Thomas, a white trader who was the adopted son of the great Yonaguska, that if Tsali's party would come in the pursuit would be called off and all other Cherokee would be permitted to stay in the Smokies, un-molested. Thomas made his way across secret paths to Euchella's hiding place at the head of Oconaluftee River, and offered the proposition. Euchella accepted the proposal, deciding it was better to sacrifice a few in order to same many. He and his band began their search for Tsali. Will Thomas reported back to General Scott. Then, knowing of Tsali's hiding place in a cave at Deep Creek, he went there alone to try to persuade the fugitive to come in and surrender rather than be hunted down by his own people. Tsali agreed to come in. He and his family were taken to Bushnell where they were tried and found guilty of murder. Tsali, his brother, and two of his sons were sentenced to be executed. Waving aside blindfolds, they were lined up and then shot by their own people, as requested, knowing that this sacrifice was for the good of all Cherokees. The old man's wife and his youngest son, Wasituna (called Washington by the whites), were spared and, after the burial of their kin, returned to their mountain home. Today the community of Bushnell and the graves of Tsali and his kinsmen are covered by the waters of Lake Fontana.

The fateful journey along the infamous "trail of tears" finally came to an end on March 26, 1839. Out West, the first order of business among the Cherokees was the dispensation of justice. Major Ridge was shot down by bullets; his son, John, as well as others who had shared in the sponsorship of the damnable Treaty of New Echota, were tomahawked.

The admission of Tennessee as the sixteenth state of the Union on June 1, 1796, and the final expulsion of the Cherokee Nation to the Oklahoma Territory on March 26, 1839, brings to a close the American-Cherokee drama on America's First Western Frontier: East Tennessee.

Great Smoky Mountains—Ancestral Home of the Cherokee Nation
Thousands of years ago these mountains were the home of the pre-historic Cherokee. Later, surviving the white man's wars, "spirits," and diseases, the Overhill Cherokees were at home in the Smokies. Today, still clinging tenaciously to their mountain homeland, the Eastern band of Cherokees live here on the Qualla Reservation.

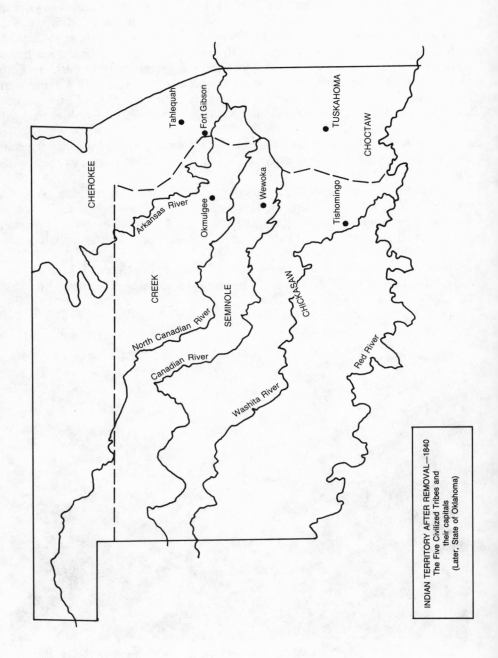

CHEROKEE

Tahlequah

Fort Gibson

TUSKAHOMA

CHOCTAW

Arkansas River

Okmulgee

Wewoka

Tishomingo

CREEK

SEMINOLE

CHICKASAW

North Canadian River

Canadian River

Washita River

Red River

INDIAN TERRITORY AFTER REMOVAL—1840
The Five Civilized Tribes and
their capitals
(Later, State of Oklahoma)

138

CADES COVE

Although the Cherokees hunted here for uncounted centuries, hardly any sign of them remain. One of their towns was located here—ruled over by Chief Old Abram of Chilhowie. By the early 1800's the heart of the Smokies, including Cades Cove, had been ceded to the whites. Today Cades Cove is an open air museum that preserves some of the material culture of several of the early settlers who lived here.

Marker showing seven clans of Cherokee Nation on Long Island of the Holston. The "Beloved Island" of the Cherokee Nation was one of the last pieces of land ceded by them to the whites. After more than one hundred years the "sacred" island was finally returned to the Nation. This marker, located across the Holston River at River Front Park in Kingsport, commemorates that event.

Four young Cherokee men who live on the Qualla Reservation today.
Left to right: George Rosario, Ed Plummer, Roho Maples and Will Laney.

Front left, Ed Plummer; Front right, Roho Maples;
Back center, Will Laney; Far left, George Rosario.

140

APPENDIX A
Grand Old Indian Families

In North America there are many Indian language families which give us tribal genealogies instead of those for individuals. In order to better understand the tribes in America during the period covered by this work, there follows a listing of a few of those language families pertinent to the areas and the period of time covered. It is not a complete list nor does it cover all tribes in all areas of North America.

THE ALGONQUIAN FAMILY

The Algonquian was a powerful family which held most of the territory east of the Mississippi, from Tennessee and Virginia on the south to Hudson Bay on the north. These Indians were the first to welcome the Dutch, English, and French traders, and were the first to fall victim to the deadly firearms of the Europeans while resisting the white advance on their villages. Not all the Algonquians lived in the forests—many lived on the plains of southern Canada, as far west as the Rocky Mountains, in the far plains of the midwest, and two tribes lived as far away as northern California. In all, there were about a hundred tribes of this family.

ATLANTIC SLOPE	CENTRAL AREA	PLAINS COUNTRY
Delaware	Illinois	Blackfoot
Powhatan	Miami	Cheuenne
	Chippewa	
	Fox	
	Ottawa	
	Shawnee	

THE IROQUOIAN FAMILY

The name Iroquois usually applies to the six tribes in New York State, yet there were other tribes in the surrounding area, not to mention five or six lesser-known groups, as well as the powerful Cherokee, who spoke languages of the Iroquoian family. Their territory was far less in scope that the Algonquian. The country these Indians claimed mainly consisted of the Mohawk Valley in New York State and the area about the Finger Lakes; with the Cherokee holding the lower Appalachians. The Iroquoian were a superior people, strong and powerful, to whom honor is due.

NORTHERN TRIBES	INDEPENDENTS	SOUTHERN
Six Nations		
Cayuga	Erie	Cherokee
Mohawk	Huron	Yuchi
Oneida	Mingo	
Onondaga	Wyandot	
Seneca		
Tuscarora		

THE MUSKHOGEAN FAMILY

One might say the Muskhogean were the elite of aboriginal days. Roughly. their territory comprised the present states of Georgia, Alabama, Mississippi, and parts of Louisiana and Tennessee—the heart of the South. Although farming was their major occupation they were a warlike people, but not as much so as the Iroquoian family. About 1830 a federation of five independent tribes was formed: the Cherokee, Choctaw, Chickasaw, Creek, and Seminole; all except the Cherokee are Muskhogean. From that time on, these people were known as the Five Civilized Tribes.

THE MUSKHOGEANS
Apalachee
Cuttawas
Chickasaw
Natchez
Choctaw
Seminole
Creek
Taensa

THE SIOUAN FAMILY

The great waters of the Mississippi was the dividing boundary between the powerful Siouan and Algonquian Families. Mostly, their territory was comprised of the prairies and the plains; however, there were a few Siouan people on the Atlantic Seaboard, and it is believed that in some remote time, long before 1492, either the Algonquian, Iroquoian, or Muskhogean drove a wedge through the Siouan territory. These coastal people were a large, powerful block of tribes holding the region of Virginia and the Carolinas. In the populous mind of today, the word ''Sioux'' seems dynamite, a symbolism of war, because among our ancestors it meant something commanding attention and thus, the Siouan family did.

DAKOTA TRIBES
Eastern Dakota
Teton-Dakota

THE ASSINIBOIN or STONEY

UPPER MISSOURI
Crow
Mandan

LOWER MISSOURI
Kansas or Kee
Osage

ATLANTIC COAST
Biloxi
Catawba
Quapaw

Appendix B
A Gallery of Early Notable Indians

ATTA-KULLA-KULLA

This wily Indian was the "Great Solon" of the Cherokee Nation for nearly half a century. He was born at the Big Island on the French Broad River around the turn of the eighteenth century. In the language of the Cherokee his name was Ata-gul-kalu, which means "Leaning Wood". He was known in his youth as Ookoo-Naka, or the White Owl, and was still called by this name when he and a small delegation of Cherokee warriors accompanied Alexander Cuming to Great Britain in 1730, where he was a big hit with King George II and the Royal Court. A man of superior abilities, Attakullakulla was recognized by the British government as emperor of the Cherokee Nation about the year 1750, and later was commonly known to the colonists as "the Little Carpenter." The whites gave him this nickname because of his artful ability to maneuver conflicting minds together, such as a wood-worker might fit pieces of wood into place smoothly, allowing him to fit parts of a peace treaty into a good, diplomatic document. He has been described as being a mere wisp of a man, small of stature, slender and delicately built, who weighed little more than a pound for each year of his life. Attakullakulla's love affair with the whites more than likely began with his visit to England and probably culminated with his rescue of John Stuart, who had been taken captive by the Cherokees in 1760 during the siege of Fort Loudoun. To save Stuart's life, the Little Carpenter purchased him from his Cherokee captor. Afterward, the elder chief took Stuart to the Overhill capitol of Echota. There, he adopted Captain Stuart, named him "Eldest Brother," and promised him enduring friendship. The brotherhood which John Stuart and Attakullakulla shared held strong until each died (for his own cause) at about the same moment during the American Revolution. The Little Carpenter was one of the most celebrated and influential chiefs among the southern tribes during his time of leadership—both as Uka (high priest) and as Civic Chief of the Cherokee Nation. He was the nephew of Old Hop, who served as Peace Chief before him, and the uncle of Old Tassel, who succeed him as Principal Chief. One of his sons was the noted Dragging Canoe, who was a half-brother to Nancy Ward. Attakullakulla died in his native country (East Tennessee) either in the Spring of 1777 or in the Summer of 1780, of natural causes, at an age above 90 years.

CORNSTALK

This principal chief was the beloved leader of the Shawnees in the middle 1700's. He resided at the village of Chillicote on the Little Miami River, in the heart of the Can-tuc-kee country. This land below the great Spay-lay-wi-thespi (Ohio) River was the sacred hunting grounds of the Shawnee tribe, and its bounty was shared by them with the Cherokees in the South. The Shawnee hunting preserve was staunchly defended through the efforts of their Peace Chief, Cornstalk, and their

War Chief, Black Fish, who were determined that no white man would be permitted to take up permanent residence there. After the Shawnees' defeat during Lord Dunmore's War, Cornstalk was committed to holding his people out of any future white warfare, and to abiding by the terms of peace agreed to in the Treaty of Camp Charlotte. As evidence of his good faith to hold his people neutral, in the Autumn of 1777 he and two companions visited Fort Randolph, which had been built upon the very site of his battle with the Virginians three years before (near the present city of Addison, Ohio). The Indians came on a mission of peace to renew their affirmations of peaceful intent, but the commander of the fort, Captain Matthew Arbuckle, decided to hold them as hostages. A few days later Cornstalk's son, Elinipsico, came to the stockade seeking information about his father. He, too, was taken hostage. Then several weeks later, a small group of irate militiamen broke into the room where the Indians were being held and—with shooting, stabbing, and clubbing—quickly dispatched the old Shawnee, his son, and their two attendants. The governors of Pennsylvania and Virginia, as well as the Continental Congress, sent urgent massages to the Shawnee trying to convince them of their deep regret for this crime. However, any apologies from the whites were useless; the murder of Cornstalk and his entourage had convinced his people of the folly of further restraint. Black Fish, who was now Principal Chief, swore revenge on all whites and for the next seventeen years the Shawnee would be the most hostile and inveterate of all Indian enemies on the western Appalachian frontier.

DRAGGING CANOE (Chenkunnasnah)

This unruly chief was called Tsi-yu-Gense-ni by the Cherokee, meaning, "he who drags the canoe." He was a courageous, violently aggressive warrior who always hated the whites and vehemently opposed the selling or leasing of any land to them. Speaking at the treaty talks on the Sycamore Shoals in 1775, he avowed that the Wataugans had dealt with only a few old men whose poverty had driven them to lease their land. He told the elder Chiefs they were taking a giant step toward the ultimate extinction of their race by signing away the hunting grounds of the Cherokee. Further, he prophesied that a black cloud hung over the Kentucky lands which the settlers had purchased and its settlement would be dark and bloody. His oratory was delivered in a deep resonate voice. This young, eminent chief was an athletic man who stood slightly over six-foot tall. There was a Roman cast to his fierce-looking face, with the scars left from smallpox only adding to its ferocity. The year following the land transactions on the Watauga, the forty-three year old War Chief with other impetuous Cherokee warriors attacked the whole arc of the white Appalachian frontier. A short time later, he and his braves withdrew from the Overhill Towns and relocated on the Chickamaugan Creek, just east of Lookout Mountain; later, they and others who had joined them became known as the Chickamaugan tribe. At the age of sixty, after an all night revelry, this "fiery follower of Mars," who had never wavered from his purpose of driving the whites from his homeland, and who had consistently refused to sign treaty deeds, was struck down by the "Grim Reaper." The great Cherokee-Chickamaugan War Chief, Dragging Canoe, second to none in the Cherokee Nation, was dead—either from all-night dancing or perhaps, as a result of wounds received during past battles. The year was 1792.

ALEXANDER McGILLIVARY

This famous Indian chieftain, like so many distinguished leaders of the Southern Tribes, was of mixed blood, being the son of the Scots trader, Lachlan McGillivary, and a halfbreed woman of an influential Creek family, whose father was a French officer at Fort Toulouse. He was born in the Creek country (present state of Alabama) at a village on the Coosa River about 1740. His mother named him Hoboi-hili-miko—Good Child King—but he was better known by the white name, Alexander McGillivary. After his mother's death sometime in the mid-1770's, Alexander became Principal Chief of the Creek Confederacy; he was probably in his early 30's at that time. It has been suggested that he was an unscrupulous man with a mixture of Scotch shrewdness, a French love of display, and an Indian secretiveness. At the onset of the American Revolution his paternal estates were seized by Georgia; therefore, he and all his warriors joined the British cause, becoming the leading instigators in the border hostilities on the western Appalachian frontier until 1790. After Great Britain lost the Revolutionary War, McGillivary put his people under the protection of Spain. He, being an educated man, became a great letter writer, keeping up a lively correspondence for several years with the English, Spanish, and Americans; playing one against the other and holding negotiations by turn in the service of all three. Because of these clever letters and his state visits, the three countries competed to supply the Creeks and showered McGillivary with favors. In 1793 while on a diplomatic mission to Pensacola in Spanish Florida, the Good Child King died from gout and other complications. After his death the Creek Confederacy broke into several factions.

JOHN LOGAN (Talgayeeta)

This tall, angular, Mingo chief was widely respected by both the whites and the Indians. Known as a great sage, his word carried much weight and he smoothed strained relationships between the two races many times. His father was a renowned friend of the white people along the shores of Cayuga Lake in New York. His wife was a Shawnee maiden whom he had married shortly after moving near the Shawnee country below the Ohio. Chief Logan's home was one of warm hospitality and friendship to all, without distinction. His village known as Mingo Town, was located at the mouth of Yellow Creek on the south side of the upper Ohio River. He was a highly skilled marksman with bow or gun, and a resourceful hunter. Logan was welcomed equally in both the councils of the different Indian tribes and the homes of the white settlers; all knew they could trust him completely. Because of this, he had refused to allow the Mingoes to participate in two early wars between the whites and Indians on the western Appalachian frontier. John Logan may have remained thus were it not for the heinous and senseless crime committed in the early Spring of 1774 which changed the heart of this mighty Mingo. At this particular time, a group of border ruffians killed several relations of his immediate family. The unprovoked, surprise attack occurring late one night at Baker's Bottom (near the present city of Wellsville, Ohio) turned Logan's heart cold. For the first time in his life, he raised his hatchet against the whites. His wrath fell with terrible vengeance upon the settlers along a line of forts and settlements in southwest Virginia and the upper Holston Valley. After several months, finally satisfying his thirst for blood, Logan and his warriors disappeared into the northern mountains of Kentucky as swiftly and silently as they had come.

MOYTOY

Chief Moytoy lived in the village of Tellico in what is now East Tennessee. He was recognized by the British as "emperor" of the Cherokee Nation in 1730. Other than this fact, he evidently was of little significance in the Old West story. Moytoy was Principal Chief of Tellico and ruled the Upper Cherokee country (Overhills) while Chief Old Hop, whom Alexander Cuming had designated as "King" of the Cherokees, ruled the Lower country from Echota into parts of northern Georgia and what later became northern Alabama. In reality, it was actually Old Hop who ruled the Cherokees and made all important decisions for them. Moytoy was one of the chiefs selected by Cuming to visit King George II in 1730 but, due to an illness of his wife, was unable to go. Soon after this, he fades from recorded white history.

OCONOSTOTA
Aganstata or Groundhop Sausage

This "Great Warrior," who ruled for over half a century, was one of the most influential chiefs of the Cherokee Nation. He was War Chief during the same period that Attakullakulla ruled as Peace Chief. He has been described as being a large athletic man, of plain manners, whose face was pitted with smallpox. Just after the Cherokee War began in 1758, he lay siege to Fort Prince George, where several Cherokee braves were being held hostage. The Fort was located near the Cherokee village of Keowee in western South Carolina. Oconostota failed to rescue the Indian sub-chiefs, and in the battle that ensued, the village of Keowee was destroyed. Oconostota became the prominent chief of the Cherokee during this war and remained so until just after the American Revolution. In 1782, very old and nearly blind, he resigned as War Chief in favor of his son, Tuskasee (Terrapin). Late that same year he made the long journey upstream from his village in the Overhill Towns to the home of his old friend, Joseph Martin, at the Long Island of the Holston, where he stayed that fall and winter. With the coming of spring, the ancient chief knew his time was at hand and, wishing to die in the beloved town of Echota, asked Marin to accompany him home, which he gladly did and stayed until death came as a release to his old friend, Oconostota. After the Cherokee burial rites accorded to ranking chiefs, the highly revered "Great Warrior" was interred in a dugout canoe along the river.

OLD TASSEL OF TORQUO
Onitositah, Thistle-head, or Kaiyahtahee

Old Tassel of Torquo, although somewhat younger, was the leading counsellor of Oconostota. He was much respected for his integrity and truth, and was a profound Indian statesman and orator. In later years he was called "Old Tassel" or "Old Corn Tassel," by the whites. He succeeded Oconostota as War Chief because the Cherokees refused to recognize the former's son, Terrapin, as the new chief, which his father had tried to ensure. Many years later after he had become an old man, Old Tassel became Principal Chief with Hanging Maw as War Chief. This nephew of Attakullakulla was a stout but mild man, rather comely with a smooth and somewhat fat face. Old Tassel was the uncle of the inventor Sequoyah, and the grandfather of the Chickamaugan chief, John Watts. At the treaty of Long Island in July of 1777, he was the principal spokesman for the Cherokee Nation. Approximately ten years later, the massacre of two white families near the Overhill Towns started rumors that a big Indian uprising was underway. Major James Hubbard of the Frankin militia decided to take advantage of this new turn of events. While on a mission to destroy the old Cherokee village of Chilhowie (presently Cades Cove in the Smokies) he persuaded Old Tassel, Hanging Maw, Old Abram, and two other Cherokee chiefs to meet him for peace talks at the house of one John Kirk, Jr. who lived a few miles south of Knoxville. Kirk's family was one of those which had been massacred by Indians, presumably Cherokee, only a few months earlier. The chiefs arrived a short time later under a flag of truce, but were betrayed. After they were seated in the house, Major Hubbard posted guards around the cabin and the door was closed. He then turned to young Kirk, handed him a hatchet and told him to take revenge for his family. Still grieving and angry, John Kirk immediately tomahawked all five Cherokee chiefs to death.

OSCEOLA

During the Creek War of 1813-14 at the Battle of Horseshoe Bend amidst a hail of rifle bullets and arrows, according to legend, a Creek mother pretending to be dead had placed her body over that of her infant son. Later, she took the boy to the Floridas where he grew up to be the renowned Seminole patriot, Osceola. This battle led by the gaunt, hawk-faced Andrew Jackson of Tennessee, crushed the military power of the Southwest Indians. At the treaty signing on March 27, 1814, Jackson forced the Creeks to cede some of their richest lands in the Mississippi Territory (about one-half of the present state of Alabama) to the United States. This treaty stripped the Creeks of a major portion of their country; the Creek Confederacy was weakened beyond repair, and members of the tribe scattered— most fleeing to the Florida peninsula where they joined with the Seminoles whose lifeways followed traditional Creek patterns. This tribe's own defense of freedom began with a war in 1817, which would last for the next forty-one years, between themselves and the United States Army. Osceola, bitterly opposing the removal of his people to a territory in the far West (later to be the state of Oklahoma) and the brutal treatment they received from the Army, became a great leader during the latter period of these wars. Due to heavy losses in the wars, the Seminoles were gradually reduced to being small scattered groups of refugees amid the saw grass and sloughs of the Everglades and Big Cypress Swamp. However, there Osceola and his people hid for decades, showing an astonishing genius in guerrilla warfare as they retreated farther and farther into the tropical swamps. In November of 1835, the U.S. Army made a surprise attack on Osceola's village, near the Great Walhoo Swamp about seven miles north of the Withlacoochee River, and during the ensuing fray a small group of soldiers seized Osceola's young wife Chechoter (Che-cho-ter) carrying her off into slavery. Two years later Chief Oscleola, Wild

Cat (who was another important war leader), and a small group of Seminoles which included several Negroes traveled to the American Fort at St. Augustine. There under a flag of truce, they met with General Jesup in order to confer with the United States Army about terms of peace. Instead of the expected council, all were captured and imprisoned despite the flag for truce. A few days later, Wild Cat and eighteen Seminoles escaped from Fort Marion, but Osceola was not as fortunate. Jesup had him placed in irons and taken to Fort Moultrie in Charleston harbor, where he died in a damp cell on January 30, 1838. Afterward, Wild Cat became the principal leader of the Seminole Resistance and the U.S. Army's "most wanted" Seminole Indian.

JOHN ROSS

This great Cherokee chief had but one-eighth Indian blood and showed little of the Indian features. His father, Daniel Ross, emigrated from Scotland shortly before the American Revolution and married a quarter-blood Cherokee woman whose father, John McDonald, and grandfather, William Shorey, were also from Scotland. Ross was born in 1790 at Ross' Landing (later called Chattanooga) where his parents kept a store, and his grandparents operated a ferry. In his youth he was known as Tsan-usdi or "Little John," but arriving at manhood was called Guwi-sguwi, the name of a large, rare migratory bird (probably the egret or swan). John Ross was a handsome, privately educated man who began his public career when barely nineteen years of age, and later he became the greatest figure of the Cherokee Nation in the nineteenth century. No danger appalled him, he never faltered in supporting what he believed to be right, and he never lost sight of the welfare of his people. His first wife, Quatia, a full-blood Cherokee, died along the infamous "Trail of Tears." Some years later he married again, this time to a white woman, Miss Stapler of Willington, Delaware. Ross' official career began in 1809, when he was intrusted with a special mission to the Arkansas Cherokees. In 1817, he was elected as a member of the Cherokee National Council and in 1819 as President of the National Committee, a position he occupied until 1827. That same year he was president of the convention which adopted the Cherokee constitution, and the following year he was elected President of the Cherokee Nation—a position he retained until the Cherokees' removal to the West. Then from 1839 to the time of his death, he was Principal Chief of the United Cherokee Nation.

SEQUOYAH

Sequoyah, inventor of the Cherokee alphabet, was a mixed blood and known among his own people as Sikwa-yi. To the whites he was known as George Gist or less correctly, Guess. His father was the white trader Nathaniel Gist—son of Christain Gist, a noted surveyor and explorer. His mother was Wurteh, a member of the Paint clan, and half-sister of Old Tassel. One of his uncles was the Little Carpenter. Some historical sources give the date of his birth as 1760, while others give 1775; probably, from Cherokee reports, it was in the latter 1760's. Either way, he was born in the village of Tuskagee just outside of old Fort Loudoun, and his early years were spent amid the turbulent storms of the American Revolution.

As he grew to manhood, he became an accomplished silversmith and an artist. Also, like most of the Cherokee warriors, he was a good hunter and a fur trader. He never attended school, and in all his life he never learned to speak, read, or write the English language. Sequoyah, aptly called the "Cadmus" of his race, was so intrigued by the whites ability to send messages by "talking leaves" that he set about devising a similar system for his own people. Because he was lame, he could not participate in as many activities as the other Cherokee males; therefore, he had more leisure time for study. After a dozen years of unwavering determination, he finally created the Cherokee syllabary, which was adopted by the Cherokee Council in 1821. This syllabary allowed his people to become literate and to preserve their heritage. In 1815 Sequoyah married Sallie Benga (Utiyu) and from the union there were four or perhaps seven children. Shortly before the signing of the infamous Treaty of New Echota (1828), he moved himself and his family to Arkansas where he lived the remainder of his life. He died in 1843 while on a personal quest for the "lost tribe of the Cherokee" in northern Mexico. His widow was given a pension of $300, the only literary pension in the United States.

NANCY WARD
(Nanyehi)

This famous Cherokee Chieftainess was nicknamed Tsistuna-gis-ke, or "Wild Rose," by her own people. She was a niece of Old Hop, ruler of the Lower Cherokee Towns, and of Attakullakulla, Peace Chief of the Cherokee Nation. She was born in 1737 or 1738 in the old Cherokee capitol of Echota on the Little Tennessee River in what is now East Tennessee. According to Cherokee histories, her mother was a full-blood Cherokee of the Wolf clan and her father a full-blood Delaware Chief. It is said that she was a strikingly beautiful woman who had a tall, erect figure. Her complexion when young was tinted like a pink-reddish, wild rose petal; hence her nickname. At womanhood her smooth skin was a tawny texture. She had regular Indian features with a prominent nose, long, silken black hair, and large piercing black eyes. She is further described as having a kindly disposition, and as being queenly and commanding in both appearance and manner. For her heroism at the Battle of Taliwa, between the Creeks and Cherokees, she was given the title of Ghigau, or "Beloved Woman," of the Cherokee Nation, finding herself revered even before the age of twenty. Nancy Ward believed in peace and strove for it all of her life, trying to save Cherokee lives as well as whites'. In later life she moved from Echota to Womankiller Ford on the Oscoee River (near the present town of Benton, Tennessee) where she operated an inn until her death. The actual date she moved is not known, but more than likely it was in the latter 1790's, for other Cherokees had moved farther south to the Amovery District of the Cherokee Nation in the Ocoee-Hiwassee area (in present Polk County) at about the same time—to escape the almost constant attacks of the frontier militias and to get away from the pressures of continuous white encroachment. Nancy Ward died at an advanced age and in ill health in either 1822 or 1824. Toward the end of her life she was affectionately called "Granny Ward" by her many descendants and neighbors. Too, she continued to be, in the minds and hearts of those who knew her, the Cherokees' "Most Beloved Woman".

According to Alderman, an interesting story about her death is told by her great grandson, Jack Hildebrand, who was four years old at the time. In his **Recollections** and a sworn statement, he tells of being in the room when "a light rose from her body, fluttered like a bird around the room, and finally flew through an open door. Those in attendance, startled by the apparition, watched until it disappeared, moving in the direction of Chota" (**Nancy Ward,** p. 83). Thus, the "Cherokee Wild Rose" passsed from life into legend. Nancy Ward's grave is located in Polk County near Benton, Tennessee; she is buried on Hancock Hill, between her son Five Killer and her brother Long Fellow, whose home sites were near hers.

JOHN WATTS

This Chickamaugan War Chief, although of mixed blood, was all Indian. The Cherokee code of ethics, laws and customs were the governing forces of his life. His father was a fur trader by the same name, and John Watts, Sr. had been among the Overhill Cherokees from a date considerably before 1763. It has been suggested that perhaps he was a soldier of the Fort Loudon garrison (1758-61). Regardless, he was familiar enough with the Cherokee language to act as interpreter between the British and Cherokee at the Treaty of Augusta in 1763. Watts' mother was a daughter of Old Tassel and his uncle was the notorious Chief Dragging Canoe. As boys, he and Sequoyah, who was his first cousin, lived in the Overhill Town of Tuskagee. There, under the strong influence of his uncle, young Watts learned organizational abilities and demonstrated leadership qualities. Sometimes, because of his grandfather's name, Old Tassel, the boy was called "Young Tassel" by the Cherokees. He was a self-educated man who could speak both languages and was considered one of the great orators of the Cherokee Nation. He has been described as astute, strong-willed, and witty. John Watts knew well the ways of the white man's diplomacy and understood their "double-dealing" peace talks. A short time after moving to Lookout Mountain with Dragging Canoe and his followers, Chief Watts established his own village, which he called Willstown, at Wills Creek below Fort Payne in Dekalb County, Alabama (about 30 miles below the Canoe's village at Lookout Mountain). Later, the site would become the capital of all the Chickamaugan towns. After the death of Dragging Canoe in 1792, Watts, called "Red-headed Will" by the whites, was determined to continue his uncle's war plans in the fight for Cherokee survival; therefore, he began a new series of bloody raids on the settlers, particularly those of the Cumberland Region. About two or three years later, finding that the Spanish authorities would no longer furnish his warriors with more supplies, War Chief John Watts suddenly did an about face. He agreed to meet with Territorial Governor Blount for peace talks on November 7, 1794, at the Tellico Block House a few miles below Knoxville. This treaty finally brought to a close the long, bitter frontier wars between the Cherokee and whites.

YONAGUSKA
Ya'nu-gun'ski or Drowning Bear

Yonaguska was a key figure in the Smoky Mountain story of the Cherokee. Although other Indians played larger roles in the history of the Cherokee Nation, none meant more than he to the Eastern Cherokees. Drowning Bear was a powerful orator and prophet who became the most prominent chief in the history of the Eastern Cherokee. He has been described as a strikingly handsome, strongly built, tall man of six foot three. As a young man he supervised the building of the council house on Soco Creek, which was the focal point of the mountain Cherokees until his death in 1839. During his life time no whiskey was allowed to be brought into, made, or sold in the Smoky Mountain Cherokee territory. As Peace Chief and counselor, Drowning Bear's principal influence among the isolated mountain Cherokee was in holding his people to the mountains, and to the old Cherokee religion and mountain traditions. In 1817, he adopted the fatherless lad William H. Thomas as his own son, giving him the Indian name of "Wil-Usdi", or "Little Will." Although only twelve, Thomas had already learned the Cherokee language as well as any white man could. He worked at the Walker trading store in Soco Valley and was a favorite among the Cherokees who were the store's principal customers. In 1821, Little Will, having learned a great deal about trading, land, law, politics, and Indians during his three years in the Walker employ, opened his own first store. The Cherokee were his primary customers and neighbors, and all the lessons he had learned served him well in building his empire and in his rise to become "tycoon of the hills." The Cherokees under Yonaguska, in 1831, appointed young Thomas as their business agent, lawyer, and clerk. As the Indians' friend, leader, and lawyer, he fought for their just rights with the Federal Government against the forced Removal. At Drowning Bear's death, Thomas was designated white chief of the Smoky Mountain Cherokee. For the next twenty-one years, from 1839 until 1860, he was deeply involved with the lives of the mountain Cherokee as well as being their lobbyist in Washington.

Appendix C
Territory of the United States of America
South of the River Ohio

(Census of 1795)

COUNTIES	Free white males, 16 years and upwards, including heads of families	Free white males under 16 years	Free white females including heads of families	All other free persons	Slaves	Total amount
Washington	2013	2578	4311	225	978	10105
Sullivan	1803	2340	3499	38	777	8457
Hawkins	2666	3279	4767	147	2472	13331
Greene	1567	2203	3350	52	466	7638
Blount	585	817	1231	00	183	2816
Jefferson	1706	1225	3021	112	776	7840
Sevier	6008	1045	1503	273	129	3578
Knox	2721	2723	3664	100	2365	11573
Tennessee	380	444	700	19	398	1941
Davidson	728	695	1192	6	992	3613
Sumner	1328	1595	2316	1	1076	6370
TOTALS:	16179	19944	29554	973	10613	77262

Source: Alderman, Pat, **The Overmountain Men,** p. 280.

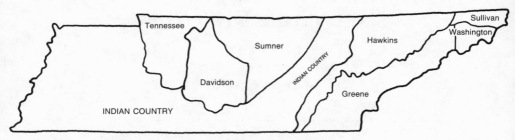

Source: Alderman, Pat, **The Overmountain Men**, p. 216.

TENNESSEE COUNTIES
of 1785
1987 — B.C. Calloway

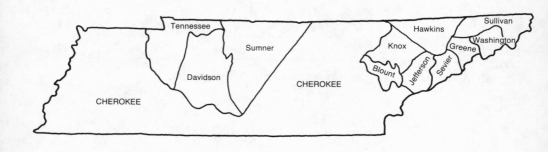

COUNTIES OF TENNESSEE
1796
B.C. Calloway — 1987

Appendix D
Early County History

This appendix contains a brief, historical summary of established counties at the time Tennessee became a state, including those counties created by the "Lost State of Franklin." The "lost state" was comprised only of present East Tennessee with seven counties. The Cumberland District with its three counties (present Middle Tennessee) was not a part of the Franklin state. There were eighty miles of Cherokee land separating the Cumberland District from the East, and these early settlers wanted their own state. The land west from the Cumberland to the Mississippi was known as the Chickasaw Country (present West Tennessee). It also was not a part of the "lost state." Nevertheless, in 1796 the Eastern, Middle and Western sections of the territory ceded south of the Ohio were all incorporated into the grand state of Tennessee with ten counties. As yet there were no counties in the western part of the new state. It was still claimed by the Chickasaws, had few settlers, and was all wilderness.

FIRST COUNTIES of EAST TENNESSEE

Blount County was created in 1795 by the second session of the Territorial Assembly. It was cut from Knox County and named for the territorial governor, William Blount, of Knoxville. Maryville, named for Governor Blount's wife Mary, originally grew from the site of John Craig's Fort, built in 1785 for protection from the Cherokees. The restored pioneer village of Cades Cove lies in the heart of a portion of this country once ruled by the Cherokees Chief, Old Abram of Chilhowie. Friendsville was established in 1796 by a small group of the Society of Friends (Quakers) from New Garden, North Carolina.

Carter County was formed in 1796 from the northeastern section of Wayne County which had been created by an act of the Franklin legislature in 1785. The county was named for Landon Carter, a Speaker of the Senate in the State of Franklin—he also served as Secretary of State. The town of Elizabethton, located at the foot of Lynn Mountain just east of Doe River in Happy Valley, was established in 1799 and named for Carter's wife, Elizabeth McLin Carter. There, Indians had an ancient village at the Watauga Old Field Flats, the Watauga Association (1772) was organized, Fort Caswell (Watauga) was built, and the Treaty of Sycamore Shoals was signed.

Grainger County was established in 1796 and named for Mary Grainger, wife of William Blount. Bean Station (1797) was located at the crossroads of the Great Indian Warpath and the Wilderness Road. It was named for William Bean, Tennessee's first permanent settler who relocated there shortly before the end of the American Revolution. The original site was covered by the waters of the TVA. Rutledge was established in 1801 and named for General George Rutledge of Sullivan County, who succeeded John Sevier as commander of the Tennessee militia.

Greene County was formed by a division of Washington County by the North Carolina legislature in 1783. For a short period of time this county encompassed all of present Tennessee except for Washington, Sullivan and Davidson counties. It was named in honor of General Nathanael Greene who commanded the Army of the South during the Revolutionary War. Greeneville, also named for the famous general, was laid off as a town in 1785 and became the permanent capital of the State of Franklin. President Andrew Johnson, who once served as the town's mayor, had a small tailor's shop here. Greeneville College was established there in 1794. Another early town in the county was Bull's Gap, named for the first settler, John Bull, who made long rifles.

Hawkins County, originally named Spencer, was created by the Franklin Assembly in 1785, being carved from a section of Sullivan and Greene counties. The following year, the North Carolina legislature ignoring the status of the State of Franklin and continuing to legislate for the westerners, took the Franklin county of Spencer and established a new county named Hawkins; actually saying they renamed it would be more correct for both counties covered the same territory. It was named in honor of Benjamin Hawkins who was a member of the Continental Congress, a U.S. Senator from North Carolina, and a signer of the deed of cession conveying that state's western territory (now Tennessee) to the Federal Government. For a period of time, the county served under two governments (Franklin and North Carolina) as two different counties. The first settlers in this county were located in Carter's Valley. Rogersville, established in 1789, was named for an Irish settler, Joseph Rogers, who had received the land from his father-in-law as a wedding gift. This was the last town in what later became the state of Tennessee to be created by the North Carolina legislature. Tennessee's first newspaper, the Knoxville Gazette (1791), was printed here.

Jefferson County originally was created as Caswell County in 1785 by the Franklin Assembly and named for Governor Caswell of North Carolina. In 1792, the Territorial Governor, William Blount, established the same territory as Jefferson County. It was named for Thomas Jefferson. Dandridge (1793) was named for Martha Dandridge Curtis, wife of President George Washington.

Knox County was created by Governor Blount in 1792 and was named for General Henry Knox, Secretary of War under President Washington. The estate of Colonel James White (called White's Fort) became the town of Knoxville in 1794. It had been named by Blount and laid out by White in 1791. It became the home of the first state capitol, the first bank and the first university.

Sevier County was originally established by the First Franklin Assembly in 1785, but was not recognized by North Carolina. Therefore, it was not until the Territorial Assembly of 1794 that Sevier County was officially created by a division of Jefferson County, and named for Governor John Sevier. Sevierville, also named for this lusty Indian fighter, was established as the county seat in the forks of Little Pigeon River about 1791. The inconspicuous, pioneer mountain village of Gatlinburg was named for one of its early settlers, Radford Gatlin, who kept a store there. Pigeon Forge was named for an ironworks operating along the Little Pigeon River and because of the numerous pigeons in the region. Great Iron Mountain (now Smoky Mountains) spreads across the southern portion of this county.

Sullivan County, created in 1779, was the second county established by North Carolina and encompassed most of the Holston settlements. It was named for General John Sullivan who was a Revolutionary War hero. Evan Shelby, one of its early settlers, operated an important way station at Sapling Grove (present Bristol, Tennessee). The county seat of Blountville established in 1792, was named for Governor William Blount. Rocky Mount (near present Johnson City) was the first territorial seat of government. John Shelby, brother of Evan, had an estate at Shoat's Ford (present Bluff City). The beloved "Sacred Island of the Cherokee" was located at the twin forks of the Holston River (present Kingsport).

Washington County, originally Washington District, was redesignated as Washington County in 1777, becoming the first county in what is now the State of Tennessee. It was the first place in the nation to honor Colonel George Washington, Commander-in-Chief of the colonial armies during the American Revolution. Jonesboro, the oldest town in the state, was chartered by the North Carolina legislature in 1779. It was named for Willie (Wylie) Jones, a man of prominence and wealth who was a good friend of the early Watauga settlers. The Boone's Creek community honors the famous long-hunter, Daniel Boone. Matthew and William Atkinson, the designers of the first Great Seal of Tennessee (1802), lived in this county.

FIRST COUNTIES OF MIDDLE TENNESSEE

Before statehood, there were only three counties in the Cumberland region. In 1788, the Assembly of North Carolina formed these counties into the Mero District, named for the Spanish governor of Louisiana and West Florida, General Don Esteban Miro (the governor's last name was misspelled in historic records "Mero" —and thus continued). The counties of the Cumberland Region were not connected with the State of Franklin, but were included with the new State of Tennessee. At the time of statehood, Tennessee County was divided into two new counties, thereby giving the new state a total of eleven.

Davidson County originally included all the Cumberland settlements which were legislated into a civil body (called Davidson County) by the North Carolina government in 1783. Its boundaries covered more than three-fourths of present Middle Tennessee. The county was named in honor of General William Lea Davidson, a native of North Carolina who was totally devoted to the cause of American freedom. He was in command of the territory of what later became Tennessee during the American Revolution. The town of Old Hickory was first called Jacksonville, but was renamed because there were so many other cities by that name and its mail was often confused. Donelson was named for John Donelson, one of the Cumberland region's early settlers, who had a farm at Clover Bottom. Nashville was first known as the French Lick and was the first town established in Middle Tennessee. The town originally grew from the area surrounding Fort Nashboro, which had been built for the settlers' protection from Indians. The French Lick was settled by James Robertson, the "Father of Tennessee," John Donelson, and other pioneer families in 1779-80. Robertson named the new settlement Nashboro after General Francis Nash who had died at the Battle of Germantown in 1777. The name was changed from Nashboro to Nashville in 1783 because of resentment toward the British. They referred to a city as a "boro," but the French who had been our allies during the American Revolution used the word "ville" for city. Therefore, Nashville means "the city of Nash." It has been the state capitol of Tennessee since 1826, its permanent site since 1843.

Sumner County was divided from Davidson County by the North Carolina Assembly in 1786 and named in honor of the Brigadire-General Jethro Sumner of North Carolina. Bledsoe's Lick was one of the first stations erected in the Cumberland Region. Although named for the early settler, Colonel Isaac Bledsoe, it was later called Castalian Springs. Cragfront (1798), the home of General James Winchester, is located here. He was one of the first men to run steamboats between Nashville and New Orleans. His home was so named because the house was built on a rock bluff above a large spring. Gallatin was established in 1802 and named for Albert Gallatin, a Swiss immigrant who served as Secretary of the Treasury under Thomas Jefferson.

Tennessee County was divided from Davidson County by the North Carolina Assembly in 1788 and named for the old Cherokee village of Tenasi. Clarksville, a hamlet located on the north bank of the Cumberland River (near the mouth of Red River) was laid off as a townsite in 1784 by Colonel John Montgomery and Colonel Martin Armstrong. Montgomery named it Clarksville in honor of his commander, George Rodgers Clark. It was the second town established in Middle Tennessee (Nashboro was the first, in 1780).

At the first state legislative meeting in Knoxville in 1796, Daniel Smith submitted the name of Tennessee for the new state. Therefore, the original County of Tennessee agreed to relinquish its name and was divided into Montgomery and Robertson counties. Montgomery County was named for Colonel John Montgomery of North Carolina, who was the founder of Clarksville and the first Sheriff of the Mero District. Robertson County was named in honor of General James Robertson who was the leader of the early Cumberland settlements and is known as the "Father of Middle Tennessee."

FIRST COUNTIES OF WEST TENNESSEE

At the time of statehood, there were no established counties in West Tennessee for it was still predominantly wilderness and claimed by the Chickasaws. After twenty-two years, the Jackson Purchase was negotiated (1818), and by it, the Chickasaws finally gave up their claim to all of West Tennessee. Afterward, settlers poured into the region, and the following year its first two counties were established.

Hardin County was created by the state legislature in 1819 and named for Colonel Joseph Hardin who had led a small group of settlers there from Greene County in that same year. Colonel Hardin himself, was the owner of 2,000 acres which he received for his Revolutionary War service. Prior to moving to the western section of the new state, he lived in East Tennessee and was Speaker of the Assembly in the State of Franklin. This county is bisected by the great Tennessee River, and numerous disputes as well as lawsuits have arisen over its boundaries. The county seat of Savannah, formerly Rudd's Ferry, was named after a city in the state of Georgia. Shiloh National Park is located in this county. The fishing towns of Saltillo and Cerro Gordo were named by soldiers returning from the Mexican War in 1848, for two of the places they had fought at in northern Mexico.

Shelby County was the second county created by the Tennessee legislature in 1819. It was named for Issac Shelby, an early settler from East Tennessee who became the first governor of Kentucky. Memphis (1826) was named for a famous city located on the Nile River in ancient Egypt. James Winchester, a famous soldier of the American Revolution and first speaker of the Tennessee Senate, suggested the name. The Chickasaw Bluffs and Mississippi River reminded him of what he had read of the Egyptian Memphis on the Nile.

CHRONOLOGY

1492 Columbus discovers New World.

1497-1600 Explorers and fishermen contact North American natives.

1500 Five Indian tribes live in Tennessee: Yuchi, southeast (present Roane and Rhea counties); Shawnee, north (Cumberland Region); Creeks, south (Middle Tennessee); Chickasaws, Chickasaw Bluffs and throughout Middle and West Tennessee; Cherokee, throughout all of Tennessee.

1540 De Soto crosses the Mississippi at or near the Fourth Chickasaw Bluff (present-day Memphis); first white man to enter Cherokee country.

1559-70 Beginnings of the league of Iroquois.

1566 Pardo, Spanish explorer, visits southeastern Tennessee.

1603-35 Early white contact with the Canadian tribes.

1607 Founding of Jamestown by English.

1608 Founding of Quebec by French.

1673 Needham and Arthur, first Englishmen to enter East Tennessee, explore the eastern wilderness and visit Overhill Cherokee villages.
Marquette and Joliet descend the Mississippi and stop at the Chickasaw Bluffs—first Europeans to see entire west coast of Tennessee.

1682 William Penn signs peace Treaty with Delawares.
La Salle builds Fort Prud'homme on First Chickasaw Bluff near mouth of Hatchie River (present Lauderdale county); first European fort in Tennessee.

1684 First European treaty made with Cherokee.

1684-1714 Charleville, a French trader, operates a trading post at Great French Lick (present-day Nashville).

1699 La Moyne, Iberville builds Fort Maurepas in the young Louisiana colony.

1700 Couture, a French trader becomes first European to travel length of Tennessee River.

1710 Eleazer Wiggan, one of the first English traders in East Tennessee, establishes trade with Overhill Cherokees.

1711-12 Remnants of Tuscarora tribe move north to join Iroquois as the sixth nation.

1715-28 Yamassee War in South Carolina destroys power of Carolina coastal Indians.

1718 John de Bienville, brother of La Moyne, Iberville, lays foundation of present New Orleans.

1721 Treaty of Charles Town (i.e., Charleton, S. C.) signed between British and Cherokee; Indians make first cession of land to the whites.

1730 Sir Alexander Cuming visits Cherokee country. At a council meeting of chiefs, he names Moytoy as "Emperor" of the Cherokee and Old Hop, "King." Group of chiefs go with him to England; one being Ookoonaka, later Attakullakulla, known to whites as Little Carpenter.

1738 First smallpox epidemic sweeps the Appalachian frontier and wipes out nearly half the Cherokee Nation.

1746 Stephen Holston builds his cabin on Tooley's River, called later Indian or Cherokee River; still later known as the Holston.

1748 Colonel Patton obtains grant from Virginia of 800,000 acres in Upper Holston Valley (presently portions of Bristol, Bluff City and Kingsport).

1749-50 Dr. Thomas Walker, agent for the Loyal Land Company of Virginia, explores upper East Tennessee and becomes the first Englishman to enter Kentucky. He was the first explorer of record to record the discovery of a gap, mountains, and great river which he named "Cumberland," in honor of the Duke of Cumberland, son of King George II.

Lawless and Hughes, men in Walker's party, are first white men to raise a cabin between the Cumberland and Ohio Rivers.

1750-51 Dr. Thomas Walker and Christopher Gist, commissioned by the Ohio Land Company of Virginia, explore vicinity of present Kingsport; Walker records camp of one Samuel Stalnaker on Reedy Creek and the finding of an elm tree with a circumference of about twenty-five feet, at a height of three feet.

1751 Pearis and Price, English fur traders, operate a trading post at the Long Island of Holston.

1754-63 French and Indian War (called Seven Years' War by Europeans).

1756 Major Andrew Lewis, with a construction crew of sixty, builds Virginia Fort near Echota.

Edmund Pendleton obtains land grant on Reedy Creek, at junction of the two forks of Holston River.

1757 South Carolina militia builds Fort Loudoun, seven miles from the abandoned Virginia Fort; first garrisoned English fort in Tennessee.

1760 Began decade of the "Long Hunters."

Murder of twenty-two Cherokees held hostage at Fort Prince George.

Daniel Boone commissioned by Henderson Company to scout East Tennessee; made hunting camps at a "bold spring" near the base of Buffalo Mountain and others a few miles farther, on a creek which today bears his name (just outside present Johnson City).

Cherokees, under Oconostota, lay siege to Fort Loudoun.

John McDonald (grandfather of Chief Ross) manages to escape Indian attacks on the whites a short distance from the fort.

The Little Carpenter after the siege of Fort Loudoun purchases the captive John Stuart and takes him to safety at the Long Island of the Holston.

Old Hop, "King" of the Cherokee Nation, reported dead by a dispatch at Fort Loudoun.

1761 Elijah (Elisha) Walden with party of Long Hunters explores Upper East Tennessee down as far as present Carter's Valley and explores the Cumberland Valley.

Fort Robinson, second English fort in Tennessee, built by the Virginia militia under Colonel Adam Stevens on the upper end of the Long Island.

Henry Timberlake and Sergeant Thomas Sumter travel through Overhill Cherokee Country.

About four hundred Cherokees arrive at Fort Robinson; sue for peace.

Island Road cut as a military route from Chilhowie,Virginia,to upper end of the Long Island of the Holston by Virginia militia under command of General Andrew Lewis.

1762 Chief Ostenaco (Man-killer), Henry Timberlake, and a small party visit King George in England.

1763 France surrenders almost all her North American empire to Great Britain. Royal Proclamation by King George III establishes Indian sanctuary and restricts westward movement of colonists.

1765 Jessie Duncan, scout, murdered by Indians; first white man to die and be buried on Tennessee soil (just outside northern part of present-day Johnson City).

1765-71 Regulation Movement in North Carolina.

1766 Andrew Greer and Caesar Dugger are trading in the Watauga hills (present-day Elizabethton).

1768 Fort Stanwix Treaty whereby northern Indians give up their claim to land in East Tennessee; extends northern Indian boundary line to meet southern Indian boundary line.

An exploring expedition moves down Holston River as far as present site of Rogersville.

A few settlers have settled at Wolf Hills (present-day Abingdon, Virginia).

Treaty of Hard Labor between English and Cherokee to legitimize some of the squatter holdings.

William Bean, first permanent white settler in Tennessee, builds a cabin along Boone's Creek near its junction with Watauga River.

First white child born in Tennessee, Russell Bean.

1769 Great northern War Chief, Pontiac, assassinated.

Daniel Boone and John Findlay (Finley) commissioned by Henderson Company to scout Kentucky.

Gilbert Christian (founder of present Kingsport) and William Anderson lead a party from the Long Island as far down as present Hawkins County, and then to junction of the Tennessee and Clinch Rivers.

Cherokees suffer defeat by Chickasaws; nearly half their warriors are killed.

1770 John Carter and Joseph Parker set up first mercantile establishment in East Tennessee just below the twin forks of Holston in a valley which today bears Carter's name (near present Rogersville).

Treaty of Lochaber signed; Cherokees cede triangle of land west of the Hard Labor cession.

James Robertson, "Father of Tennessee," builds his cabin at "Watauga Old-field Flats" near the Doe River (present Elizabethton).

1771 Amos Eaton (Heaton) builds Eaton's Station on a ridge above Island Flats (east of present Kingsport, now known as Chestnut Ridge).

Donelson surveys south edge of Lochaber cession.

Evan Shelby settles on tract of land he called Sapling Grove; builds a combination fort, way station, and trading post on hill there (present corner of Seventh and Anderson streets in Bristol, Tennessee).

John Shelby, brother of Evan, settles at Shoat's Ford (present-day Bluff City).

Gilbert Christian seizes part of Pendleton grant and stakes claim of 250 acres at mouth of Reedy Creek, officially recorded in 1782.

Battle of Alamance ends Regulation movement; many regulators flee to the Watauga.

Jacob Brown establishes his Nolichucky settlemenmt (about mid-way between present-day Jonesboro and Erwin).

1772 The Wataugans and Cherokees sign lease agreement.

Jacob Brown and Cherokees agree to lease of Nolichucky land.

Watauga Association is formed; first constitution west of the Appalachians and the first free and independent government in the New World.

1773 "Boston Tea Party."

Watauga Road laid out; starting from Wolf Hills, it ran south to the Long Island and then west to the flats of Sycamore Shoals.

1774 Colonel William Preston surveys Fincastle county, Virginia.

Lord Dunmore's War with the Shawnee.

First Continental Congress meets in Philadelphia.

King's Mill Fort built on north fork of Reedy Creek.

1775-83 The American Revolution.

1775 Henderson's Transylvania Purchase; biggest real estate deal in American history, comprising nearly all of present-day Kentucky.

Jacob Brown obtains deeds to his Nolichucky "empire."

Inhabitants of Watauga and Nolichucky designate themselves the Washington District in an area claimed by North Carolina.

Daniel Boone and forty axemen blaze the "Wilderness Trail" starting from Long Island of the Holston and continuing to the Cumberland Gap.

Pittsburg Conference; Indians exchange neutrality pledge for an American pledge to accept the Ohio River as a permanent boundary between them.

Three settlements being established in Kentucky: Boonesboro, Harrodburg, and Fort Logan (St. Aspen).

Long Island of Holston becomes Pendleton District.

Fort Caswell, sometimes called Fort Watauga, built at the Sycamore Shoals (present city of Elizabethton).

1776 Virginia declares herself a free and independent state.

Transylvania becomes Kentucky County, Virginia.

Delegation of northern Indians arrive at Overhill Towns for war talks.

Nancy Ward sends white trader, Isaac Thomas, to warn settlers of planned Cherokee attack.

Cherokee war parties, with some Creek warriors, attack whole arc of the white frontier.

Dragging Canoe engages in Battle of Island Flats; first warfare of the Revolution west of the mountains.

Old Abram lays siege to Fort Caswell.

Mrs. William Bean captured by foraging Indians.

Four-state invasion of the Cherokee Nation by white militias.

Dragging Canoe, other chiefs, and a party of hostile braves move to Chickamauga Creek (near present Chattanooga); later these Indians are known as the Chickamaugans.

Fort Patrick Henry built near site of old Fort Robinson.

Declaration of Independence signed in Philadelphia.

1777 Looney's Fort built by Moses Looney, on Island Road near Fall Creek.

David Crockett, grandfather of celebrated Davy Crockett, is killed by Chickamaugans at Crockett Creek (near present Rogersville).

Samuel Moore and Benjamin Linn, young hunters, sent as spies to the Illinois territory, to scout the country for General John Sullivan.

Great Island Treaty signed. Land titles of Wataugans legitimized, new boundaries agreed upon, and Cherokees retain title to The Long Island of the Holston.

Washington District becomes Washington County, with boundaries co-extensive with present State of Tennessee.

Chief Cornstalk brutally murdered by whites at Fort Randolph (near present-day Addison in Gallia County, Ohio).

Joseph Martin, Virginia Indian agent, establishes trading post on the Great Island.

Blackfish and Shawnee warriors invade Kentucky.

First fourth of July celebration on Tennessee soil and in all the West occurs at Fort Patrick Henry.

Riverfront area opposite west end of famous Long Island becomes known as "Boatyard District."

Chief Attakullakulla (Little Carpenter) dies of natural causes in his own country.

1778 Virginia compensates Henderson and Company for loss of Transylvania lands with 200,000 acres on Green River in Kentucky.

Daniel Boone captured, adopted by Chief Blackfish, and given Indian name, "Big Turtle."

General John Sullivan lays waste to Iroquois country and destroys power of the Six Nations.

Tidence Lane organizes and builds Buffalo Ridge Baptist Church; suggested by some to be the first Baptist Church in Tennessee (located in present Gray Community).

1779 Colonel Evan Shelby descends Tennessee River and destroys all eleven Chickamaugan towns.

Indian agent John Stuart dies in Pensacola, Florida.

Pendleton District becomes Sullivan County.

Jonesborough established; first town in Tennessee and oldest town west of the mountains—county seat of Washington County.

James Robertson, "Father of Middle Tennessee," leads group of settlers overland from the Long Island of the Holston to the Cumberland region.

John Donelson's flotilla begins descent of Holston River, from Fort Patrick Henry on the way to Cumberland Country.

Construction of Fort Nashborough begins.

Another smallpox epidemic hits Cherokee Nation; 2,500 die.

1780 Rev. Samuel Doak builds Doak's school; later it is named Martin's Academy; first educational institute west of the mountains (in 1795 it became Washington College).

Rev. Doak organizes Salem Church, first Presbyterian Church in Tennessee. John Sevier, or "Nolichucky Jack," scourges Cherokee towns on Little Tennessee and Hiwassee Rivers.

Benedict Arnold commits treason.

Settlers at Nashborough draw up Cumberland Compact.

Battle of King's Mountain occurs.

1782 Great Cherokee Chief Oconostota dies at Echota.

North Carolina grants Henderson 190,000 acres in Powell Valley to compensate for his Transylvania land losses. Also gave 10,000 acres in the Clinch River Valley to John Carter and his new partner for their losses.

John Sevier defeats Chickamaugans and burns all their towns.

John Donelson is killed by Indians.

Matthew Talbot organizes "Watauga River Church" (locally known as, and still called today, Sinking Creek Baptist Church); oldest church in Tennessee occupying its original location and foundation.

Nancy Ward moves to home of son-in-law, Joseph Martin, on Long Island.

1783 Robertson and Chickasaw Treaty signed; Chickasaws give up their claim to land in Middle Tennessee.

North Carolina divides Washington to form Greene County.

Cumberland settlements become district of Davidson; formed by North Carolina.

1784 Alexander McGillivray, chief of Creeks, forms alliance with Spain.

"Colbert Pirate Gang" operates on the Mississippi.

Name of Nashborough changes to Nashville and town laid off.

North Carolina cedes western lands to United States but repeals act the following year.

State of Franklin established; constitution adopted.

1785 First Franklin Legislature meets at Greeneville; John Sevier elected governor and four new counties created in upper East Tennessee.

Valentine Sevier, brother of John, undertook settling of the Great Bend of Tennessee River.

Franklin and North Carolina both claim jurisdiction in East Tennessee resulting in two governments operating in the same state.

Davy Crockett born at Limestone, between Jonesborough and Greeneville.

1786 Hawkins County erected from the Franklin County of Spencer.

General James White builds White's Fort, later to become Knoxville.

1787 United States Constitution adopted.

1788 Franklin Legislature meets at Greeneville for last time.

Road built from White's Fort to Nashville.

Battle of Franklin on Tipton-Haynes farm at Sinking Creek (just outside present-day Johnson City).

Three distinguished Cherokee chiefs, Old Tassel, Abram, and Hanging Maw, are brutally murdered by Sevier's henchmen under a flag of truce.

Government of Franklin collapses.

1789 Mero District created in Cumberland region.

General George Washington inaugurated as President.

North Carolina cedes her western lands to United States.

1790 "Territory of the United States South of the River Ohio" created; it consisted of most all of the present state of Tennessee.

Vermont admitted as fourteenth state.

First United States territorial census taken.

William Blount appointed Territorial governor and chose home of William Cobb, Rocky Mount, as his capital (north of present-day Johnson City).

1791 Streets for Knoxville laid out.

Treaty of Holston between Cherokees and United States signed; new boundaries agreed upon, annual payment agreed on for cessions, and Cherokees come under protection of United States.

Tennessee's first newspaper, Knoxville Gazette, published at Rogersville.

1792 Blount chooses White's Fort as new capital and renamed site Knoxville.

Kentucky admitted as fifteenth state. Isaac Shelby becomes governor.

Fiery Chickamaugan chief Dragging Canoe dies.

Creeks, Choctaws and Chickamaugans go on warpath.

Half-breed John Watts, of Willstown, elected as new War Chief of Chickamaugan Cherokees.

1793 "Mad Anthony" Wayne (Revolutionary veteran) breaks the power of northwestern Indian tribes.

The Whiskey Rebellion enacted; excise tax on spirits.

1795 Blount County carved from Knox.

Walton Road from Knoxville to Nashville completed across Cumberland Plateau.

Towns of Blountville in Sullivan County, Sevierville in Sevier County, Greeneville in Greene County, and Clarksville in Montgomery County were chartered; they were then and are now seats of the county governments.

Census of Southwest Territory taken; population 77,262 of which 10,613 were slaves—more than enough to apply for statehood.

Daniel Smith submits name Tennessee for new state.

The Cumberland County by name of Tennessee agrees to relinquish its name to the new state and becomes Montgomery and Robertson counties.

1796 First General Assembly meets in Knoxville and first state constitution is adopted; state capital until 1812 and again between 1818-1825.

John Sevier, first state governor inaugurated; served until 1801 and again from 1803-1809.

William Blount and William Cocke elected as first United States Senators, re-elected four months later.

May 31, Tennessee admitted as sixteenth state of the union.

Andrew Jackson elected as first United States Congressman.

1803 United States buys the Louisiana colony from France.

William King of the Virginia saltworks, buys two and a half acres of land along riverbank in Boat Yard District from Robert Christian, son of Gilbert (across river from the Long Island).

Ohio becomes a state.

Agents of William King build King's Boat Yard; first organized freighting company west of the mountains.

1805 Third Treaty of Tellico signed by Cherokees and United States; settlements of East and Middle Tennessee now united.

Chickasaws sell 335,000 acres of land south of Duck River to the United States for $22,000.

Richard Christian, son of Gilbert, lays out Christian's Ville Boat Yard along the Island Road.

1806 Fisk Female Academy established in Overton county; it is the first school for girls in the South.

Blount College at Knoxville, renamed East Tennessee College and later, named the University of Tennessee.

1809 James Shelby, son of Evan, sells Sapling Grove to James King who renames the site "King's Meadows"; later it is named Bristol.

1812-14 War of 1812 between the United States and Great Britain.

1812 Nashville become state capital until 1815; in 1835 it will be designated as the capital of Tennessee.

1814 Battle of Horseshoe Bend (present state of Alabama).

Andrew Jackson, with some Cherokee warriors, defeated the Creeks putting an end to the Creek Wars.

Hartford Convention destroys power of the Federalist party in the United States.

Arkansas Territory organized.

1815 John Sevier, an old Wataugan, dies near Fort Decatur, Georgia.

1818 Jackson directs campaign against Seminoles and drives the Spanish garrison from Pensacola.

Spain cedes the Floridas to United States.

State capital moves back to Knoxville until 1825.

Tusculum College established at Greeneville.

1819 "Manumission Intelligence" later, "Emancipator," first anti-slavery paper in the United States published at Jonesborough.

Cherokees relinquish their claim to heart of Great Smoky Mountains; land now legally open to white settlement.

City of Memphis laid out.

1821 Jackson appointed Territorial Governor of Florida.

Sequoyah's syllabary accepted by Cherokee National Council.

1822 Ross' Rossville and Christian's Christianville become Kingsport.

Jackson elected United States Senator.

1825 Murfreesboro serves as state capital until 1835.

Nashoba, Frances White's colony for freed slaves, established in Shelby County, near Germantown.

1827 Sam Houston resigns his governorship; first Tennessee governor ever to resign for personal reasons. He goes into voluntary exile among Cherokees in Arkansas.

East Tennessee College becomes second university in the state.

Davy Crockett elected to Congress as a representative of the western states.

Cherokees adopt a national constitution with John Ross as president of the nation.

1828 Andrew Jackson elected President; center of political power has now crossed the Appalachians.

Indian Removal Act put through Congress.

Cherokees establish national newspaper, ''Cherokee Phoenix,'' in New Echota, Georgia.

1833 Epidemic of Asiatic cholera sweeps over Tennessee. Large cities paralyzed and many small towns almost depopulated.

1835-42 Seminole Wars in Florida.

1835 Nashville becomes the permanent state capital and new state constitution is adopted.

Treaty of Echota signed by Major Ridge, a handfull of Cherokees and the United States; Cherokees given two years to move West.

1836 Sam Houston and other Tennesseans lead Texans in their war for independence from Mexico.

1838 Great removal of Cherokees from Tennessee begun.

Tsali and kin executed at Bushnell; they sacrificed their lives so mountain Cherokees could stay in the hills of Tennessee and western North Carolina.

1838-39 The ''Trail of Tears'' to the West causes death of more than 4,000 Cherokees.

1839 Major Ridge and other sponsors of Echota Treaty are executed by fellow Cherokees in the West.

BIBLIOGRAPHY

Books

Abernathy, Thomas Perkins. **From Frontier to Plantation in Tennessee.** Alabama: University of Alabama Press, 1967, pp. 1-220.

Addington, Robert M. **History of Scott County, Virginia.** Kingsport, Tennessee: Kingsport Press, Inc., 1979, pp. 7-38, 50-58, 72-78, 82-87 and 156-161.

Alderman, Pat. **Nancy Ward.** Johnson City, Tennessee: The Overmountain Press, 1978.

Alderman, Pat. **The Overmountain Men.** Erwin and Johnson City, Tennessee: Wingreen Co., Inc. and Kinkead Printing Company, 1958.

Burt, Jessie and Robert B. Ferguson. **Indians of the Southeast: Then and Now.** Nashville and New York: Abingdon Press, 1973.

Caruso, John Anthony. **The Appalachian Frontier.** New York: Bobbs-Merrill Co., Inc., 1959.

Clark, Thomas D. **Frontier America.** New York: Charles Scribner's Sons, 1959.

Cotterill, R.S. **The Southern Indians.** Oklahoma: University of Oklahoma Press, 1954.

Dixon, Max. **The Wataugans.** Tennessee American Revolution Bicentennial Commission, 1976.

Dunlop, Richard. **Doctors of the American Frontier.** Garden City, N.Y.: Doubleday & Company, 1965.

Eckert, Allan W. **The Frontiersmen.** Boston, Mass.: Little, Brown, and Company, 1967.

Filson, John. **The Discovery, Settlement and Present State of Kentucky.** New York, New York, Corinth Books, Inc., 1962.

Fink, Paul M. **Jonesborough: The First Century of Tennessee's First Town.** Washington, D.C.: Dept of Housing and Urban Development, 1972.

Frome, Michael. **Strangers in High Places.** Knoxville: University of Tennessee Press, 1980, pp. 5-80.

Gerson, Noel B. **Franklin, America's "Lost State."** New York: Crowell-Collier Press, 1968.

Hartley, William and Ellen. **Osceola The Unconquered Indian.** New York: Hawthorn Books, Inc., 1973.

Haywood, John. **The Civil and Political History of the State of Tennessee From Its Earliest Settlement Up to the Year 1796.** Knoxville, Tennessee: Tenase Company, 1969.

Haywood, John. **Natural and Aboriginal History of Tennessee.** Knoxville, Tennessee: University of Tennessee Press, 1959.

Jacobs, Wilbur R. **Dispossessing the American Indian.** New York, N.Y.: Charles Scribner's Sons, 1972.

Joiner, Henry M. **Tennessee Then and Now.** Alabama: Southern Textbook Publishers, Inc., 1983, pp. 1-300.

Josephy, Alvin M., Jr. **The Indian Heritage of America.** New York, N.Y.: Alred A. Knopf, Inc., 1980, pp. 10-55, 81-109, 278-285 and 295-344.

Kincaid, Robert L. **The Wilderness Road.** Harrogate, Tennessee: Lincoln Memorial University Press, 1955.

Lay, Elery A. Dr. **An Industrial Commercial History of the Tri-Cities in Tennessee-Virginia.** Kingsport, Tennessee: Lay Publications, 1982, pp. 3-9, 21-29 and 37-39.

Merritt, Frank. **Early History of Carter County.** Knoxville, Tennessee: Archer and Smith Publishing Co., 1950, pp. 1-147.

Mooney, James. **Myths of the Cherokee.** Washington: Government Printing Office, 1970.

Ramsey, J.G.M., A.M. and M.D. **Annals of Tennessee.** Kingsport, Tennessee: Kingsport Press, 1926.

Randolph, J. Ralph. **British Traders Among the Indians, 1660- 1763.** Norman, Oklahoma, 1973.

Rosenstiel, Annette. **Red and White.** New York, N.Y.: University Books, 1983.

Snow, Dean. **The Archaeology of North America.** New York, N.Y.: The Viking Press, 1976, pp. 7-82.

The Sullivan County Historical Commission and Associations, **Historic Sites of Sullivan County.** Kingsport, Tennessee: The Kingsport Press, 1976, pp. 41-43, 115, 192-194 and 215-217.

Taylor, Oliver. **Historic Sullivan.** Bristol, Tennessee: The King Printing Company. 1909.

Thomas, M. N. Lewis and Madeline Kneberg. **Tribes That Slumber.** Knoxville, Tennessee: University of Tennessee Press, 1977.

West, C. W. "Dub." **The Mysteries of Sequoyah.** Muskogee, Oklahoma: Muscogee Publishing Co., 1975.

White, Jon Manchip. **Everyday Life of the North American Indian.** New York: Holmes and Meier Publishers, Inc., 1980.

Williams, Samuel Cole. **Dawn of Tennessee Valley and Tennessee History.** Johnson City, Tennessee: The Watauga Press, 1937.

Williams, Samuel Cole. **History of Johnson City and Its Environs.** Johnson City, Tennessee: The Watauga Press, 1940, pp. 9-26.

Williams, Samuel Cole. **The Lost State of Franklin.** Johnson City, Tennessee: The Watauga Press, 1924.

Williams, Samuel Cole. **Memoirs of Lt. Henry Timberlake, 1756-1765.** Marietta, Georgia: Continental Book Company, 1948.

Wissler, Clark, **Indians of the United States.** New York: Doubleday, Doran and Co., Inc., 1940, pp. 55-180.

Woodward, Grace Steele, **The Cherokees.** Oklahoma: University of Oklahoma Press, 1963.

Magazines

Fink, Paul. "Jacob Brown of Nolichucky," **Tennessee Historical Quarterly,** 21 (1962), pp. 235-50.

"Historic Jonesborough," **Travelhost,** (June 27, 1982), p. 15.

La Fay, Howard. "George Washington: The Man Behind the Myths," **National Geographic,** Vol. 150, No. 1, (July, 1976), pp. 90-111.

Parris, John, "The Tsali Legend," **Now and Then,** Vol. 3, No. 3, (Autumn, 1986), p. 15.

Stinson, Bryon, "The Watauga Association," **American History Illustrated,** (April, 1973), pp. 20-32.

Atlases and Gazetteers

Encyclopedia Britannica World Atlas. Chicago: Encyclopedia Britannica, Inc., 1960.

Hammond's World Atlas and Gazetteer. New York: C.S. Hammond & Co., 1943.

Pamphlets

At Home in the Smokies. National Park Handbook 125, Washington, D. C.: U.S. Department of the Interior, 1984.

Cades Cove. Gatlinburg, Tennessee: Great Smoky Mountain Natural History Association, 1980.

The Cherokees Past and Present. Cherokee, North Carolina: Cherokee Publications, 1970.

Upper East Tennessee and Southwest Virginia. Kingsport, Tennessee: Edwards and Associates Advertising, 1978.

Individuals

From Boone's Creek: Kenneth and Ruth Hodges. Raphael and Stella Martin.

From Gray Station: Mr. Norman Calloway. Mrs. Lucille Deakins. Mrs. Peggy Hensley. Mrs. Zella Sifford.

From Elizabethton: Mr. and Mrs. Ralph Baird.

From Kingsport: Mr. Loyd B. Anderson (Memoirs).

From Kingsport: Mrs. Dora F. Anderson.

From Rogersville: Mrs. Nell Hybarger.

Newspapers

The Historical News (Hiram, Georgia), July 1988.

"Remembering The 'State of Franklin,' " **The Greenville Sun,** October 7, 1986.

Taylor, Oliver. "Kingsport Tennessee," **Kingsport Times,** October 20, 1920.

INDEX

*Indian Tribes
**Indian Villages/Towns

182